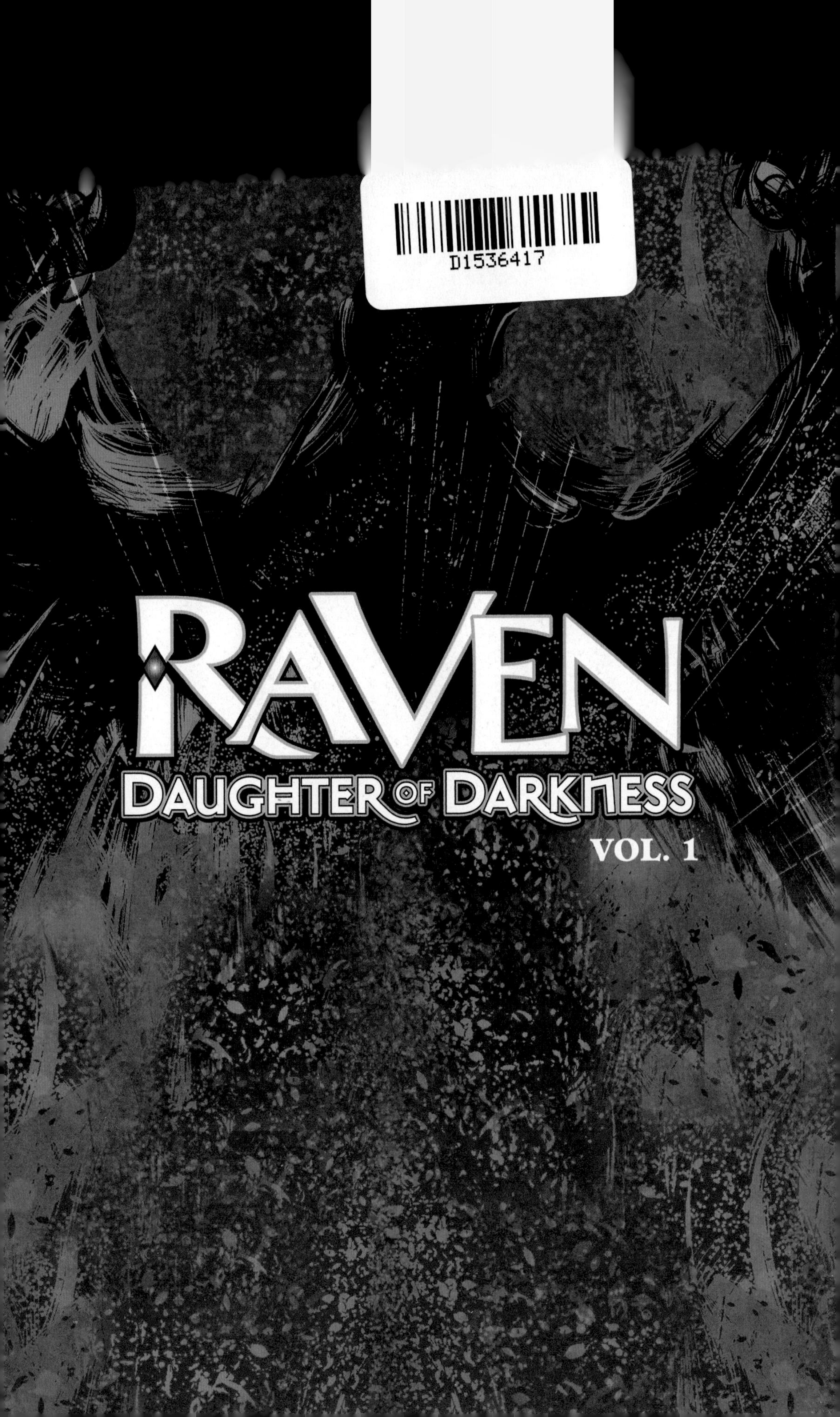
RAVEN
DAUGHTER OF DARKNESS
VOL. 1

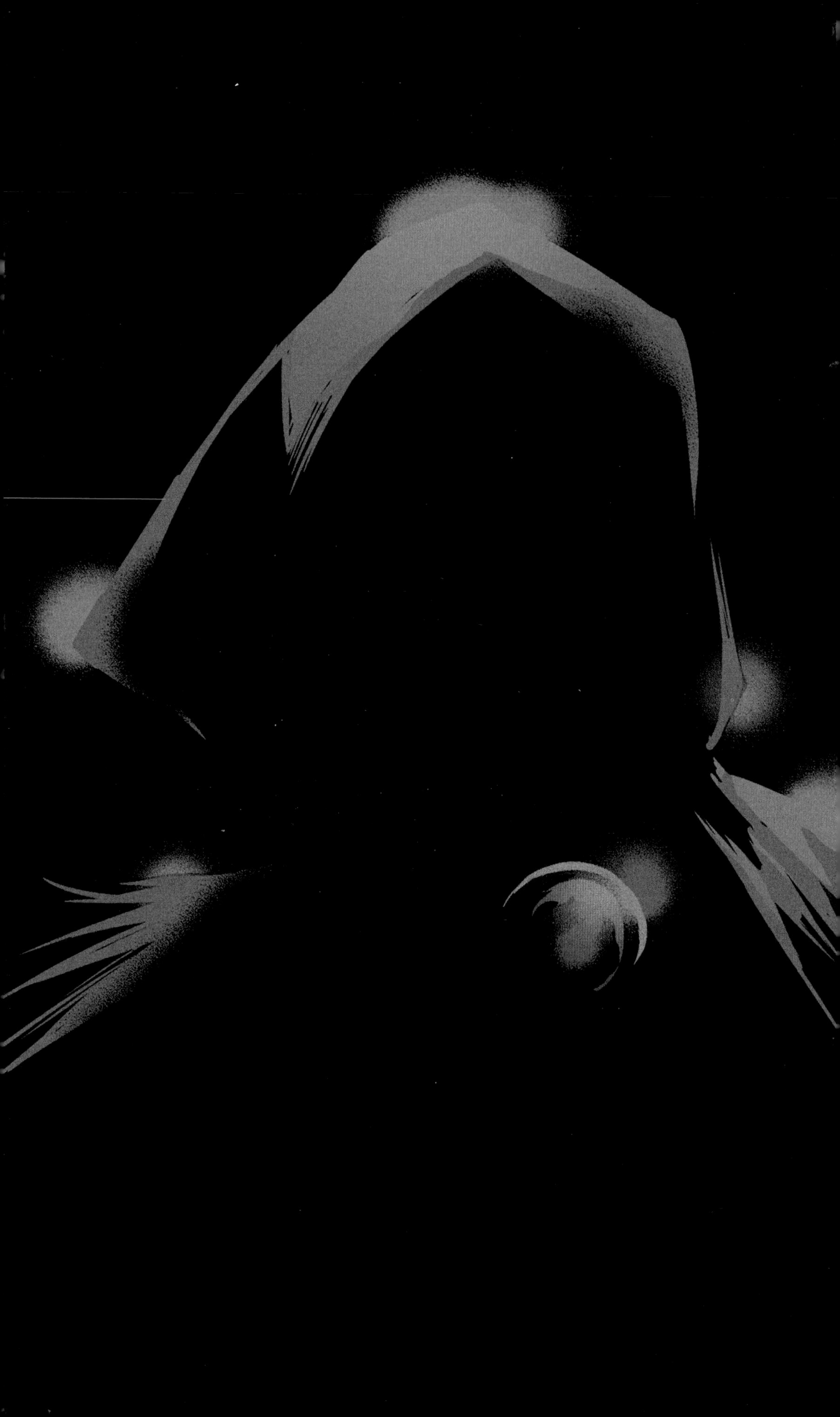

RAVEN
DAUGHTER OF DARKNESS
VOL. 1

MARV WOLFMAN
writer

POP MHAN
artist

LOVERN KINDZIERSKI
colorist

SAIDA TEMOFONTE
letterer

YANICK PAQUETTE
collection cover artist

RAVEN created by MARV WOLFMAN and GEORGE PÉREZ

JOEY CAVALIERI Editor – Original Series • MICHAEL McCALISTER Assistant Editor – Original Series
JEB WOODARD Group Editor – Collected Editions • ERIKA ROTHBERG Editor – Collected Edition
STEVE COOK Design Director – Books • SHANNON STEWART Publication Design

BOB HARRAS Senior VP – Editor-in-Chief, DC Comics • PAT McCALLUM Executive Editor, DC Comics

DAN DiDIO Publisher • JIM LEE Publisher & Chief Creative Officer
AMIT DESAI Executive VP – Business & Marketing Strategy, Direct to Consumer & Global Franchise Management
BOBBIE CHASE VP & Executive Editor, Young Reader & Talent Development • MARK CHIARELLO Senior VP – Art, Design & Collected Editions
JOHN CUNNINGHAM Senior VP – Sales & Trade Marketing • BRIAR DARDEN VP – Business Affairs
ANNE DePIES Senior VP – Business Strategy, Finance & Administration • DON FALLETTI VP – Manufacturing Operations
LAWRENCE GANEM VP – Editorial Administration & Talent Relations • ALISON GILL Senior VP – Manufacturing & Operations
JASON GREENBERG VP – Business Strategy & Finance • HANK KANALZ Senior VP – Editorial Strategy & Administration
JAY KOGAN Senior VP – Legal Affairs • NICK J. NAPOLITANO VP – Manufacturing Administration
LISETTE OSTERLOH VP – Digital Marketing & Events • EDDIE SCANNELL VP – Consumer Marketing
COURTNEY SIMMONS Senior VP – Publicity & Communications • JIM (SKI) SOKOLOWSKI VP – Comic Book Specialty Sales & Trade Marketing
NANCY SPEARS VP – Mass, Book, Digital Sales & Trade Marketing • MICHELE R. WELLS VP – Content Strategy

RAVEN: DAUGHTER OF DARKNESS VOL. 1

Published by DC Comics. Compilation and all new material Copyright © 2018 DC Comics. All Rights Reserved.
Originally published in single magazine form in RAVEN: DAUGHTER OF DARKNESS 1-6. Copyright © 2018 DC Comics. All Rights Reserved. All characters,
their distinctive likenesses and related elements featured in this publication are trademarks of DC Comics.
The stories, characters and incidents featured in this publication are entirely fictional.
DC Comics does not read or accept unsolicited submissions of ideas, stories or artwork.

DC Comics, 2900 West Alameda Ave., Burbank, CA 91505
Printed by Times Printing, LLC, Random Lake, WI. 9/14/18. First Printing.
ISBN: 978-1-4012-8473-2

Library of Congress Cataloging-in-Publication Data is available.

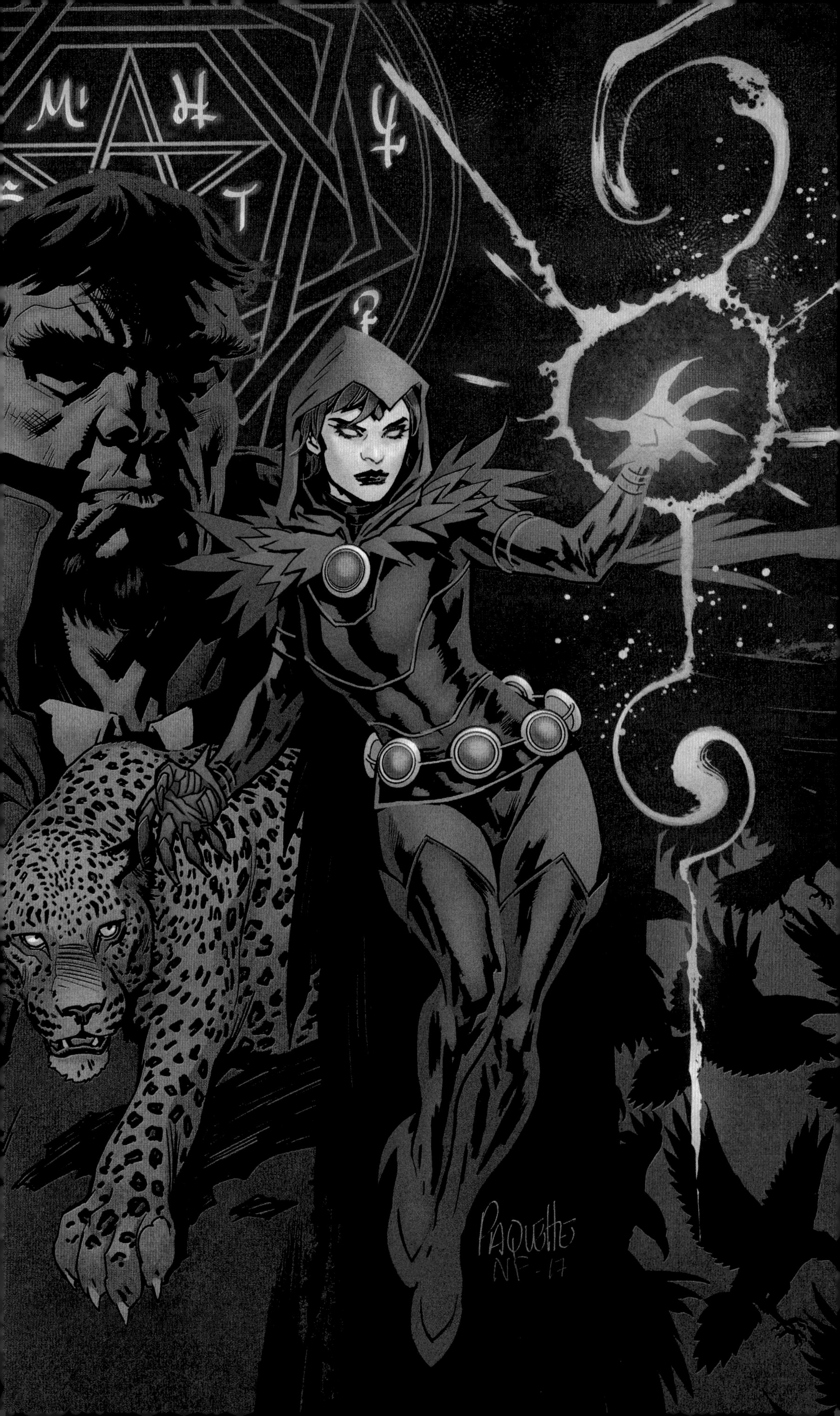
PAQUETTE
NF-17

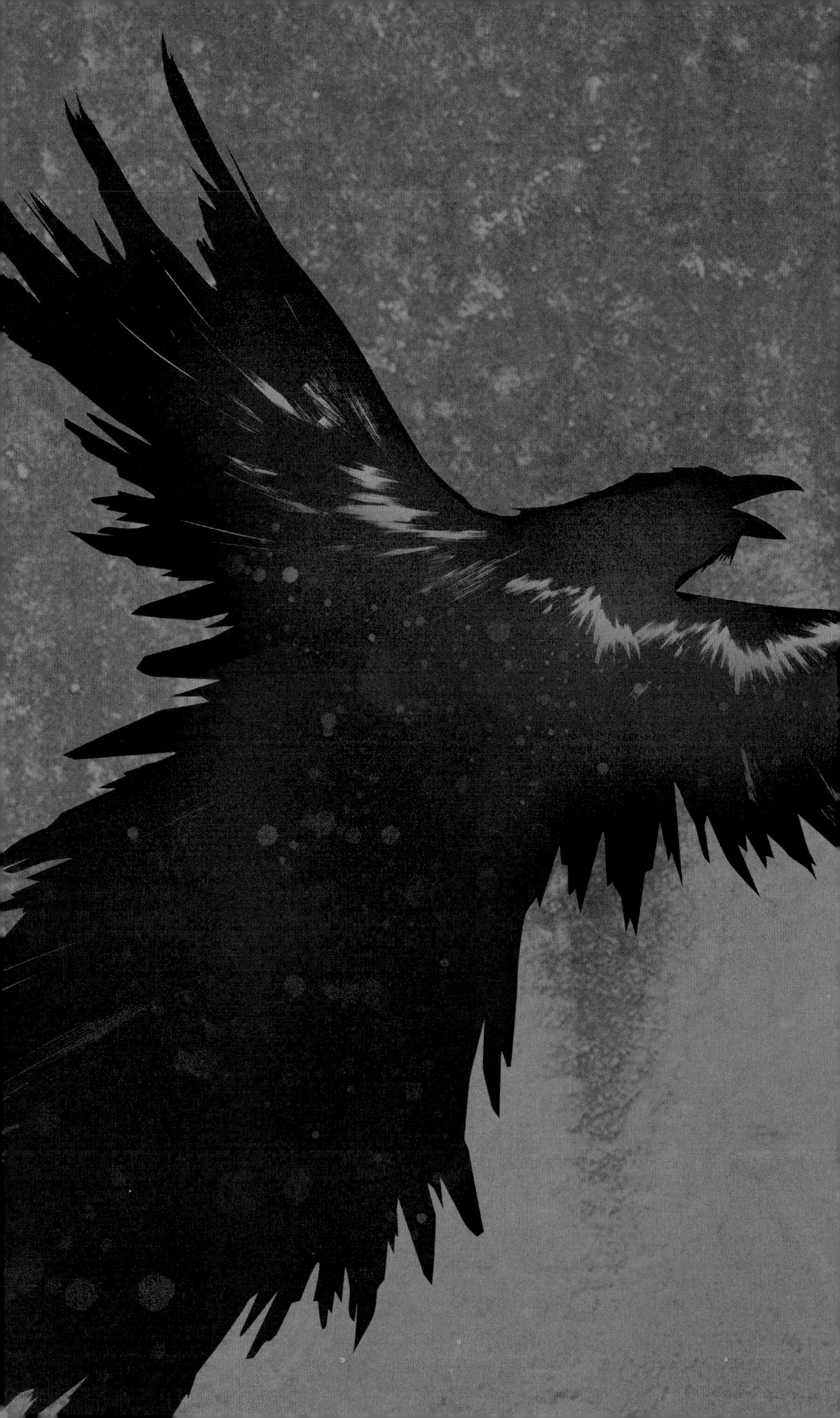

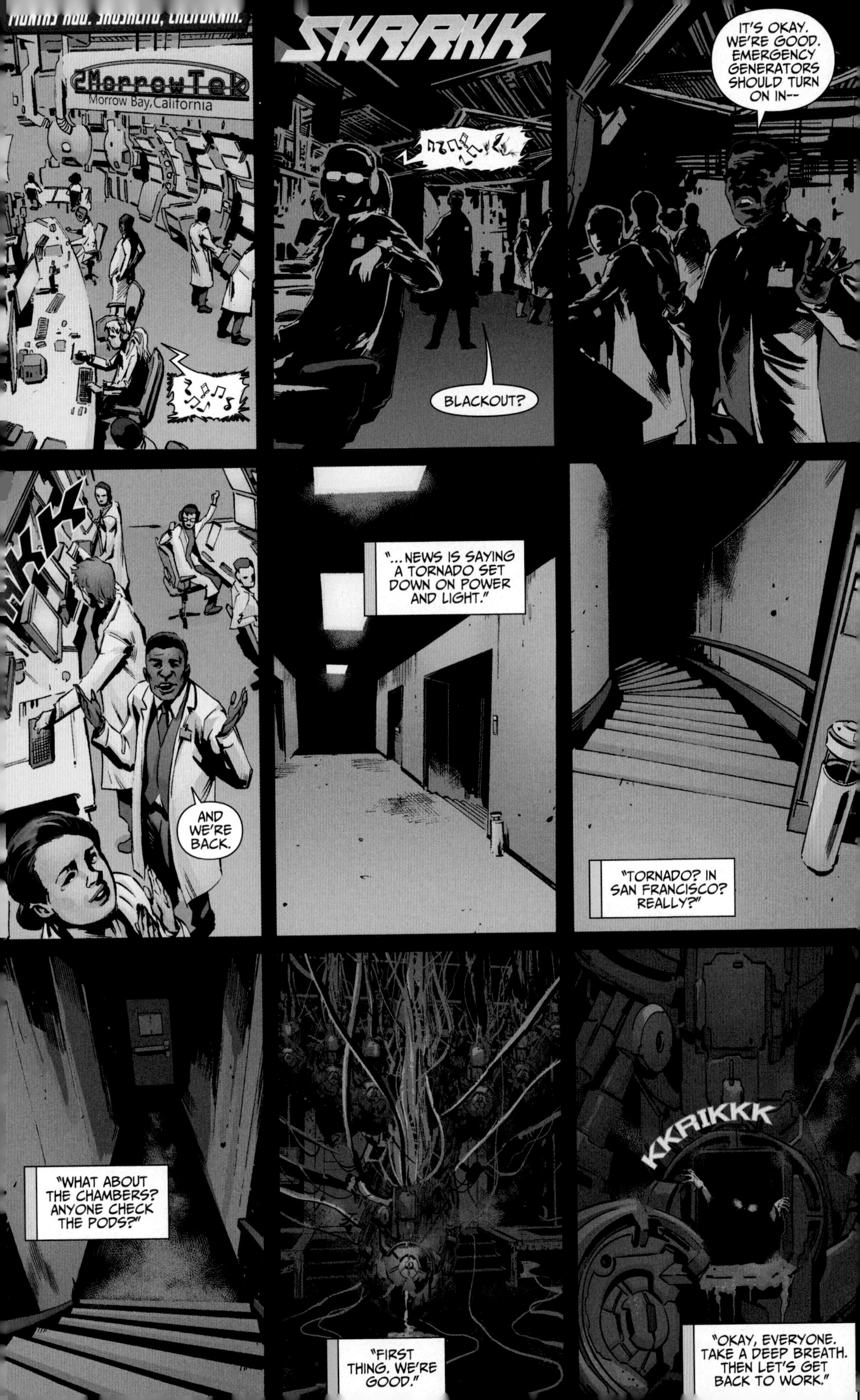
2MorrowTek
Morrow Bay, California
SKRKK
BLACKOUT?
IT'S OKAY. WE'RE GOOD. EMERGENCY GENERATORS SHOULD TURN ON IN--
AND WE'RE BACK.
"...NEWS IS SAYING A TORNADO SET DOWN ON POWER AND LIGHT."
"TORNADO? IN SAN FRANCISCO? REALLY?"
"WHAT ABOUT THE CHAMBERS? ANYONE CHECK THE PODS?"
"FIRST THING. WE'RE GOOD."
KKRIKKK
"OKAY, EVERYONE. TAKE A DEEP BREATH. THEN LET'S GET BACK TO WORK."

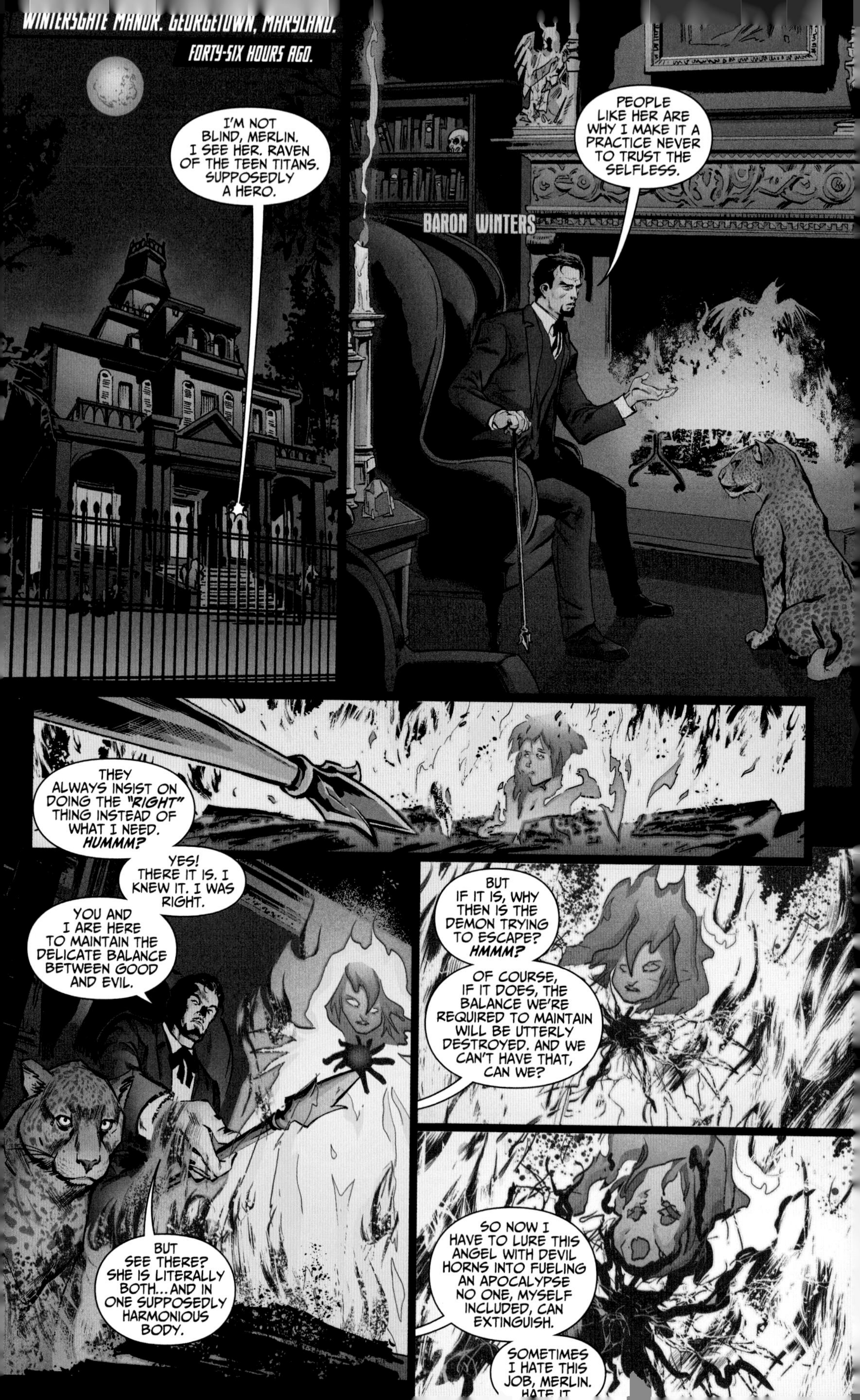
WINTERSGATE MANOR. GEORGETOWN, MARYLAND.
FORTY-SIX HOURS AGO.
I'M NOT BLIND, MERLIN. I SEE HER. RAVEN OF THE TEEN TITANS. SUPPOSEDLY A HERO.
BARON WINTERS
PEOPLE LIKE HER ARE WHY I MAKE IT A PRACTICE NEVER TO TRUST THE SELFLESS.
THEY ALWAYS INSIST ON DOING THE "RIGHT" THING INSTEAD OF WHAT I NEED. HUMMM?
YES! THERE IT IS. I KNEW IT. I WAS RIGHT.
YOU AND I ARE HERE TO MAINTAIN THE DELICATE BALANCE BETWEEN GOOD AND EVIL.
BUT SEE THERE? SHE IS LITERALLY BOTH...AND IN ONE SUPPOSEDLY HARMONIOUS BODY.
BUT IF IT IS, WHY THEN IS THE DEMON TRYING TO ESCAPE? HMMM?
OF COURSE, IF IT DOES, THE BALANCE WE'RE REQUIRED TO MAINTAIN WILL BE UTTERLY DESTROYED. AND WE CAN'T HAVE THAT, CAN WE?
SO NOW I HAVE TO LURE THIS ANGEL WITH DEVIL HORNS INTO FUELING AN APOCALYPSE NO ONE, MYSELF INCLUDED, CAN EXTINGUISH.
SOMETIMES I HATE THIS JOB, MERLIN.

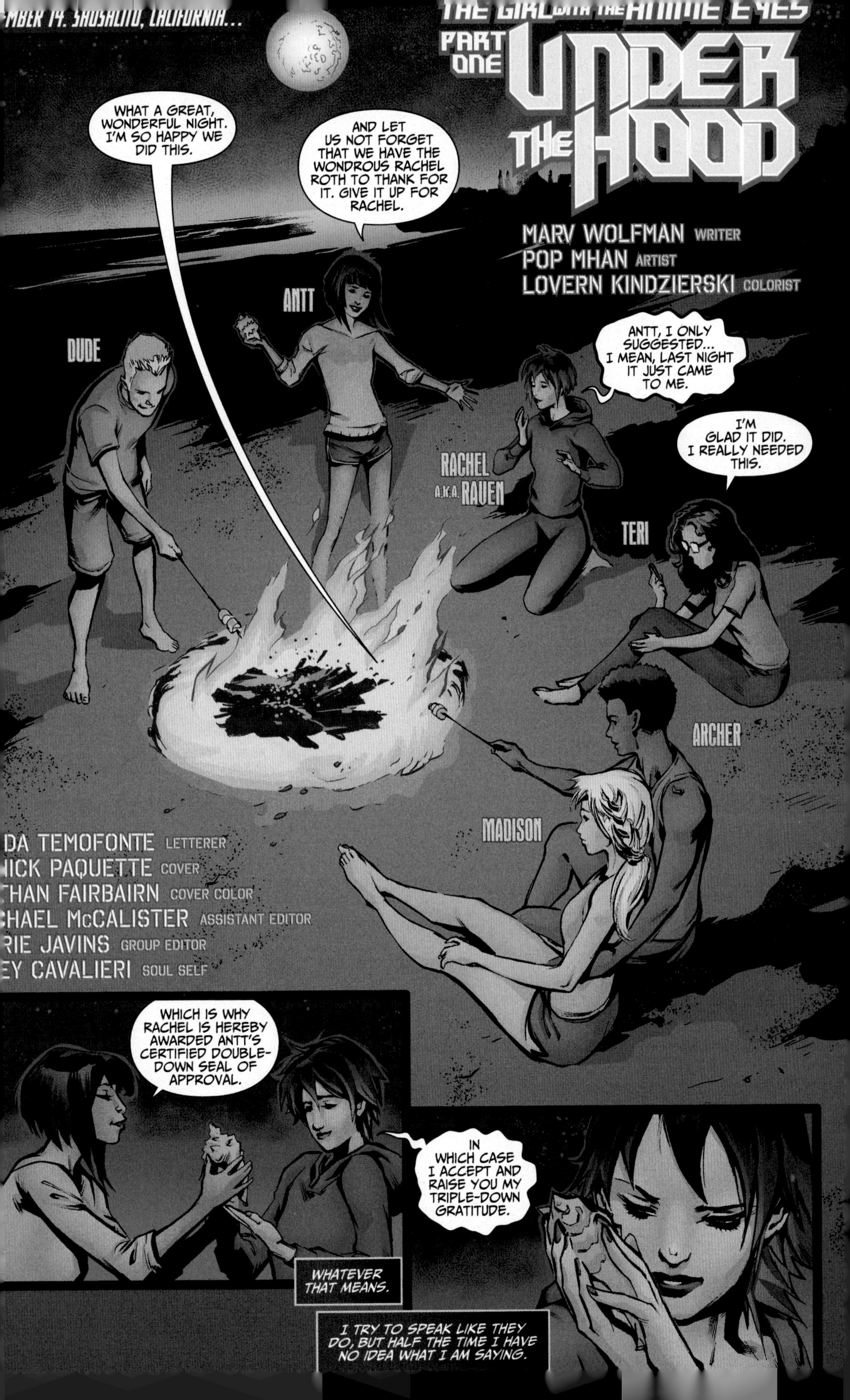

MBER 14. SAUSALITO, CALIFORNIA...
THE GIRL WITH THE ANIME EYES
PART ONE
UNDER THE HOOD
MARV WOLFMAN WRITER
POP MHAN ARTIST
LOVERN KINDZIERSKI COLORIST
WHAT A GREAT, WONDERFUL NIGHT. I'M SO HAPPY WE DID THIS.
AND LET US NOT FORGET THAT WE HAVE THE WONDROUS RACHEL ROTH TO THANK FOR IT. GIVE IT UP FOR RACHEL.
ANTT
DUDE
ANTT, I ONLY SUGGESTED... I MEAN, LAST NIGHT IT JUST CAME TO ME.
I'M GLAD IT DID. I REALLY NEEDED THIS.
RACHEL A.K.A. RAVEN
TERI
ARCHER
MADISON
DA TEMOFONTE LETTERER
ICK PAQUETTE COVER
THAN FAIRBAIRN COVER COLOR
HAEL McCALISTER ASSISTANT EDITOR
RIE JAVINS GROUP EDITOR
EY CAVALIERI SOUL SELF
WHICH IS WHY RACHEL IS HEREBY AWARDED ANTT'S CERTIFIED DOUBLE-DOWN SEAL OF APPROVAL.
IN WHICH CASE I ACCEPT AND RAISE YOU MY TRIPLE-DOWN GRATITUDE.
WHATEVER THAT MEANS.
I TRY TO SPEAK LIKE THEY DO, BUT HALF THE TIME I HAVE NO IDEA WHAT I AM SAYING.

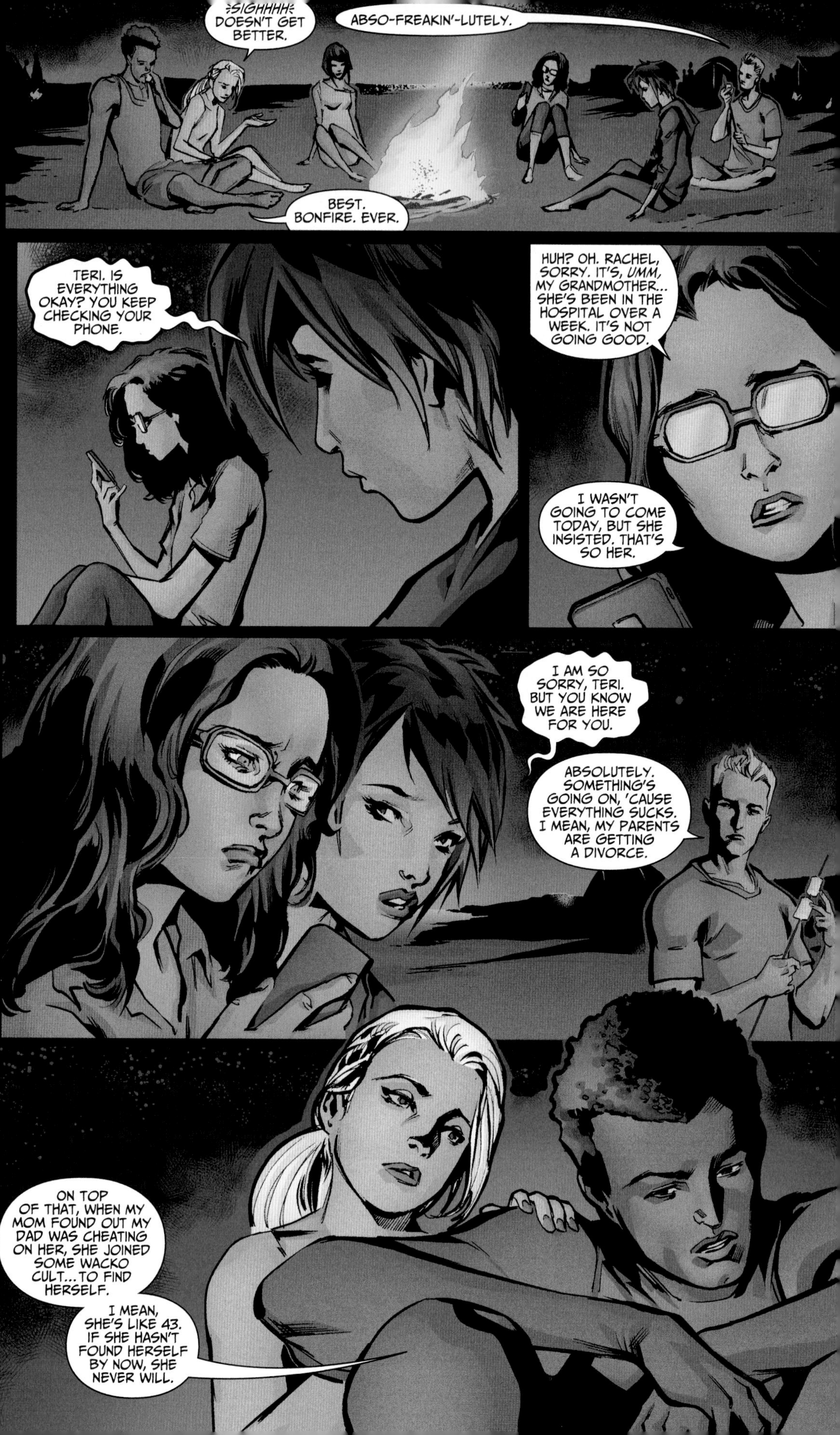

SIGHHHH
DOESN'T GET BETTER.
ABSO-FREAKIN'-LUTELY.
BEST. BONFIRE. EVER.
TERI. IS EVERYTHING OKAY? YOU KEEP CHECKING YOUR PHONE.
HUH? OH. RACHEL, SORRY. IT'S, *UMM*, MY GRANDMOTHER... SHE'S BEEN IN THE HOSPITAL OVER A WEEK. IT'S NOT GOING GOOD.
I WASN'T GOING TO COME TODAY, BUT SHE INSISTED. THAT'S SO HER.
I AM SO SORRY, TERI. BUT YOU KNOW WE ARE HERE FOR YOU.
ABSOLUTELY. SOMETHING'S GOING ON, 'CAUSE EVERYTHING SUCKS. I MEAN, MY PARENTS ARE GETTING A DIVORCE.
ON TOP OF THAT, WHEN MY MOM FOUND OUT MY DAD WAS CHEATING ON HER, SHE JOINED SOME WACKO CULT...TO FIND HERSELF.
I MEAN, SHE'S LIKE 43. IF SHE HASN'T FOUND HERSELF BY NOW, SHE NEVER WILL.

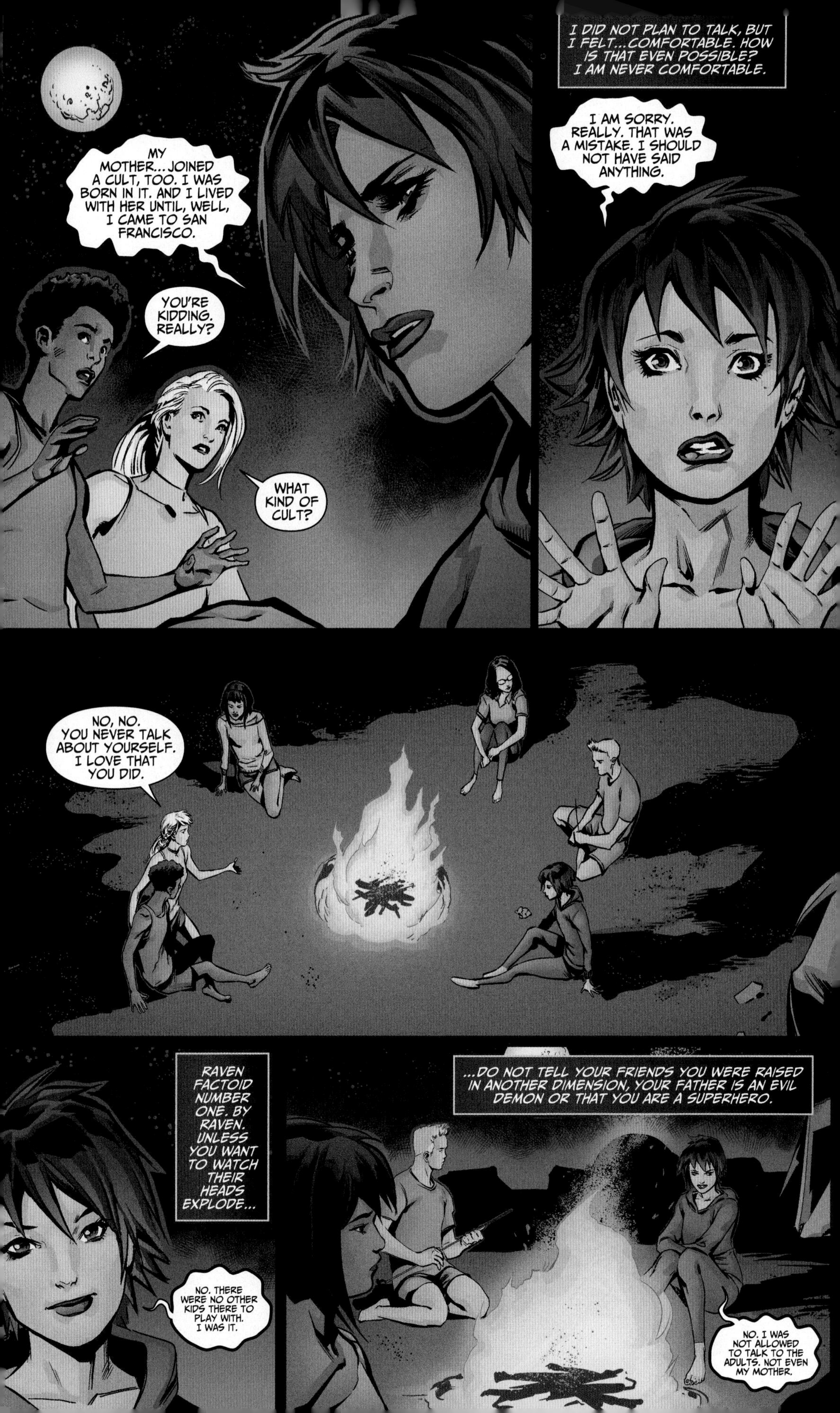
MY MOTHER... JOINED A CULT, TOO. I WAS BORN IN IT. AND I LIVED WITH HER UNTIL, WELL, I CAME TO SAN FRANCISCO.
YOU'RE KIDDING. REALLY?
WHAT KIND OF CULT?
I DID NOT PLAN TO TALK, BUT I FELT...COMFORTABLE. HOW IS THAT EVEN POSSIBLE? I AM NEVER COMFORTABLE.
I AM SORRY. REALLY. THAT WAS A MISTAKE. I SHOULD NOT HAVE SAID ANYTHING.
NO, NO. YOU NEVER TALK ABOUT YOURSELF. I LOVE THAT YOU DID.
RAVEN FACTOID NUMBER ONE. BY RAVEN. UNLESS YOU WANT TO WATCH THEIR HEADS EXPLODE...
NO. THERE WERE NO OTHER KIDS THERE TO PLAY WITH. I WAS IT.
...DO NOT TELL YOUR FRIENDS YOU WERE RAISED IN ANOTHER DIMENSION, YOUR FATHER IS AN EVIL DEMON OR THAT YOU ARE A SUPERHERO.
NO. I WAS NOT ALLOWED TO TALK TO THE ADULTS. NOT EVEN MY MOTHER.

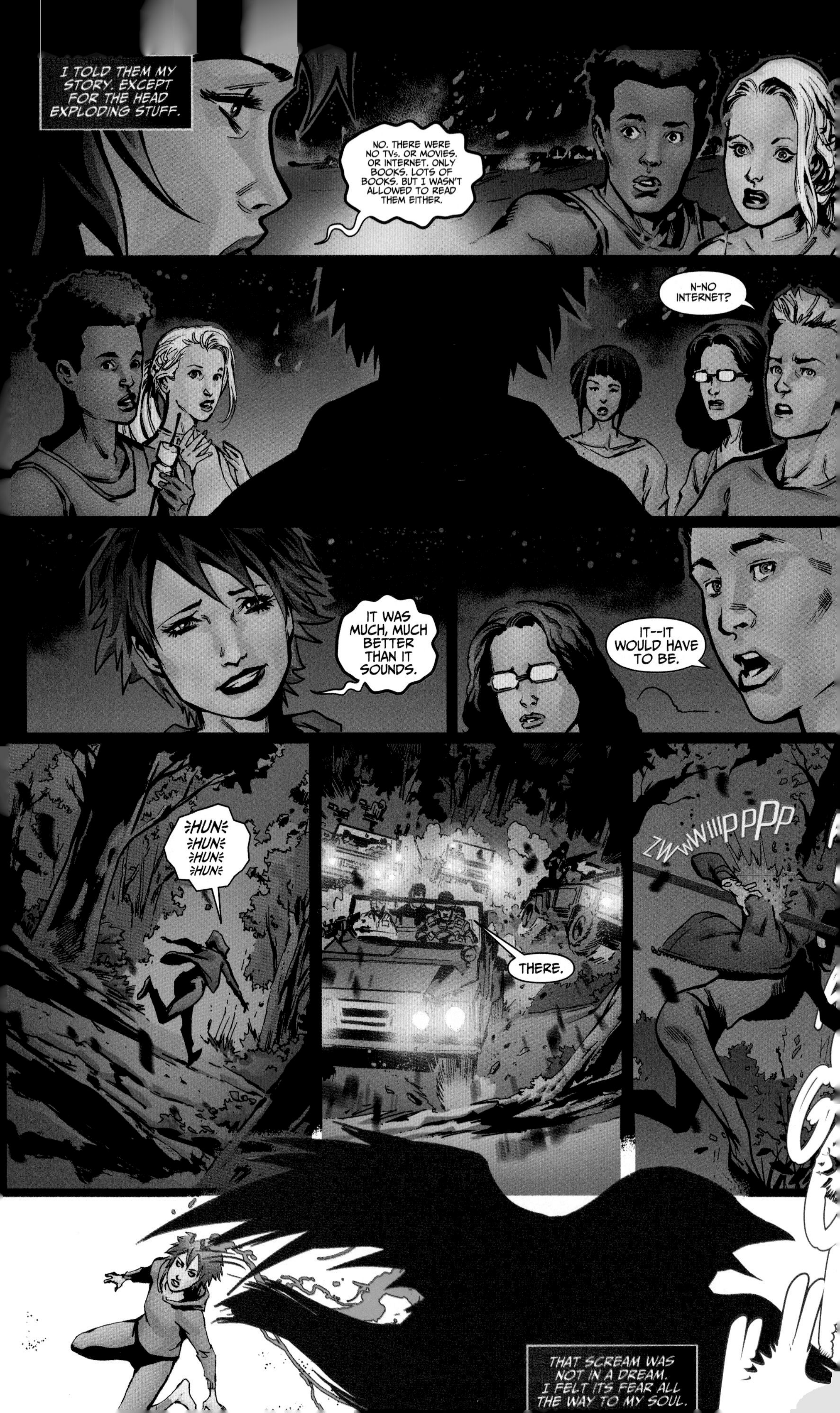
I TOLD THEM MY STORY. EXCEPT FOR THE HEAD EXPLODING STUFF.
NO. THERE WERE NO TVs. OR MOVIES. OR INTERNET. ONLY BOOKS. LOTS OF BOOKS. BUT I WASN'T ALLOWED TO READ THEM EITHER.
N-NO INTERNET?
IT WAS MUCH, MUCH BETTER THAN IT SOUNDS.
IT--IT WOULD HAVE TO BE.
HUN HUN HUN HUN HUN
THERE.
ZWWWIIIPPPP
THAT SCREAM WAS NOT IN A DREAM. I FELT ITS FEAR ALL THE WAY TO MY SOUL.

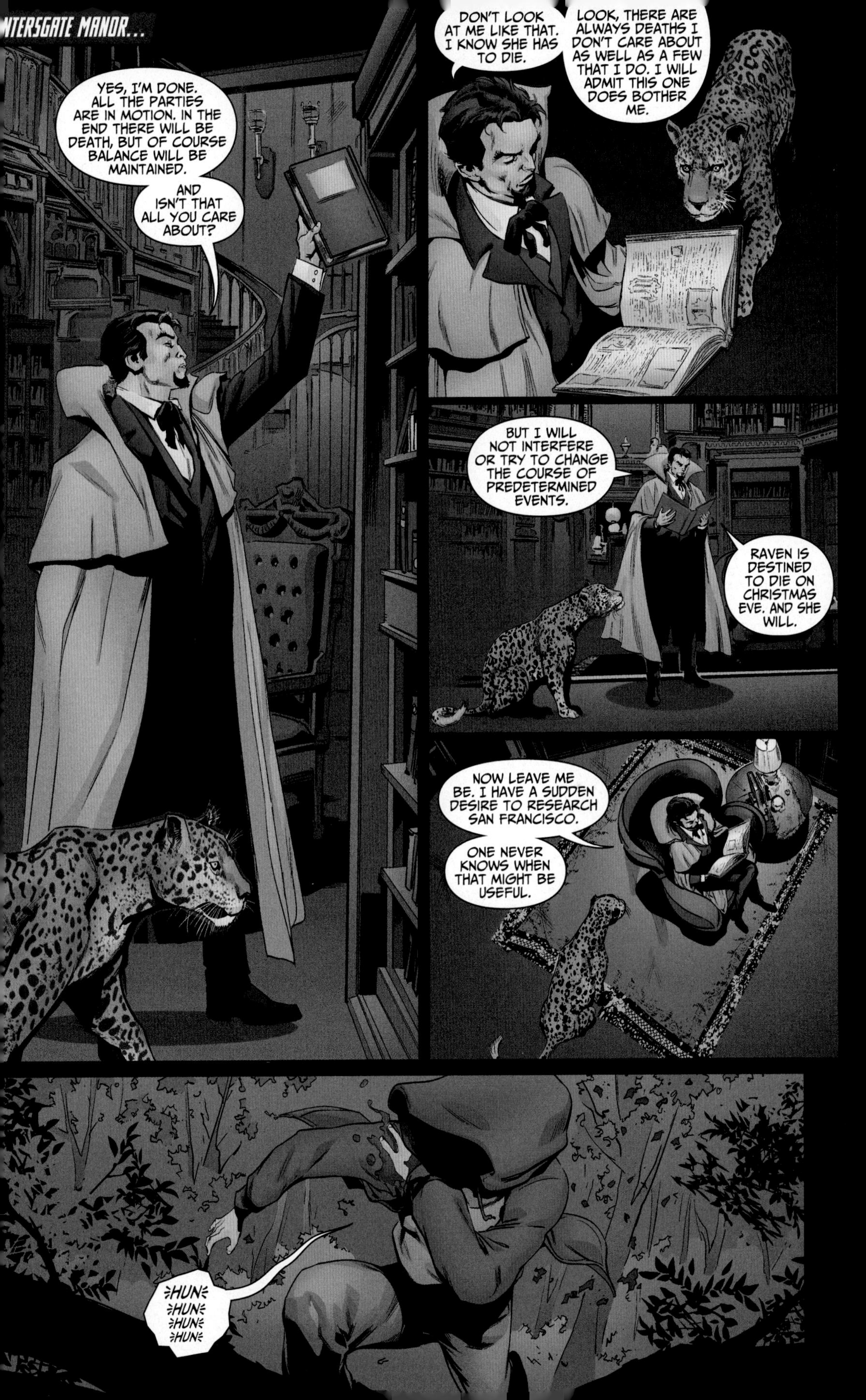
NTERSGATE MANOR...
YES, I'M DONE. ALL THE PARTIES ARE IN MOTION. IN THE END THERE WILL BE DEATH, BUT OF COURSE BALANCE WILL BE MAINTAINED.
AND ISN'T THAT ALL YOU CARE ABOUT?
DON'T LOOK AT ME LIKE THAT. I KNOW SHE HAS TO DIE.
LOOK, THERE ARE ALWAYS DEATHS I DON'T CARE ABOUT AS WELL AS A FEW THAT I DO. I WILL ADMIT THIS ONE DOES BOTHER ME.
BUT I WILL NOT INTERFERE OR TRY TO CHANGE THE COURSE OF PREDETERMINED EVENTS.
RAVEN IS DESTINED TO DIE ON CHRISTMAS EVE. AND SHE WILL.
NOW LEAVE ME BE. I HAVE A SUDDEN DESIRE TO RESEARCH SAN FRANCISCO.
ONE NEVER KNOWS WHEN THAT MIGHT BE USEFUL.
HUN HUN HUN HUN

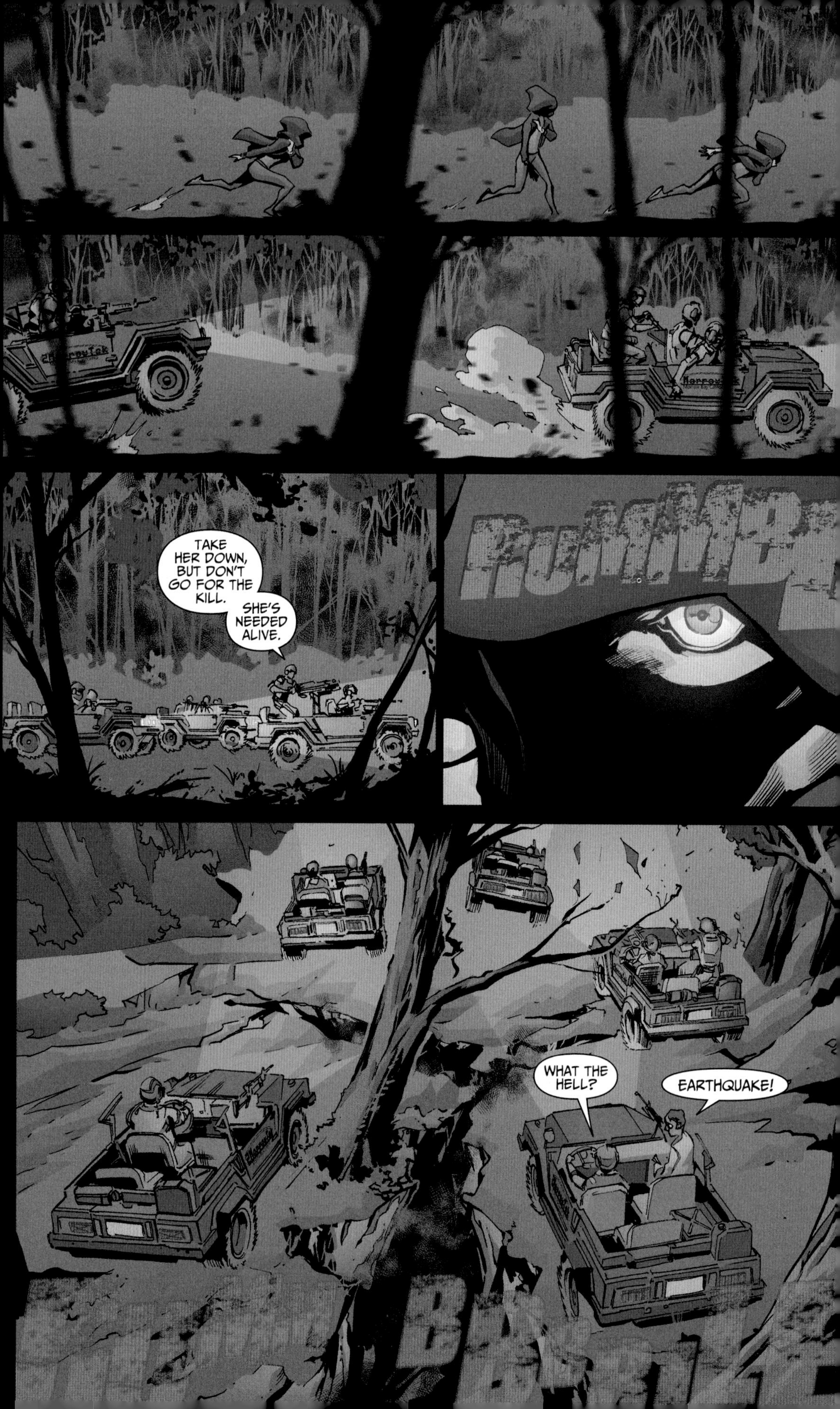
TAKE HER DOWN, BUT DON'T GO FOR THE KILL.
SHE'S NEEDED ALIVE.
WHAT THE HELL?
EARTHQUAKE!

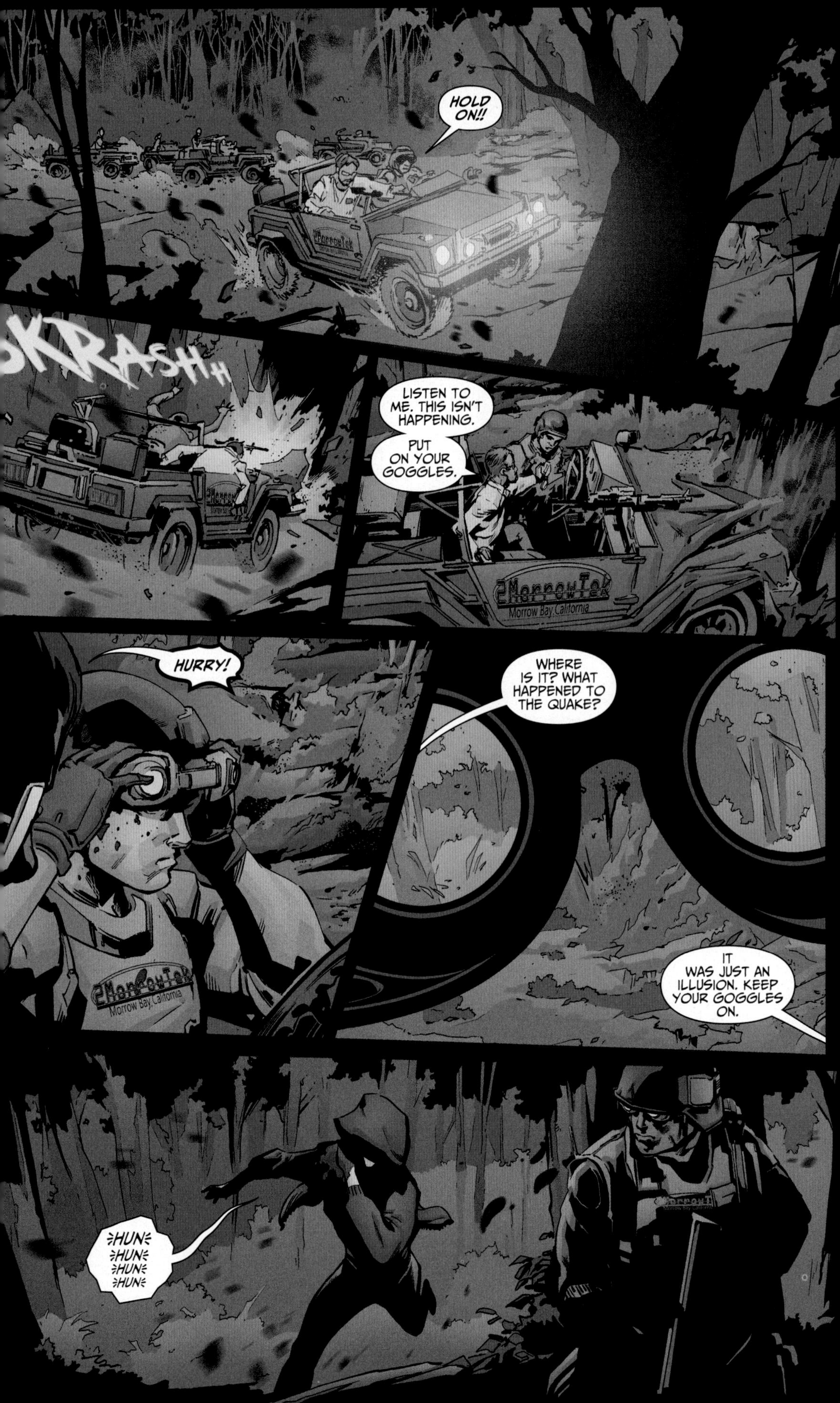

HOLD ON!!
SKRASHH
2MorrowTek
LISTEN TO ME. THIS ISN'T HAPPENING.
PUT ON YOUR GOGGLES.
2MorrowTek
Morrow Bay, California
HURRY!
WHERE IS IT? WHAT HAPPENED TO THE QUAKE?
2MorrowTek
Morrow Bay, California
IT WAS JUST AN ILLUSION. KEEP YOUR GOGGLES ON.
HUN HUN HUN HUN

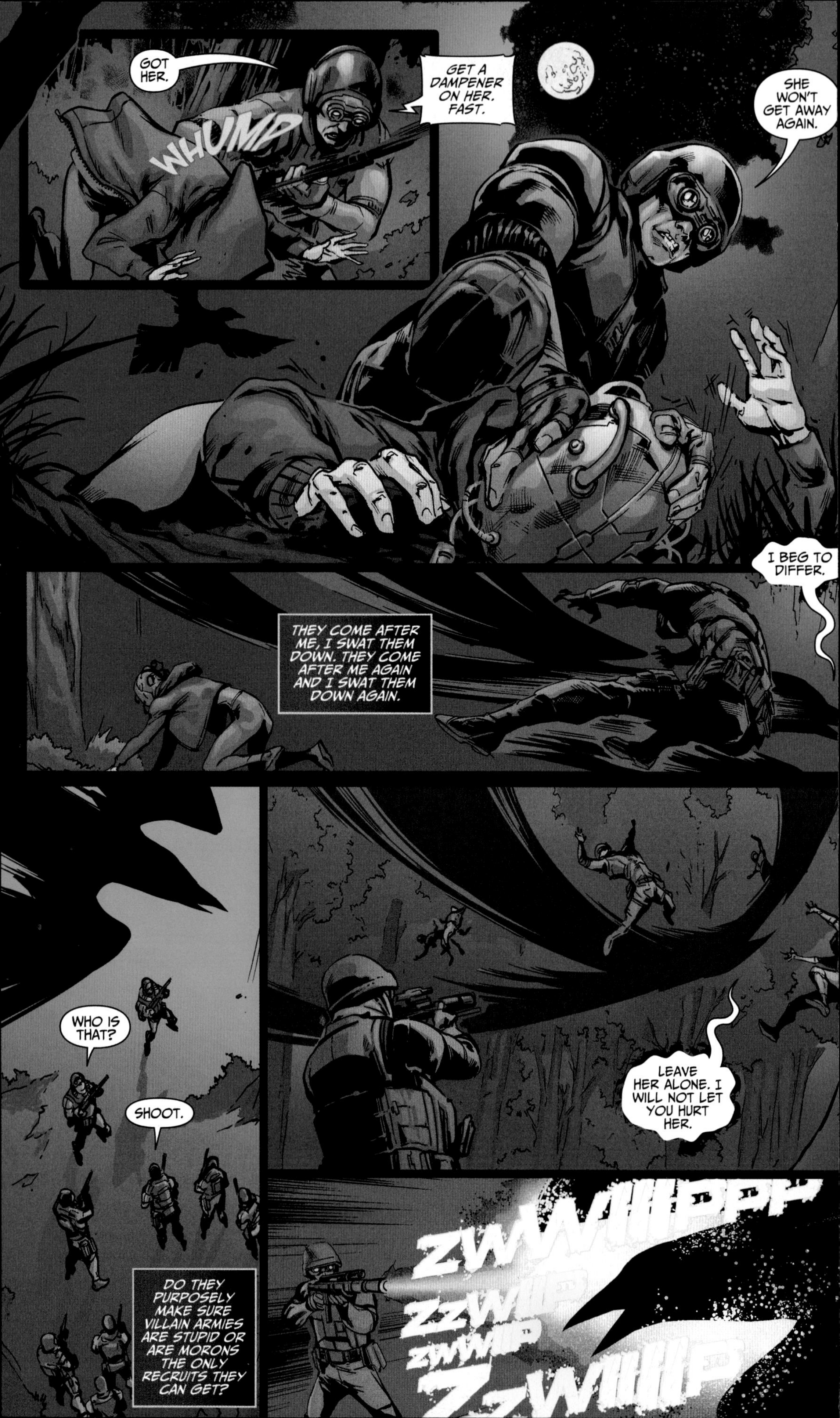
GOT HER.
WHUMP
GET A DAMPENER ON HER. FAST.
SHE WON'T GET AWAY AGAIN.
I BEG TO DIFFER.
THEY COME AFTER ME, I SWAT THEM DOWN. THEY COME AFTER ME AGAIN AND I SWAT THEM DOWN AGAIN.
WHO IS THAT?
SHOOT.
DO THEY PURPOSELY MAKE SURE VILLAIN ARMIES ARE STUPID OR ARE MORONS THE ONLY RECRUITS THEY CAN GET?
LEAVE HER ALONE. I WILL NOT LET YOU HURT HER.
ZWHHPPP
ZZWHIP
ZWWHIP
ZZWHHP

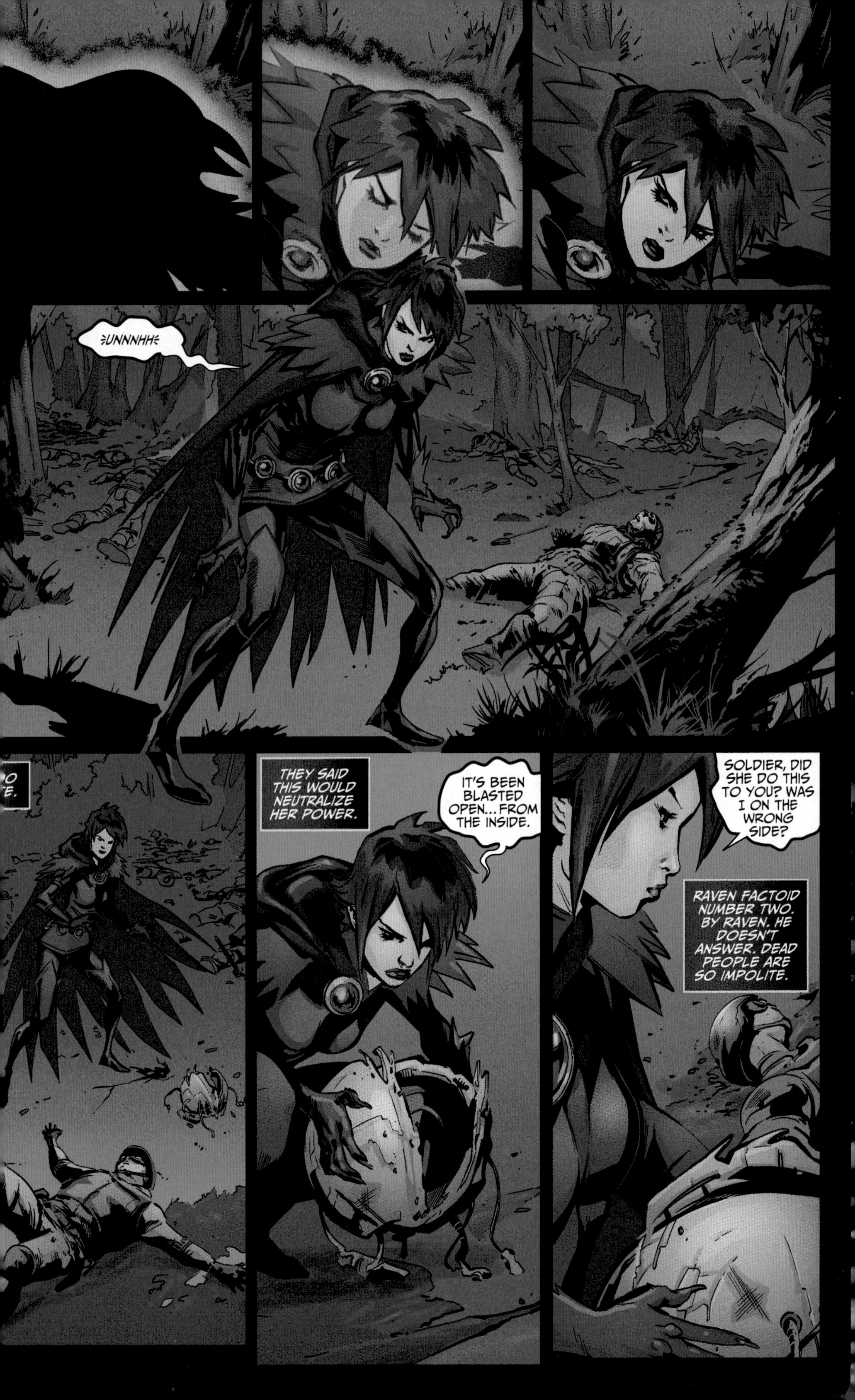
UNNNHH
THEY SAID THIS WOULD NEUTRALIZE HER POWER.
IT'S BEEN BLASTED OPEN... FROM THE INSIDE.
SOLDIER, DID SHE DO THIS TO YOU? WAS I ON THE WRONG SIDE?
RAVEN FACTOID NUMBER TWO. BY RAVEN. HE DOESN'T ANSWER. DEAD PEOPLE ARE SO IMPOLITE.

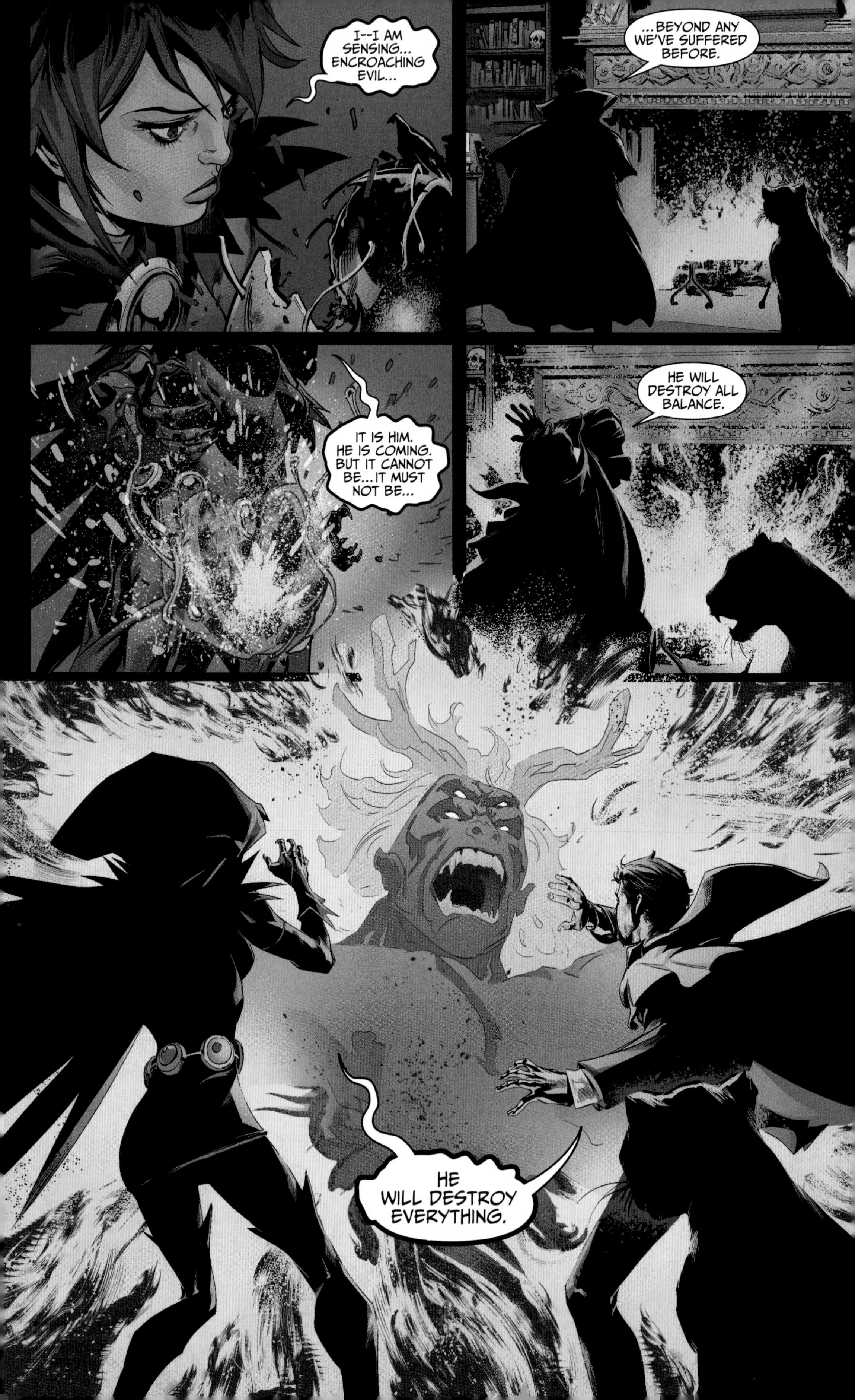
I--I AM SENSING... ENCROACHING EVIL...
...BEYOND ANY WE'VE SUFFERED BEFORE.
IT IS HIM. HE IS COMING. BUT IT CANNOT BE...IT MUST NOT BE...
HE WILL DESTROY ALL BALANCE.
HE WILL DESTROY EVERYTHING.

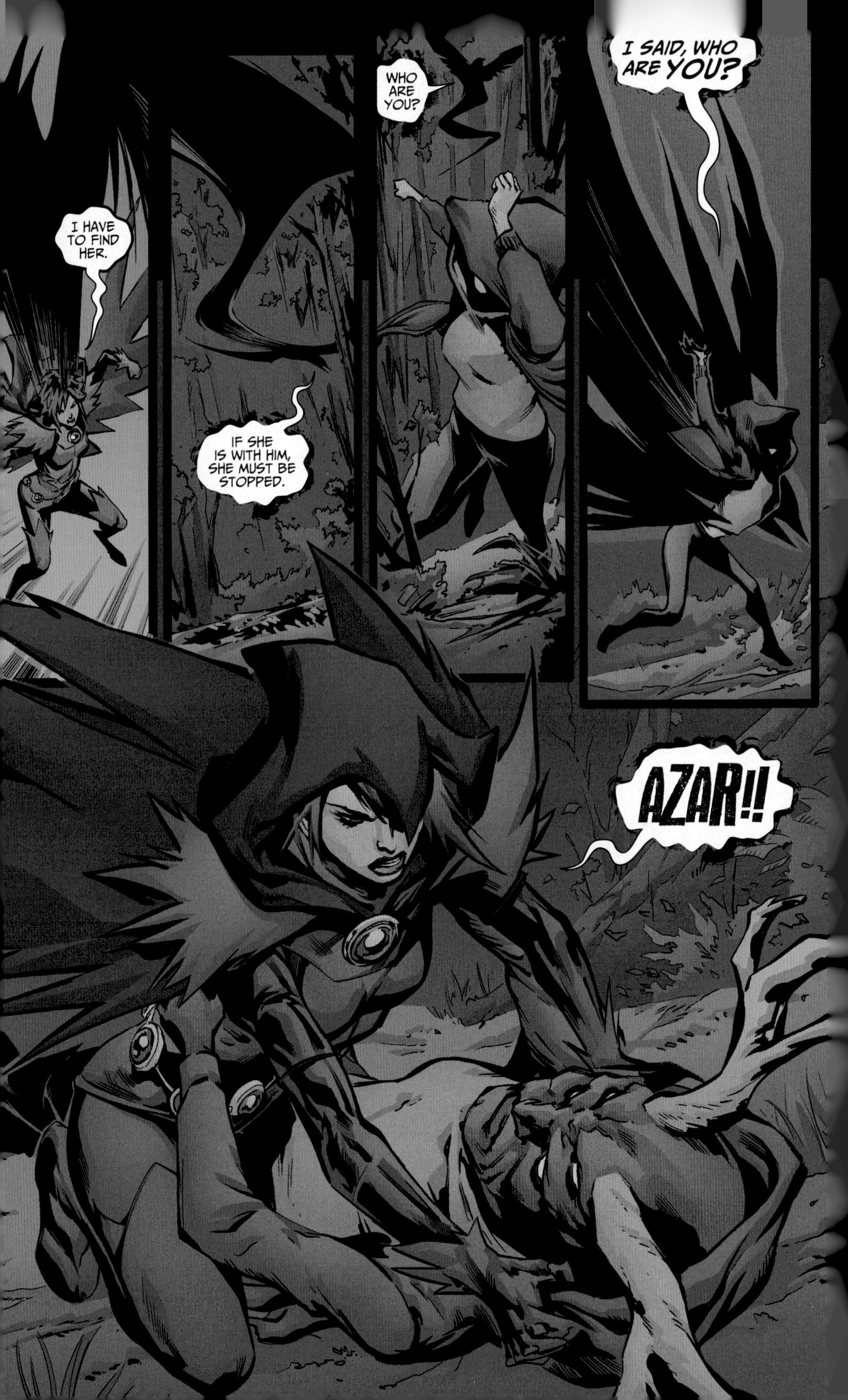
I HAVE TO FIND HER.
IF SHE IS WITH HIM, SHE MUST BE STOPPED.
WHO ARE YOU?
I SAID, WHO ARE YOU?
AZAR!!

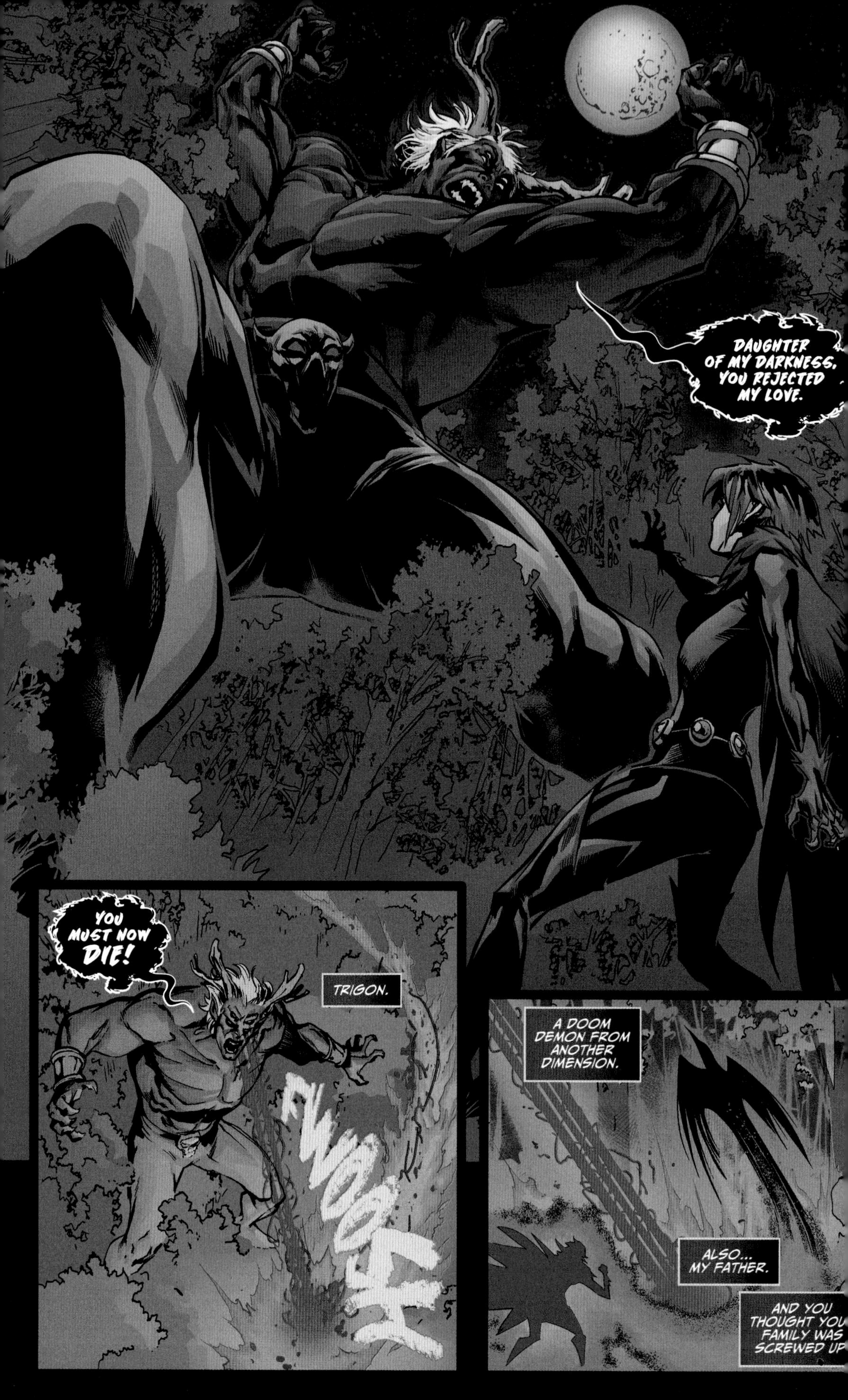
DAUGHTER OF MY DARKNESS, YOU REJECTED MY LOVE.
YOU MUST NOW DIE!
TRIGON.
FWOOOSH
A DOOM DEMON FROM ANOTHER DIMENSION.
ALSO... MY FATHER.
AND YOU THOUGHT YOU FAMILY WAS SCREWED UP

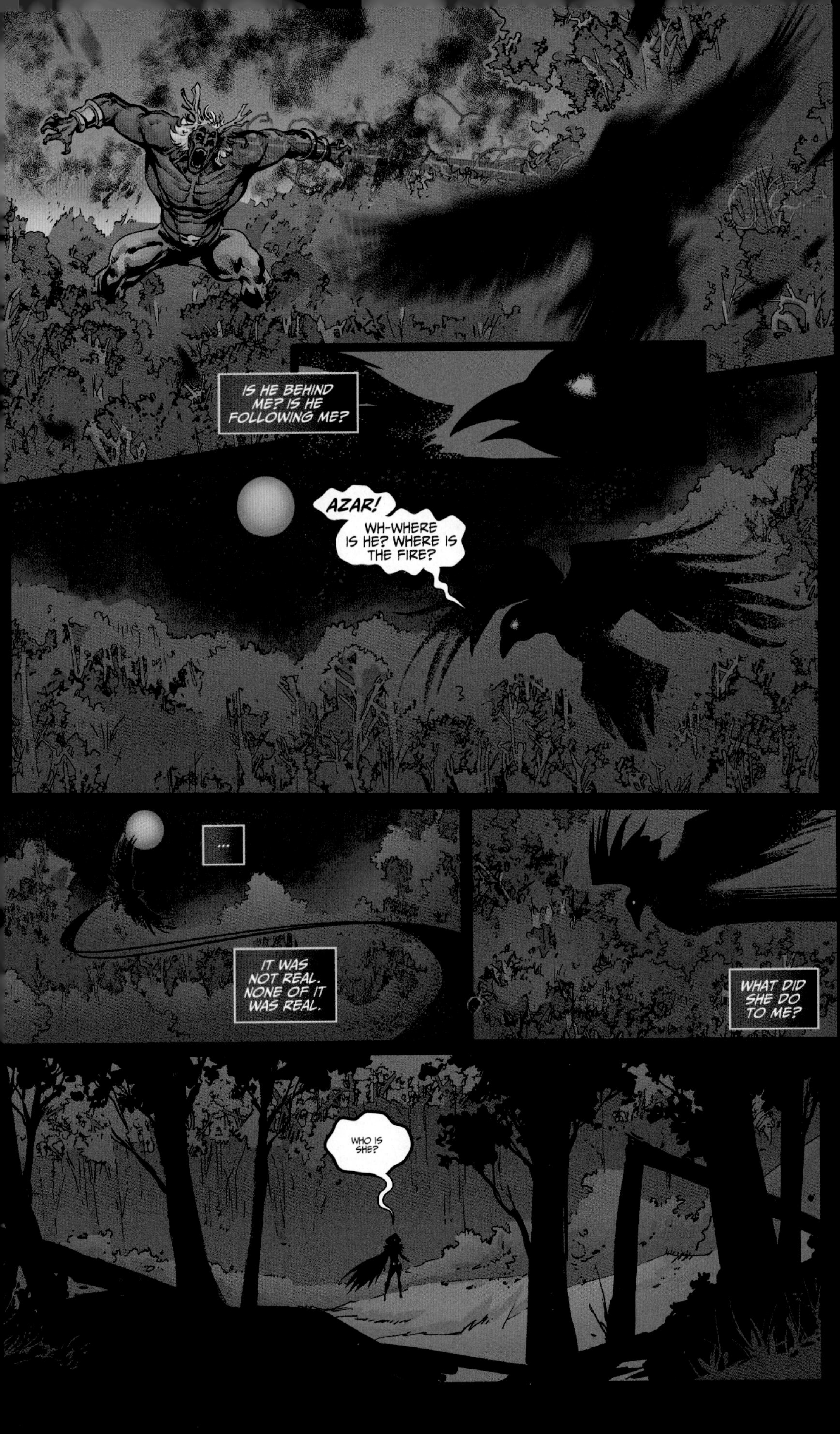
IS HE BEHIND ME? IS HE FOLLOWING ME?
AZAR!
WH-WHERE IS HE? WHERE IS THE FIRE?
...
IT WAS NOT REAL. NONE OF IT WAS REAL.
WHAT DID SHE DO TO ME?
WHO IS SHE?

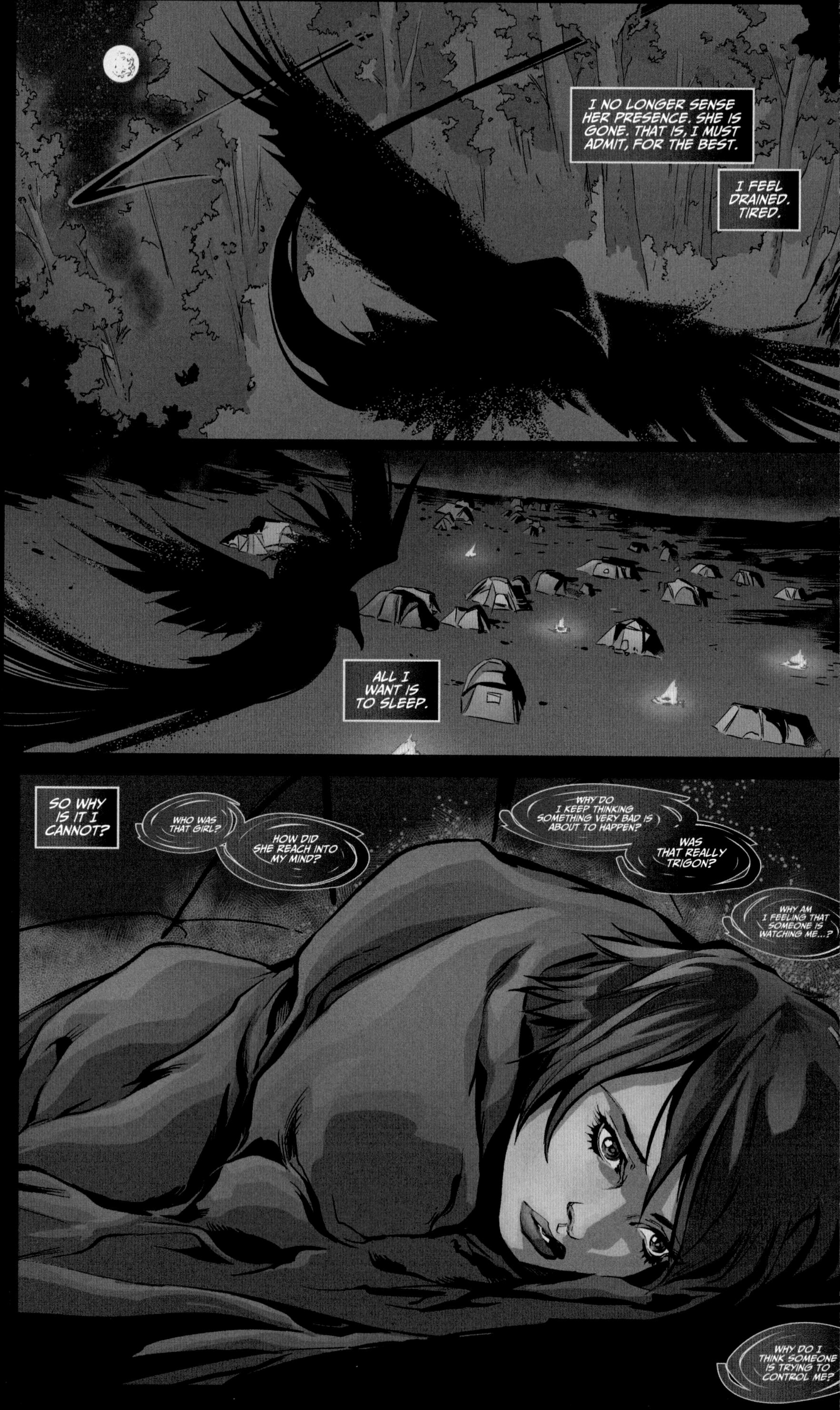

I NO LONGER SENSE HER PRESENCE. SHE IS GONE. THAT IS, I MUST ADMIT, FOR THE BEST.
I FEEL DRAINED. TIRED.
ALL I WANT IS TO SLEEP.
SO WHY IS IT I CANNOT?
WHO WAS THAT GIRL?
HOW DID SHE REACH INTO MY MIND?
WHY DO I KEEP THINKING SOMETHING VERY BAD IS ABOUT TO HAPPEN?
WAS THAT REALLY TRIGON?
WHY AM I FEELING THAT SOMEONE IS WATCHING ME...?
WHY DO I THINK SOMEONE IS TRYING TO CONTROL ME?

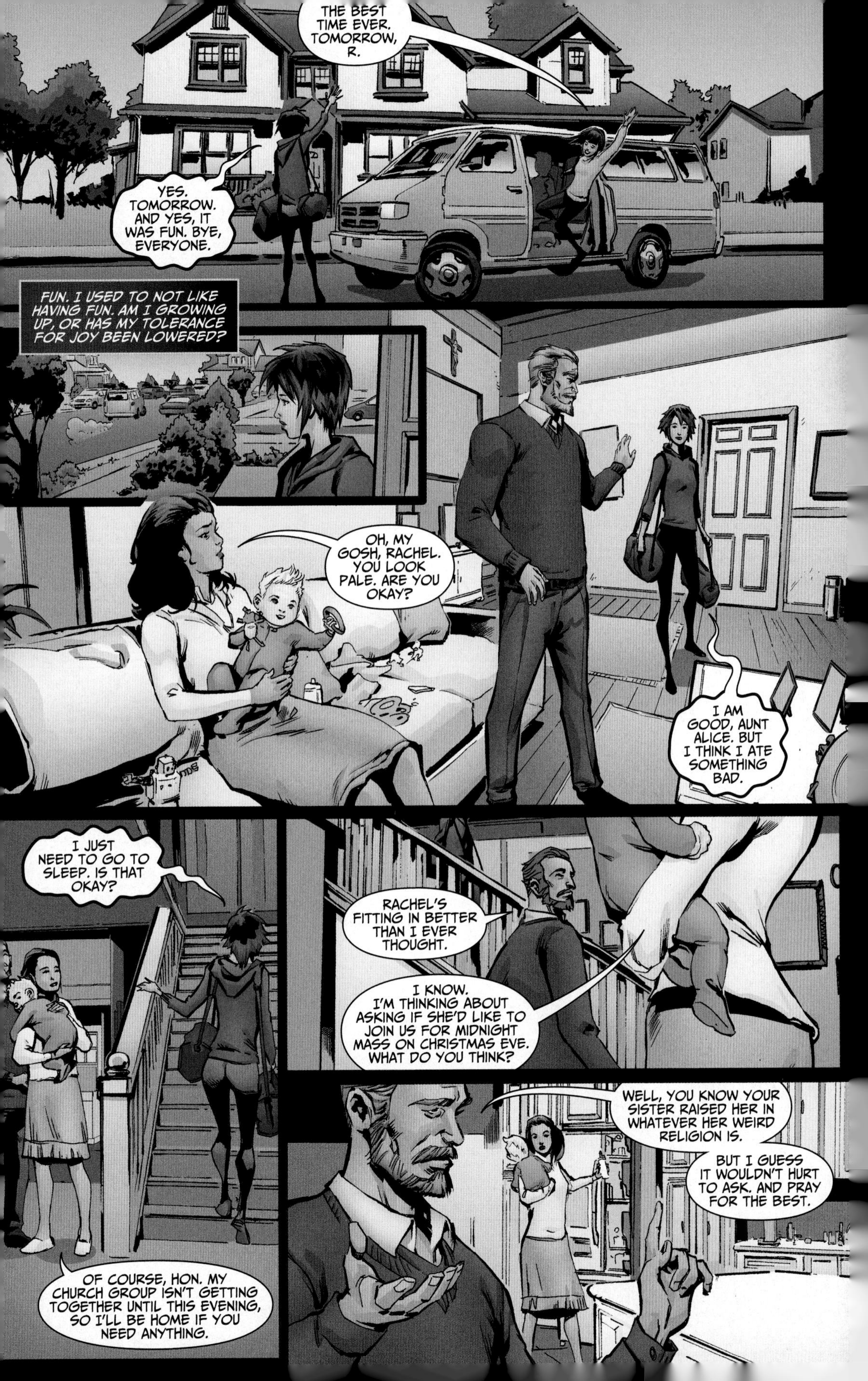
THE BEST TIME EVER. TOMORROW, R.
YES. TOMORROW. AND YES, IT WAS FUN. BYE, EVERYONE.
FUN. I USED TO NOT LIKE HAVING FUN. AM I GROWING UP, OR HAS MY TOLERANCE FOR JOY BEEN LOWERED?
OH, MY GOSH, RACHEL. YOU LOOK PALE. ARE YOU OKAY?
I AM GOOD, AUNT ALICE. BUT I THINK I ATE SOMETHING BAD.
I JUST NEED TO GO TO SLEEP. IS THAT OKAY?
OF COURSE, HON. MY CHURCH GROUP ISN'T GETTING TOGETHER UNTIL THIS EVENING, SO I'LL BE HOME IF YOU NEED ANYTHING.
RACHEL'S FITTING IN BETTER THAN I EVER THOUGHT.
I KNOW. I'M THINKING ABOUT ASKING IF SHE'D LIKE TO JOIN US FOR MIDNIGHT MASS ON CHRISTMAS EVE. WHAT DO YOU THINK?
WELL, YOU KNOW YOUR SISTER RAISED HER IN WHATEVER HER WEIRD RELIGION IS.
BUT I GUESS IT WOULDN'T HURT TO ASK. AND PRAY FOR THE BEST.

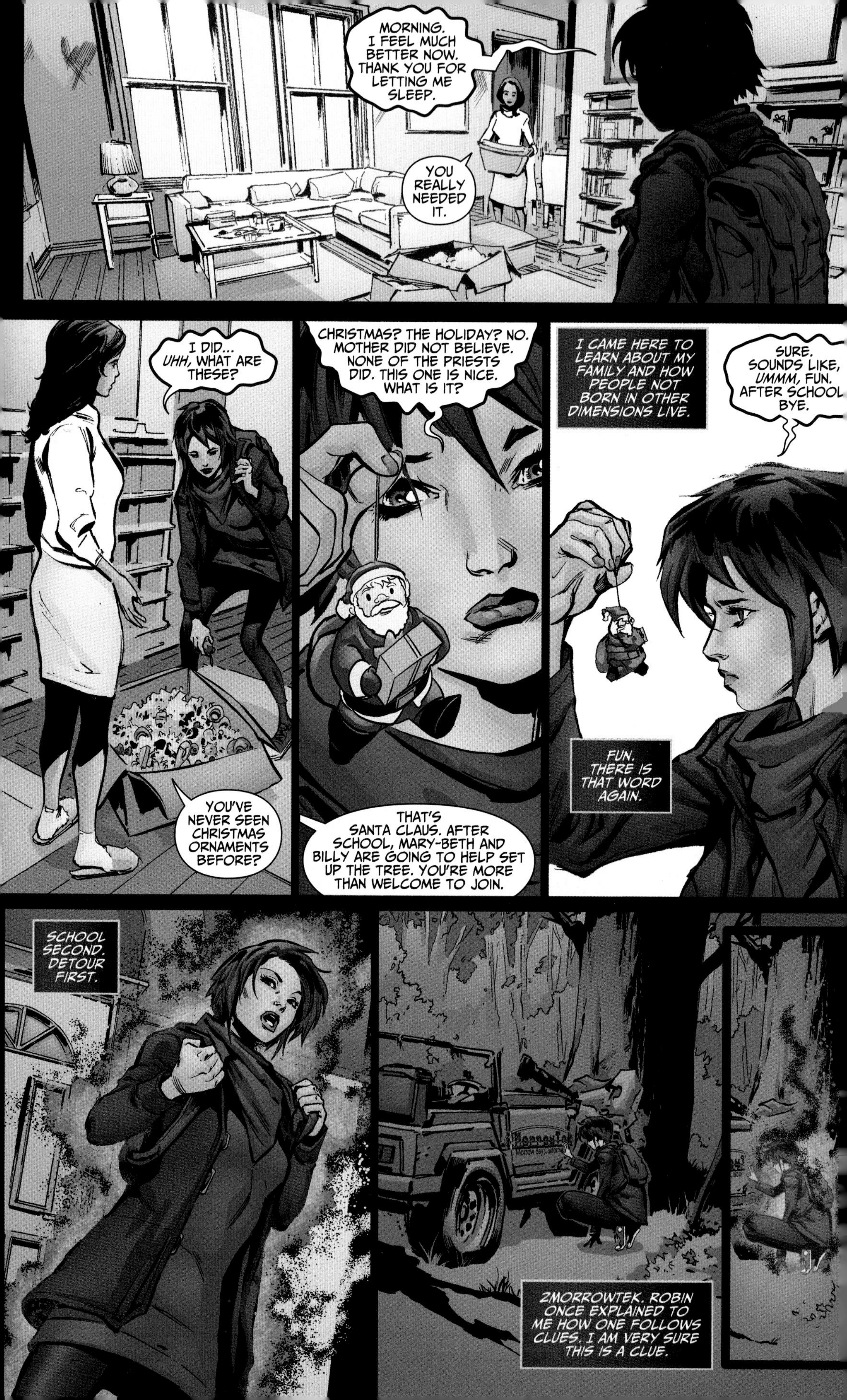
MORNING. I FEEL MUCH BETTER NOW. THANK YOU FOR LETTING ME SLEEP.
YOU REALLY NEEDED IT.
I DID... UHH, WHAT ARE THESE?
YOU'VE NEVER SEEN CHRISTMAS ORNAMENTS BEFORE?
CHRISTMAS? THE HOLIDAY? NO. MOTHER DID NOT BELIEVE. NONE OF THE PRIESTS DID. THIS ONE IS NICE. WHAT IS IT?
THAT'S SANTA CLAUS. AFTER SCHOOL, MARY-BETH AND BILLY ARE GOING TO HELP SET UP THE TREE. YOU'RE MORE THAN WELCOME TO JOIN.
I CAME HERE TO LEARN ABOUT MY FAMILY AND HOW PEOPLE NOT BORN IN OTHER DIMENSIONS LIVE.
SURE. SOUNDS LIKE, UMMM, FUN. AFTER SCHOOL BYE.
FUN. THERE IS THAT WORD AGAIN.
SCHOOL SECOND. DETOUR FIRST.
2MORROWTEK. ROBIN ONCE EXPLAINED TO ME HOW ONE FOLLOWS CLUES. I AM VERY SURE THIS IS A CLUE.

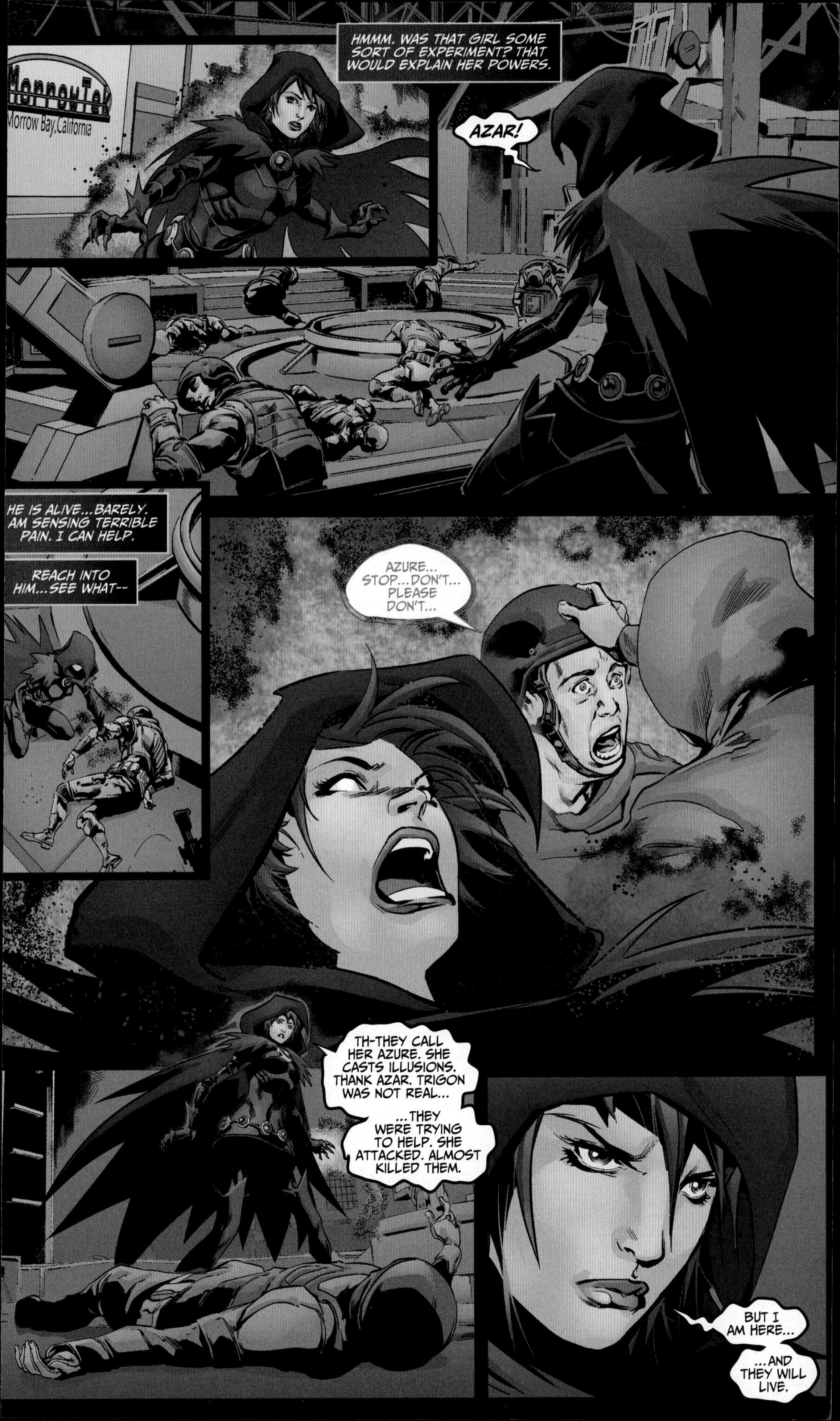

MorrowTek
Morrow Bay, California
HMMM. WAS THAT GIRL SOME SORT OF EXPERIMENT? THAT WOULD EXPLAIN HER POWERS.
AZAR!
HE IS ALIVE...BARELY. AM SENSING TERRIBLE PAIN. I CAN HELP.
REACH INTO HIM...SEE WHAT--
AZURE... STOP...DON'T... PLEASE DON'T...
TH-THEY CALL HER AZURE. SHE CASTS ILLUSIONS. THANK AZAR. TRIGON WAS NOT REAL...
...THEY WERE TRYING TO HELP. SHE ATTACKED. ALMOST KILLED THEM.
BUT I AM HERE...
...AND THEY WILL LIVE.

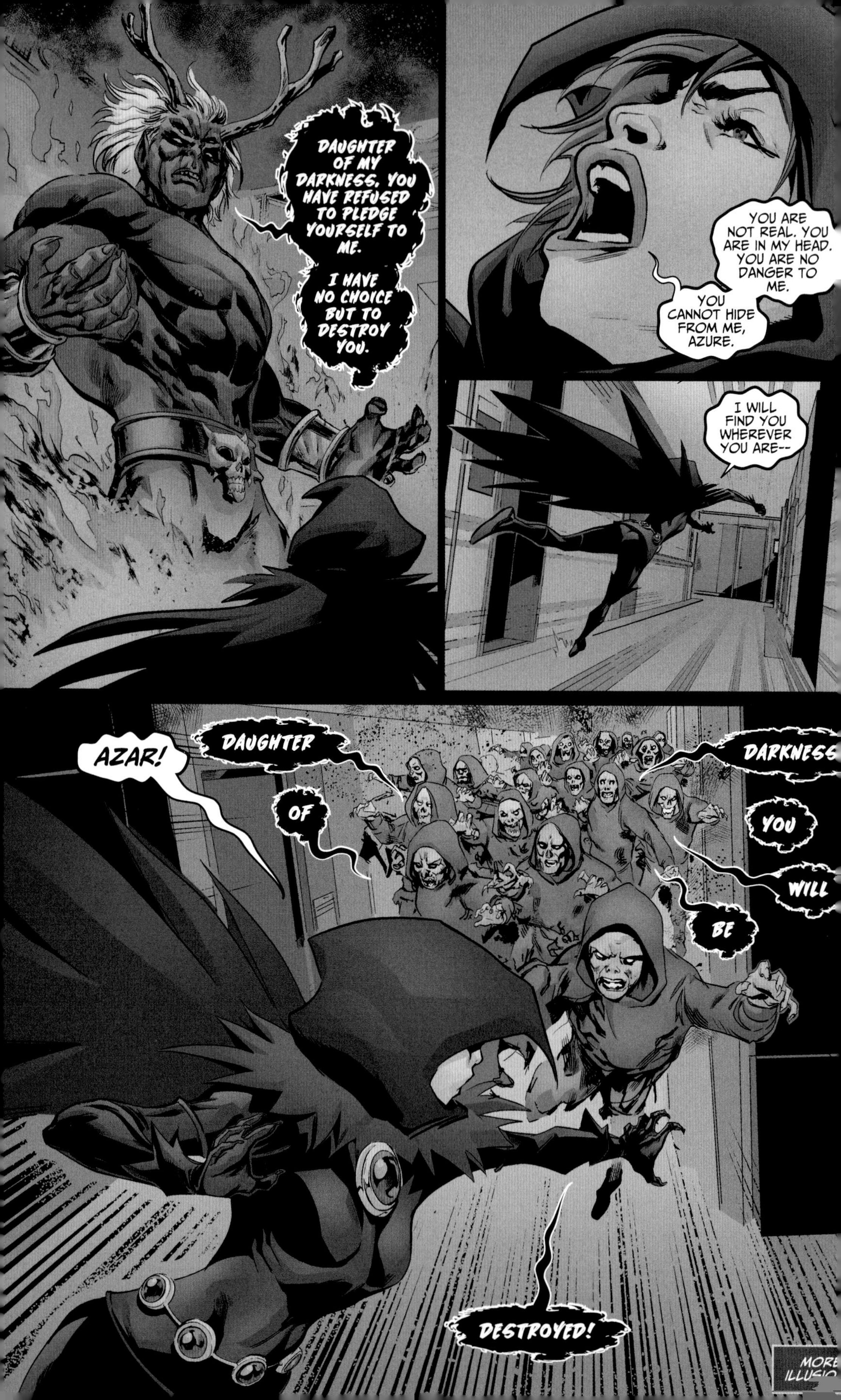
DAUGHTER OF MY DARKNESS. YOU HAVE REFUSED TO PLEDGE YOURSELF TO ME.
I HAVE NO CHOICE BUT TO DESTROY YOU.
YOU ARE NOT REAL. YOU ARE IN MY HEAD. YOU ARE NO DANGER TO ME.
YOU CANNOT HIDE FROM ME, AZURE.
I WILL FIND YOU WHEREVER YOU ARE--
AZAR!
DAUGHTER
OF
DARKNESS
YOU
WILL
BE
DESTROYED!

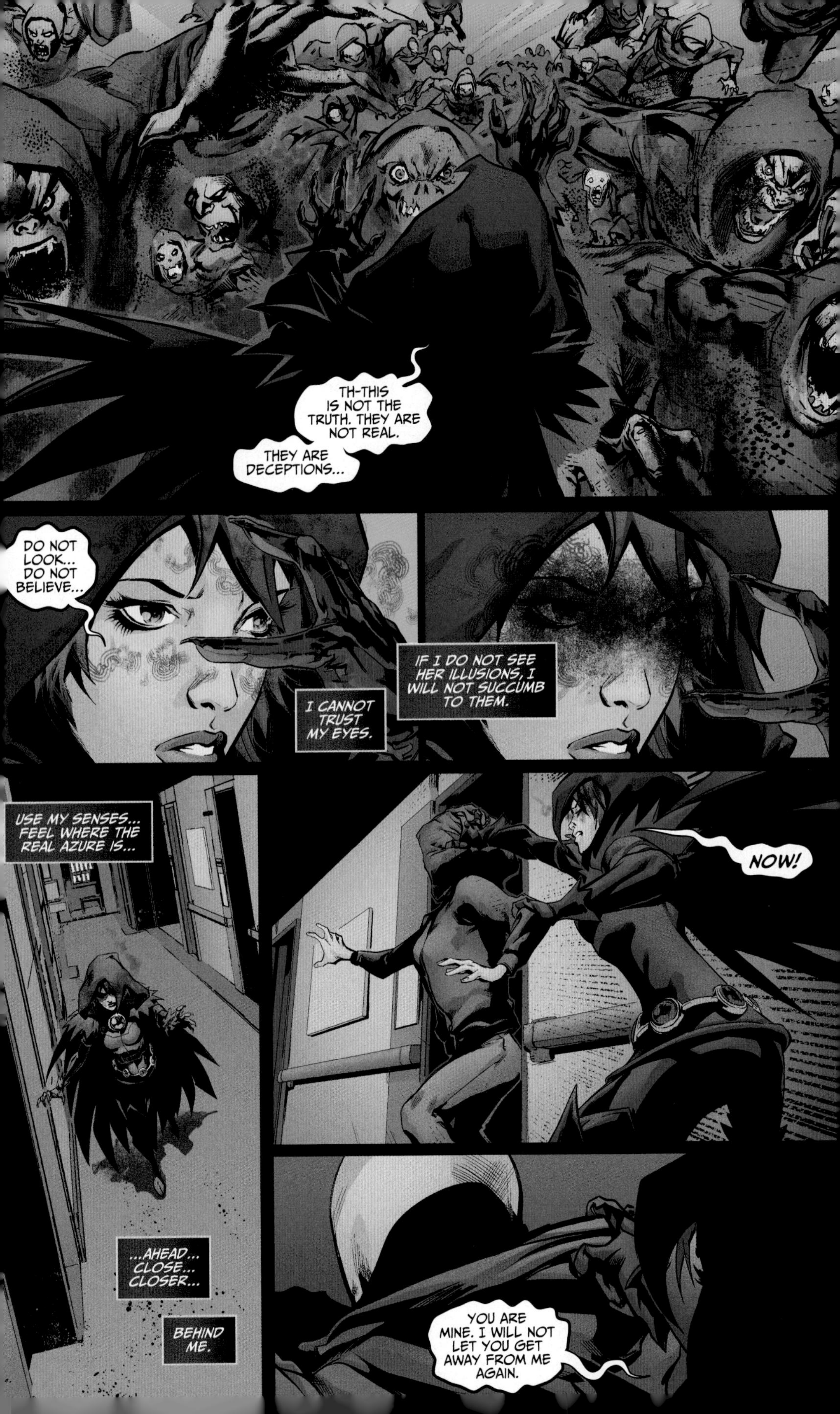
TH-THIS IS NOT THE TRUTH. THEY ARE NOT REAL.
THEY ARE DECEPTIONS...
DO NOT LOOK... DO NOT BELIEVE...
I CANNOT TRUST MY EYES.
IF I DO NOT SEE HER ILLUSIONS, I WILL NOT SUCCUMB TO THEM.
USE MY SENSES... FEEL WHERE THE REAL AZURE IS...
...AHEAD... CLOSE... CLOSER...
BEHIND ME.
NOW!
YOU ARE MINE. I WILL NOT LET YOU GET AWAY FROM ME AGAIN.

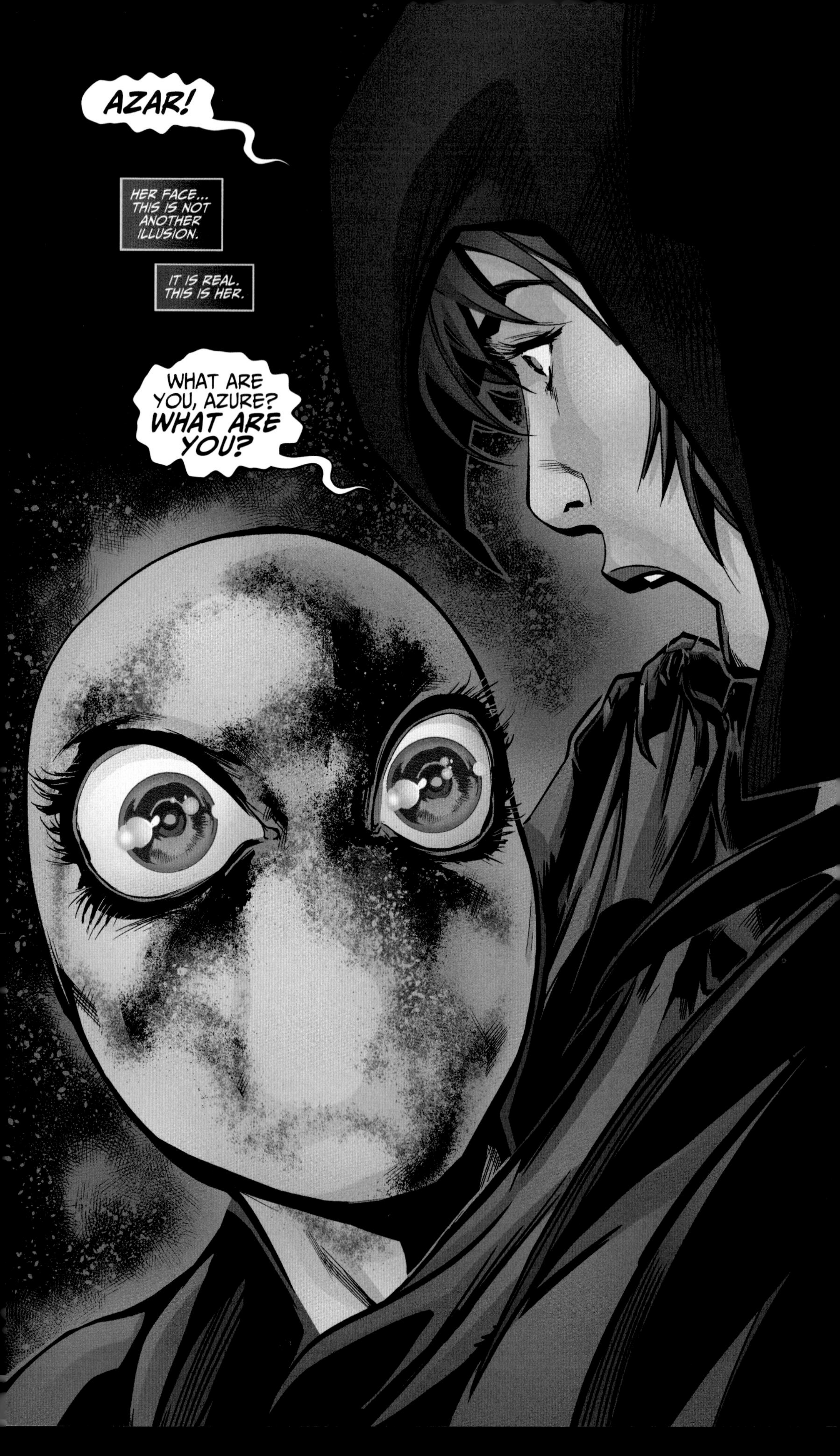
AZAR!
HER FACE... THIS IS NOT ANOTHER ILLUSION.
IT IS REAL. THIS IS HER.
WHAT ARE YOU, AZURE? WHAT ARE YOU?

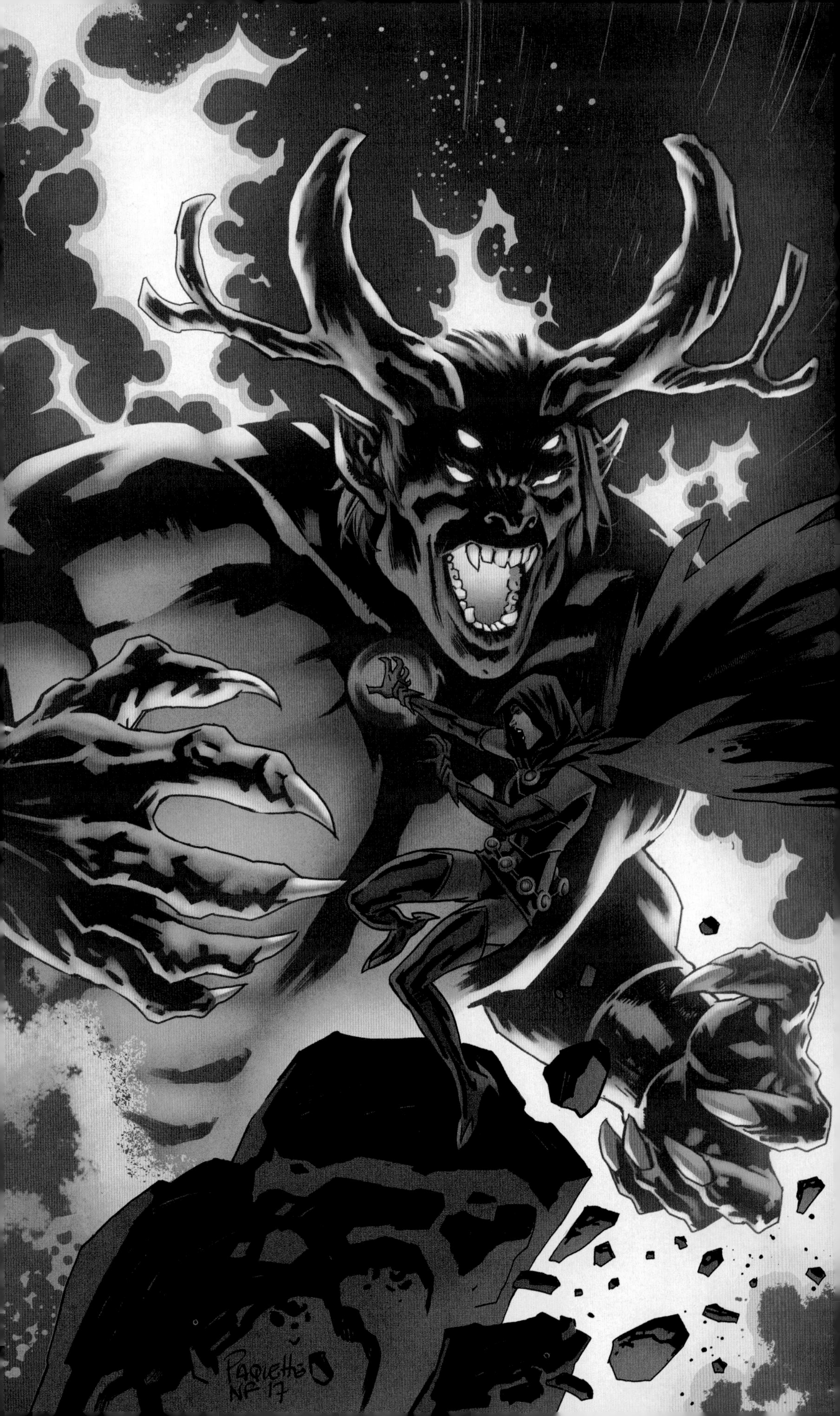

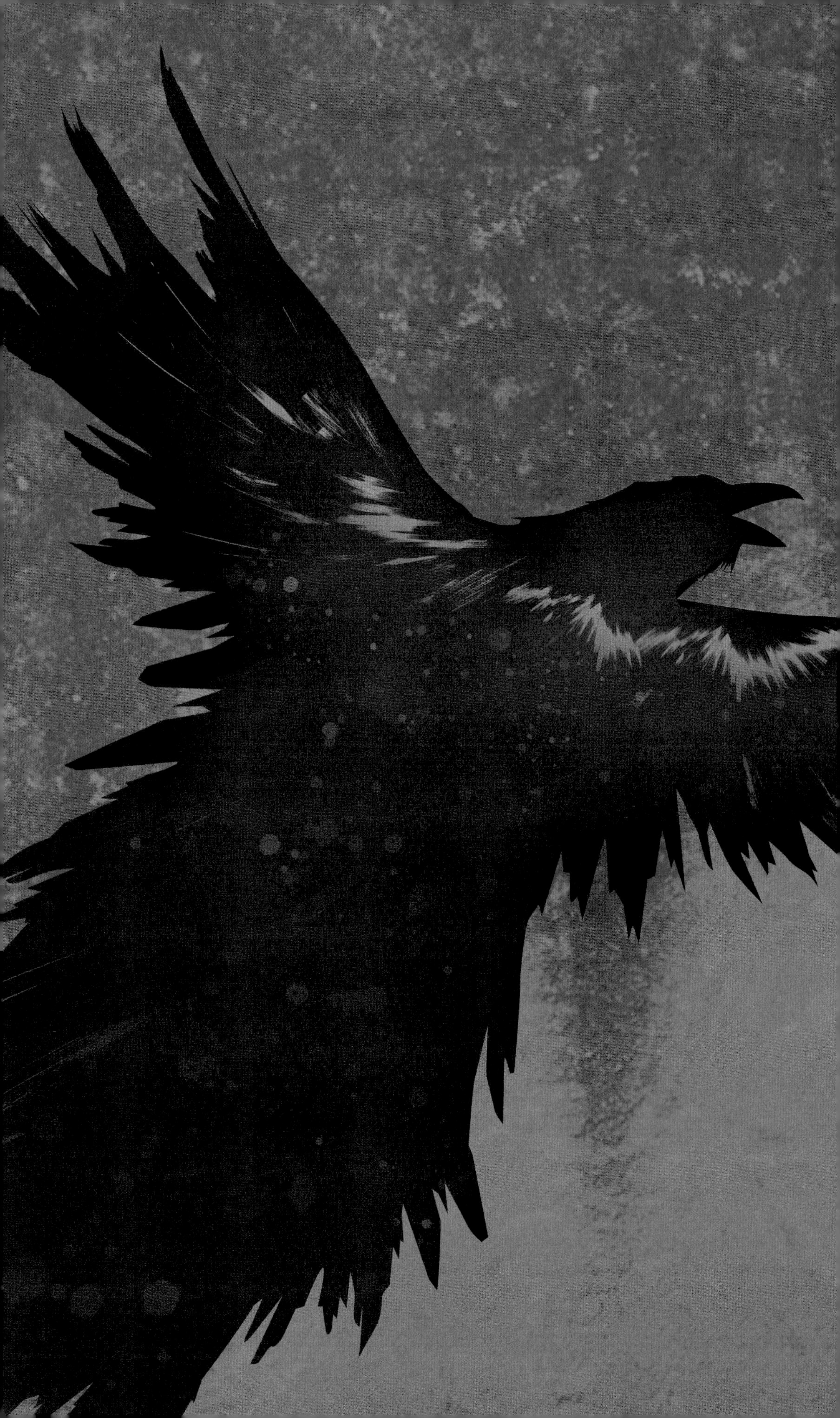

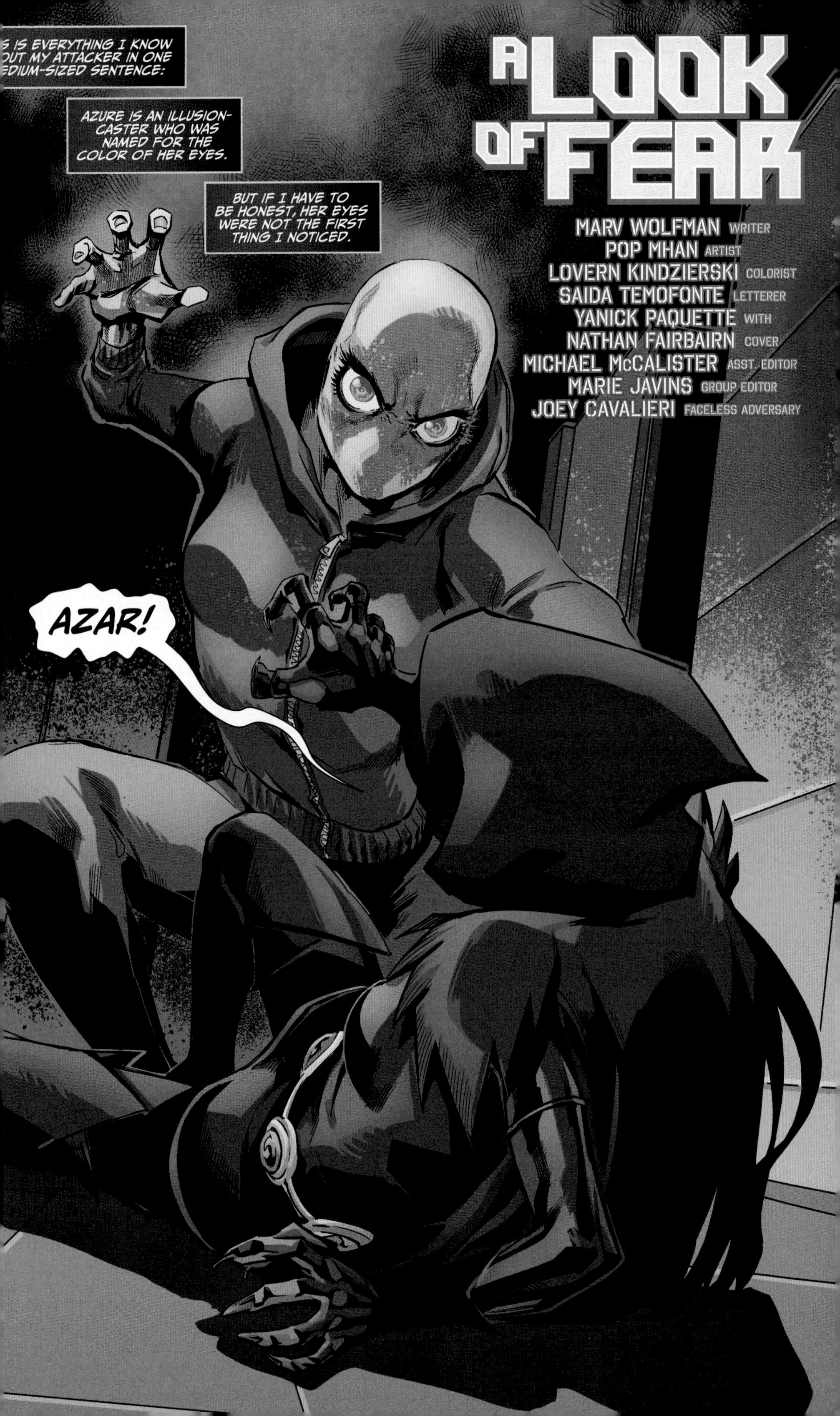

S IS EVERYTHING I KNOW
OUT MY ATTACKER IN ONE
EDIUM-SIZED SENTENCE:
AZURE IS AN ILLUSION-CASTER WHO WAS NAMED FOR THE COLOR OF HER EYES.
BUT IF I HAVE TO BE HONEST, HER EYES WERE NOT THE FIRST THING I NOTICED.
A LOOK OF FEAR
MARV WOLFMAN WRITER
POP MHAN ARTIST
LOVERN KINDZIERSKI COLORIST
SAIDA TEMOFONTE LETTERER
YANICK PAQUETTE WITH
NATHAN FAIRBAIRN COVER
MICHAEL McCALISTER ASST. EDITOR
MARIE JAVINS GROUP EDITOR
JOEY CAVALIERI FACELESS ADVERSARY
AZAR!

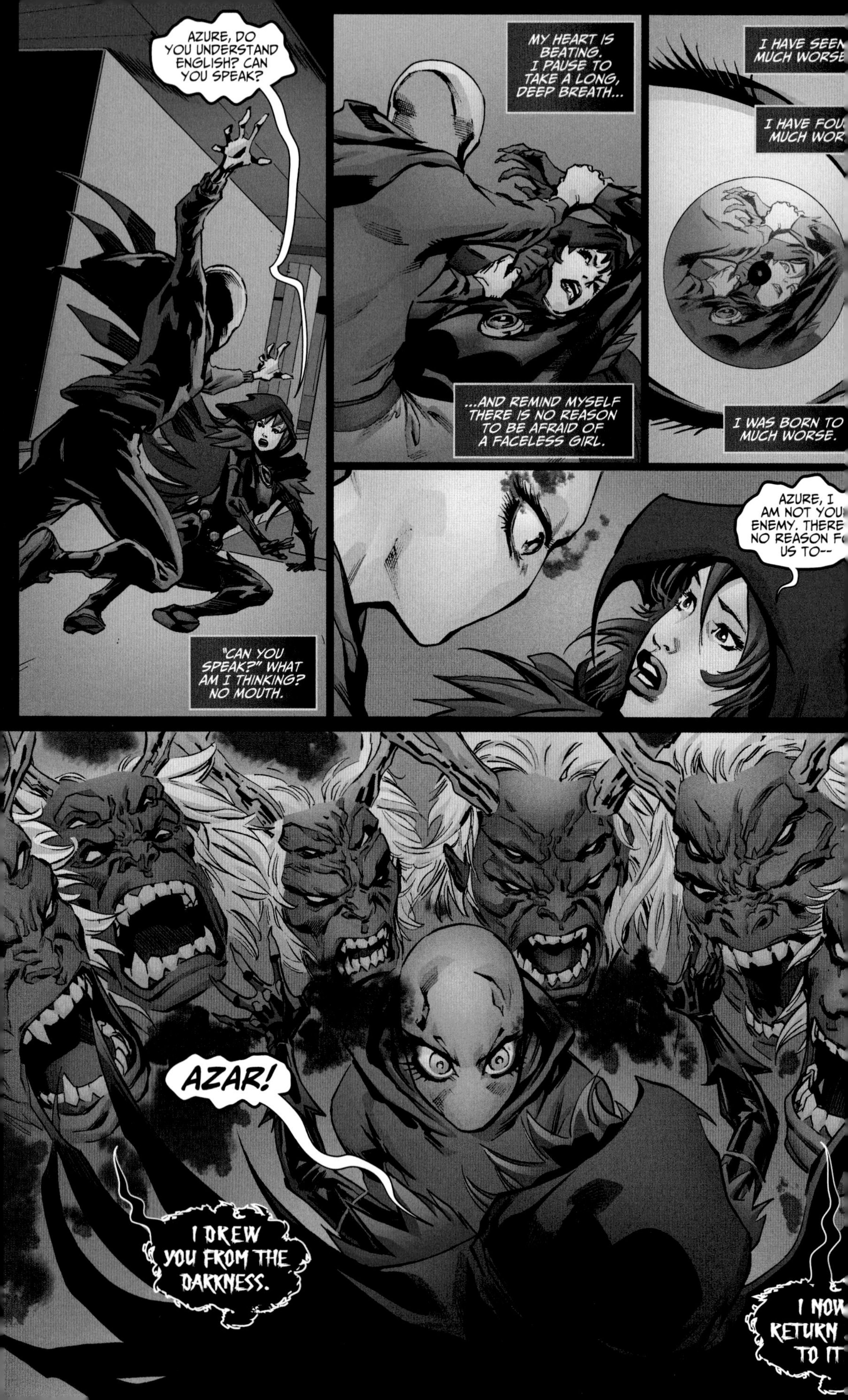
AZURE, DO YOU UNDERSTAND ENGLISH? CAN YOU SPEAK?
"CAN YOU SPEAK?" WHAT AM I THINKING? NO MOUTH.
MY HEART IS BEATING. I PAUSE TO TAKE A LONG, DEEP BREATH...
...AND REMIND MYSELF THERE IS NO REASON TO BE AFRAID OF A FACELESS GIRL.
I HAVE SEEN MUCH WORSE
I HAVE FOU MUCH WOR
I WAS BORN TO MUCH WORSE.
AZURE, I AM NOT YOU ENEMY. THERE NO REASON F US TO--
AZAR!
I DREW YOU FROM THE DARKNESS.
I NOW RETURN TO IT

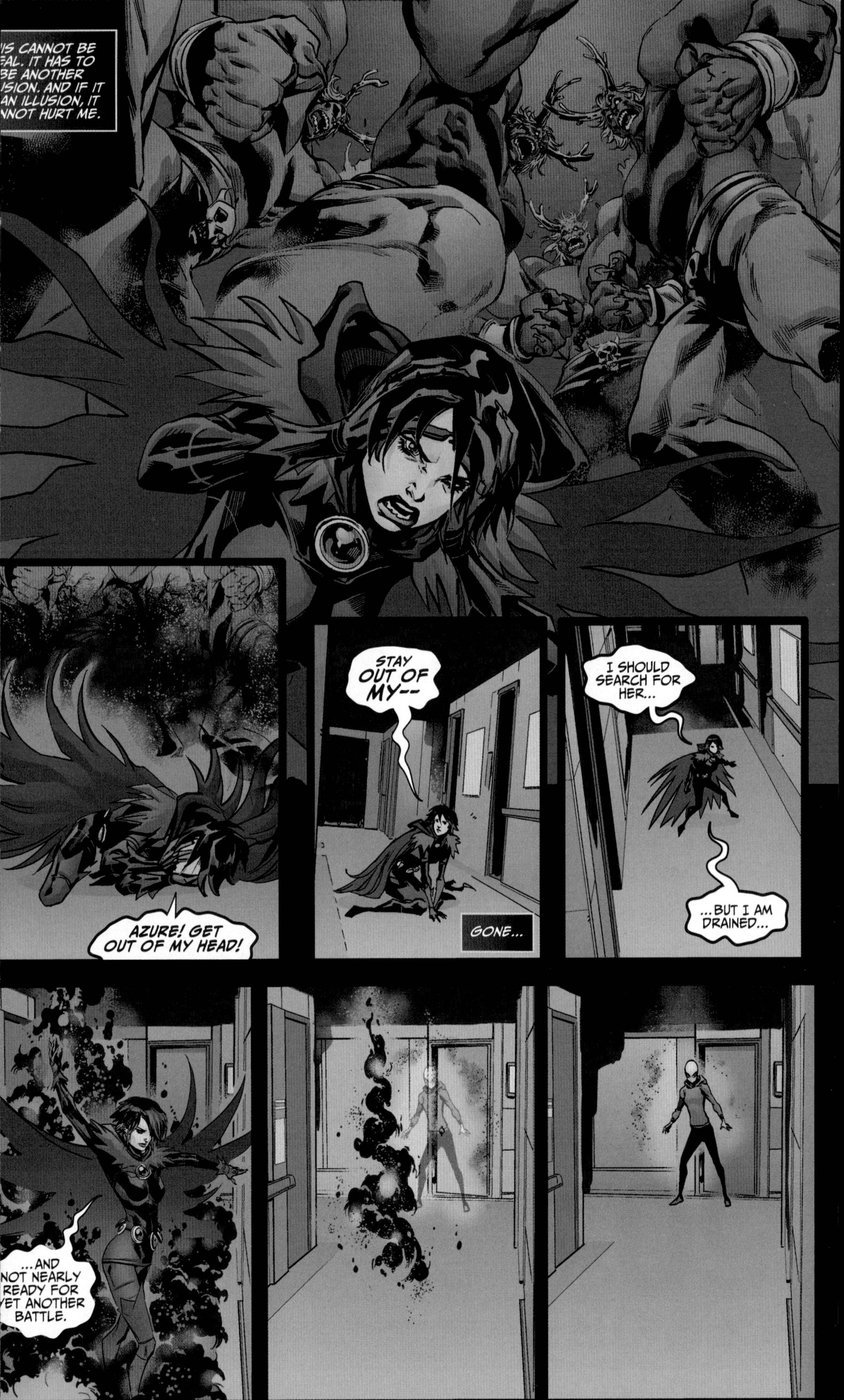
IS CANNOT BE
EAL. IT HAS TO
BE ANOTHER
ISION. AND IF IT
AN ILLUSION, IT
NNOT HURT ME.
AZURE! GET OUT OF MY HEAD!
STAY OUT OF MY--
GONE...
I SHOULD SEARCH FOR HER...
...BUT I AM DRAINED...
...AND NOT NEARLY READY FOR YET ANOTHER BATTLE.

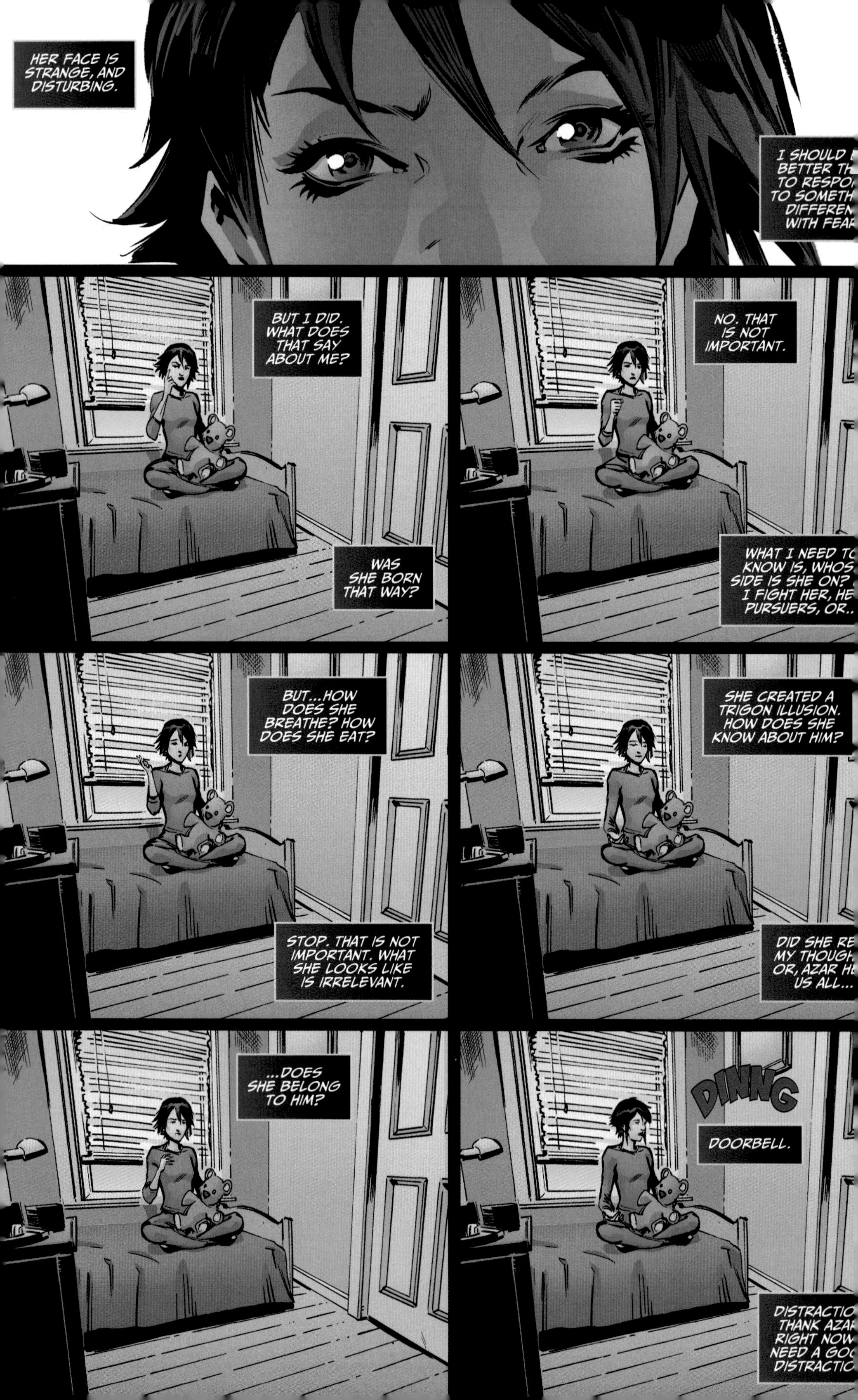
HER FACE IS STRANGE, AND DISTURBING.
BUT I DID. WHAT DOES THAT SAY ABOUT ME?
WAS SHE BORN THAT WAY?
NO. THAT IS NOT IMPORTANT.
BUT...HOW DOES SHE BREATHE? HOW DOES SHE EAT?
STOP. THAT IS NOT IMPORTANT. WHAT SHE LOOKS LIKE IS IRRELEVANT.
SHE CREATED A TRIGON ILLUSION. HOW DOES SHE KNOW ABOUT HIM?
...DOES SHE BELONG TO HIM?
DINNG
DOORBELL.

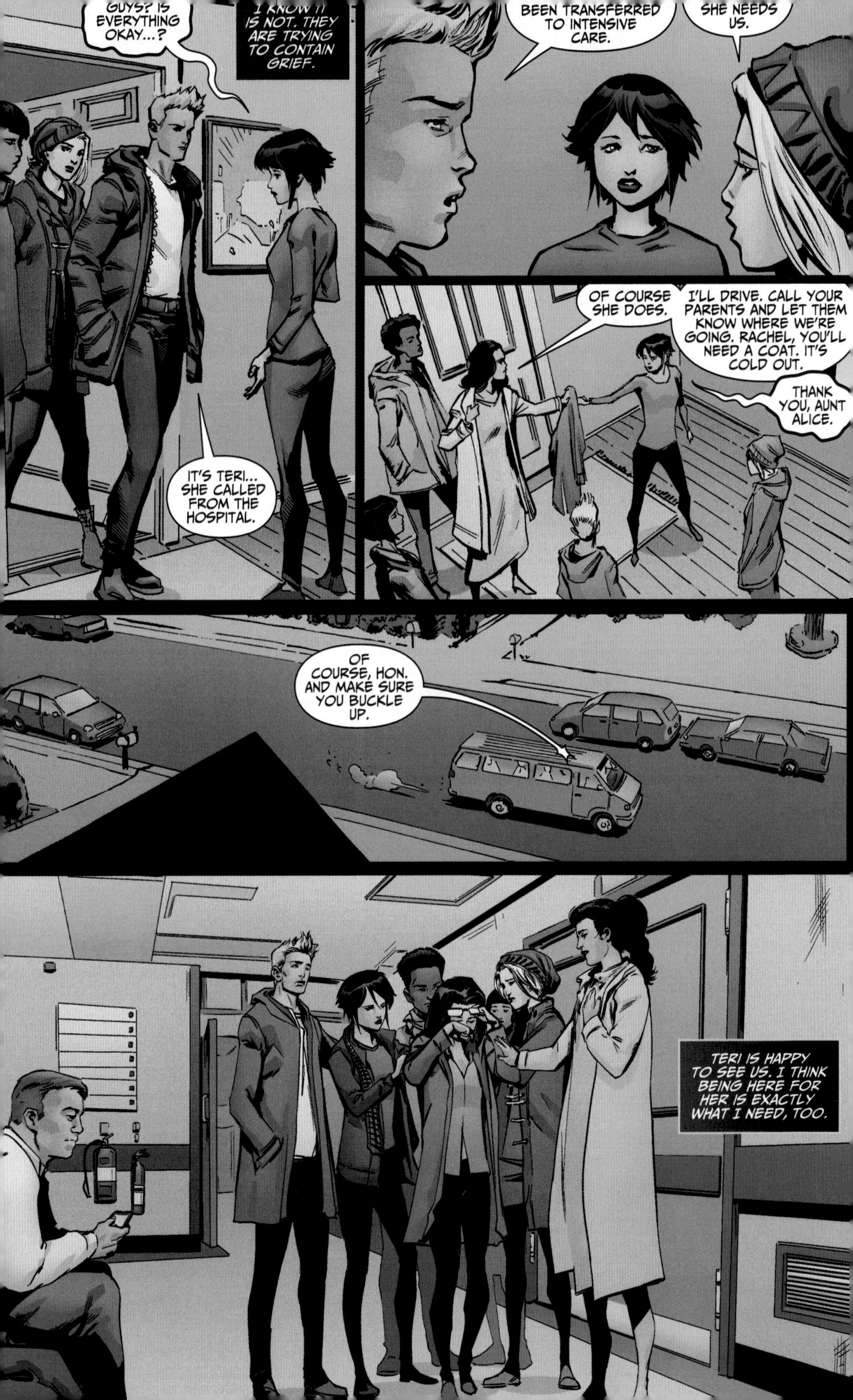
GUYS? IS EVERYTHING OKAY...?
I KNOW IT IS NOT. THEY ARE TRYING TO CONTAIN GRIEF.
IT'S TERI... SHE CALLED FROM THE HOSPITAL.
BEEN TRANSFERRED TO INTENSIVE CARE.
SHE NEEDS US.
OF COURSE SHE DOES.
I'LL DRIVE. CALL YOUR PARENTS AND LET THEM KNOW WHERE WE'RE GOING. RACHEL, YOU'LL NEED A COAT. IT'S COLD OUT.
THANK YOU, AUNT ALICE.
OF COURSE, HON. AND MAKE SURE YOU BUCKLE UP.
TERI IS HAPPY TO SEE US. I THINK BEING HERE FOR HER IS EXACTLY WHAT I NEED, TOO.

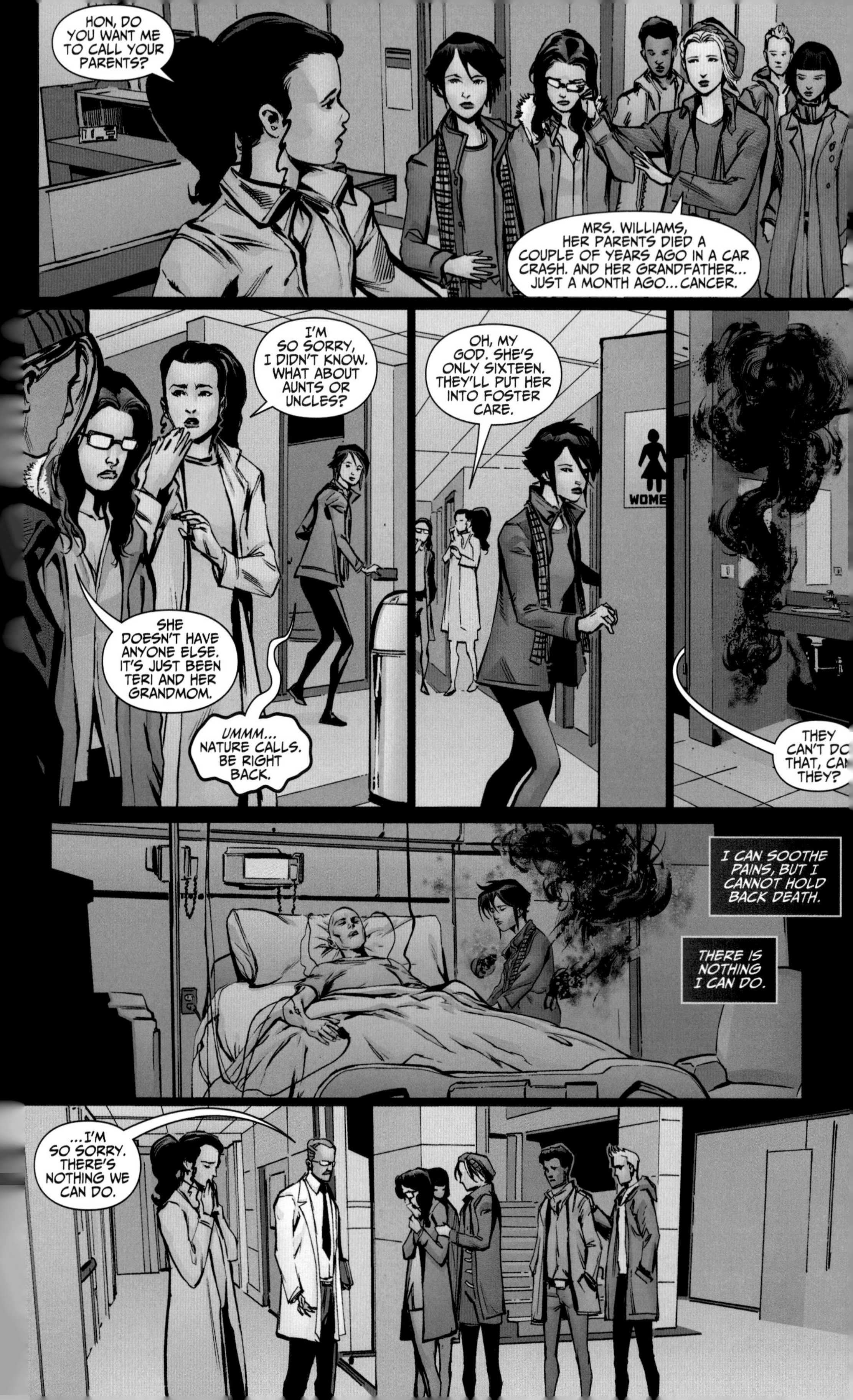
HON, DO YOU WANT ME TO CALL YOUR PARENTS?
MRS. WILLIAMS, HER PARENTS DIED A COUPLE OF YEARS AGO IN A CAR CRASH. AND HER GRANDFATHER... JUST A MONTH AGO... CANCER.
I'M SO SORRY, I DIDN'T KNOW. WHAT ABOUT AUNTS OR UNCLES?
SHE DOESN'T HAVE ANYONE ELSE. IT'S JUST BEEN TERI AND HER GRANDMOM.
UMMM... NATURE CALLS. BE RIGHT BACK.
OH, MY GOD. SHE'S ONLY SIXTEEN. THEY'LL PUT HER INTO FOSTER CARE.
WOME
THEY CAN'T DO THAT, CAN THEY?
I CAN SOOTHE PAINS, BUT I CANNOT HOLD BACK DEATH.
THERE IS NOTHING I CAN DO.
...I'M SO SORRY. THERE'S NOTHING WE CAN DO.

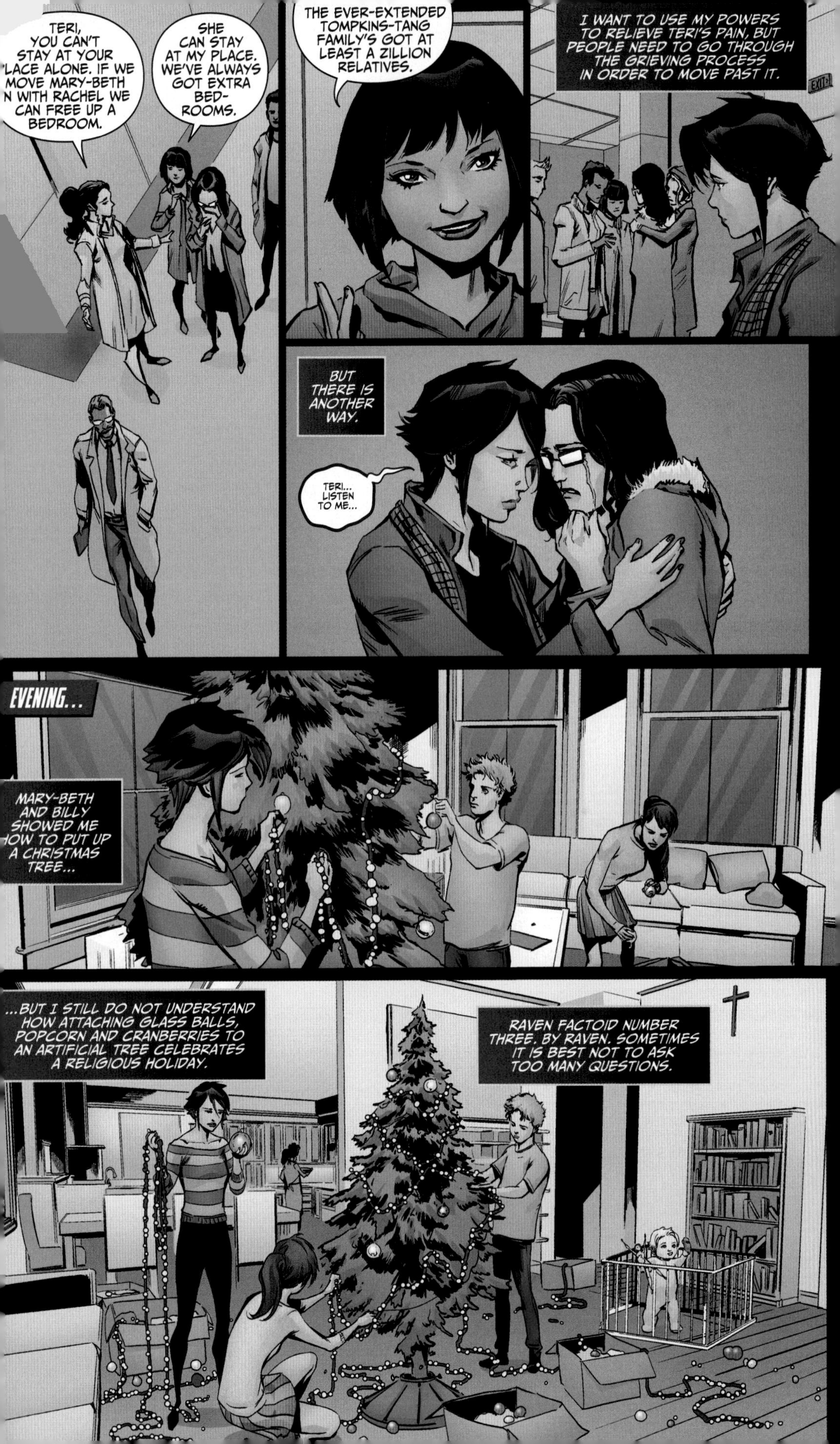
TERI, YOU CAN'T STAY AT YOUR PLACE ALONE. IF WE MOVE MARY-BETH IN WITH RACHEL WE CAN FREE UP A BEDROOM.
SHE CAN STAY AT MY PLACE. WE'VE ALWAYS GOT EXTRA BED-ROOMS.
THE EVER-EXTENDED TOMPKINS-TANG FAMILY'S GOT AT LEAST A ZILLION RELATIVES.
I WANT TO USE MY POWERS TO RELIEVE TERI'S PAIN, BUT PEOPLE NEED TO GO THROUGH THE GRIEVING PROCESS IN ORDER TO MOVE PAST IT.
EXIT
BUT THERE IS ANOTHER WAY.
TERI... LISTEN TO ME...
EVENING...
MARY-BETH AND BILLY SHOWED ME HOW TO PUT UP A CHRISTMAS TREE...
...BUT I STILL DO NOT UNDERSTAND HOW ATTACHING GLASS BALLS, POPCORN AND CRANBERRIES TO AN ARTIFICIAL TREE CELEBRATES A RELIGIOUS HOLIDAY.
RAVEN FACTOID NUMBER THREE. BY RAVEN. SOMETIMES IT IS BEST NOT TO ASK TOO MANY QUESTIONS.

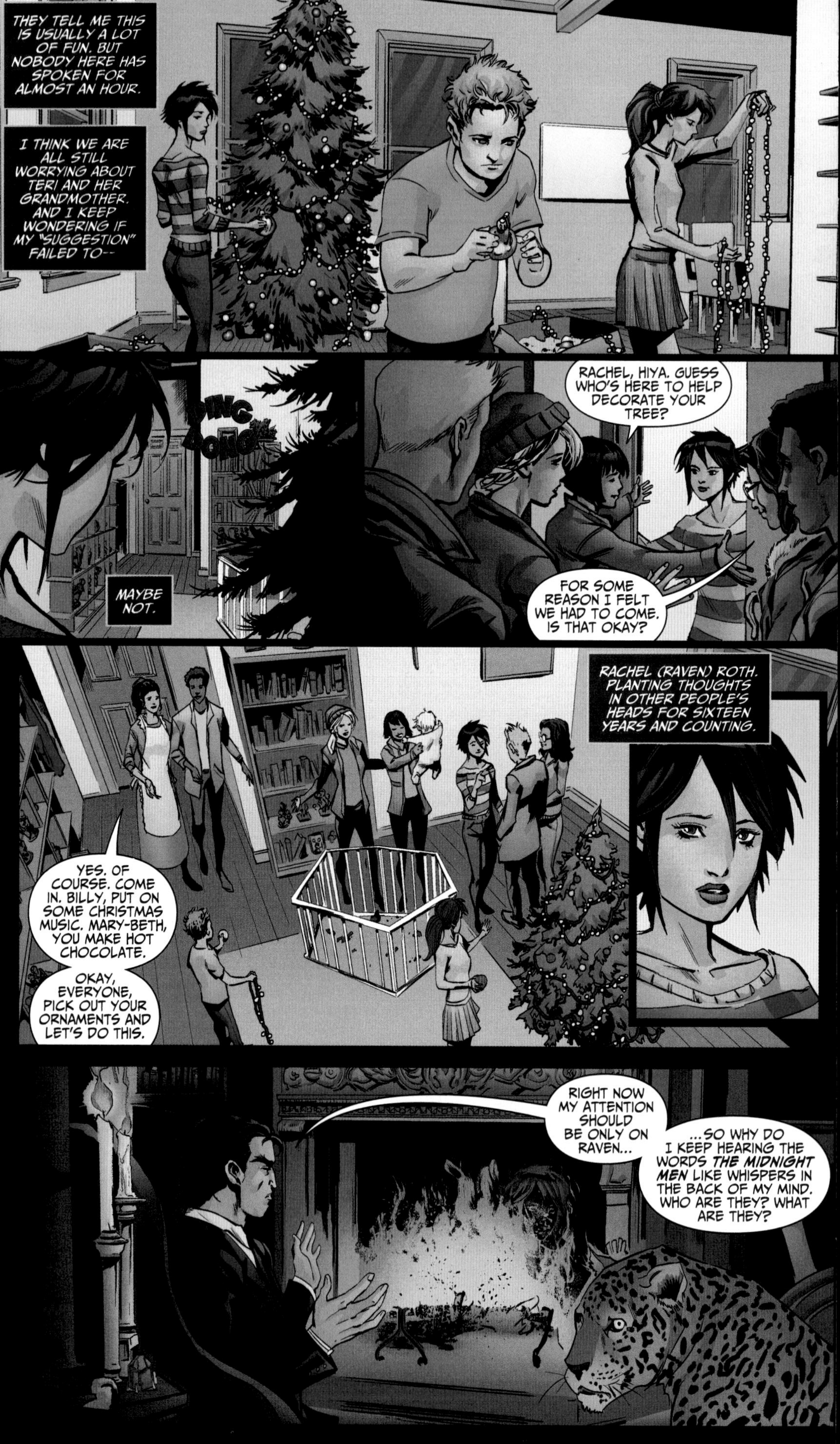
THEY TELL ME THIS IS USUALLY A LOT OF FUN. BUT NOBODY HERE HAS SPOKEN FOR ALMOST AN HOUR.
I THINK WE ARE ALL STILL WORRYING ABOUT TERI AND HER GRANDMOTHER. AND I KEEP WONDERING IF MY "SUGGESTION" FAILED TO--
DING DONG
MAYBE NOT.
RACHEL, HIYA. GUESS WHO'S HERE TO HELP DECORATE YOUR TREE?
FOR SOME REASON I FELT WE HAD TO COME. IS THAT OKAY?
YES. OF COURSE. COME IN. BILLY, PUT ON SOME CHRISTMAS MUSIC. MARY-BETH, YOU MAKE HOT CHOCOLATE.
OKAY, EVERYONE, PICK OUT YOUR ORNAMENTS AND LET'S DO THIS.
RACHEL (RAVEN) ROTH. PLANTING THOUGHTS IN OTHER PEOPLE'S HEADS FOR SIXTEEN YEARS AND COUNTING.
RIGHT NOW MY ATTENTION SHOULD BE ONLY ON RAVEN...
...SO WHY DO I KEEP HEARING THE WORDS THE MIDNIGHT MEN LIKE WHISPERS IN THE BACK OF MY MIND. WHO ARE THEY? WHAT ARE THEY?

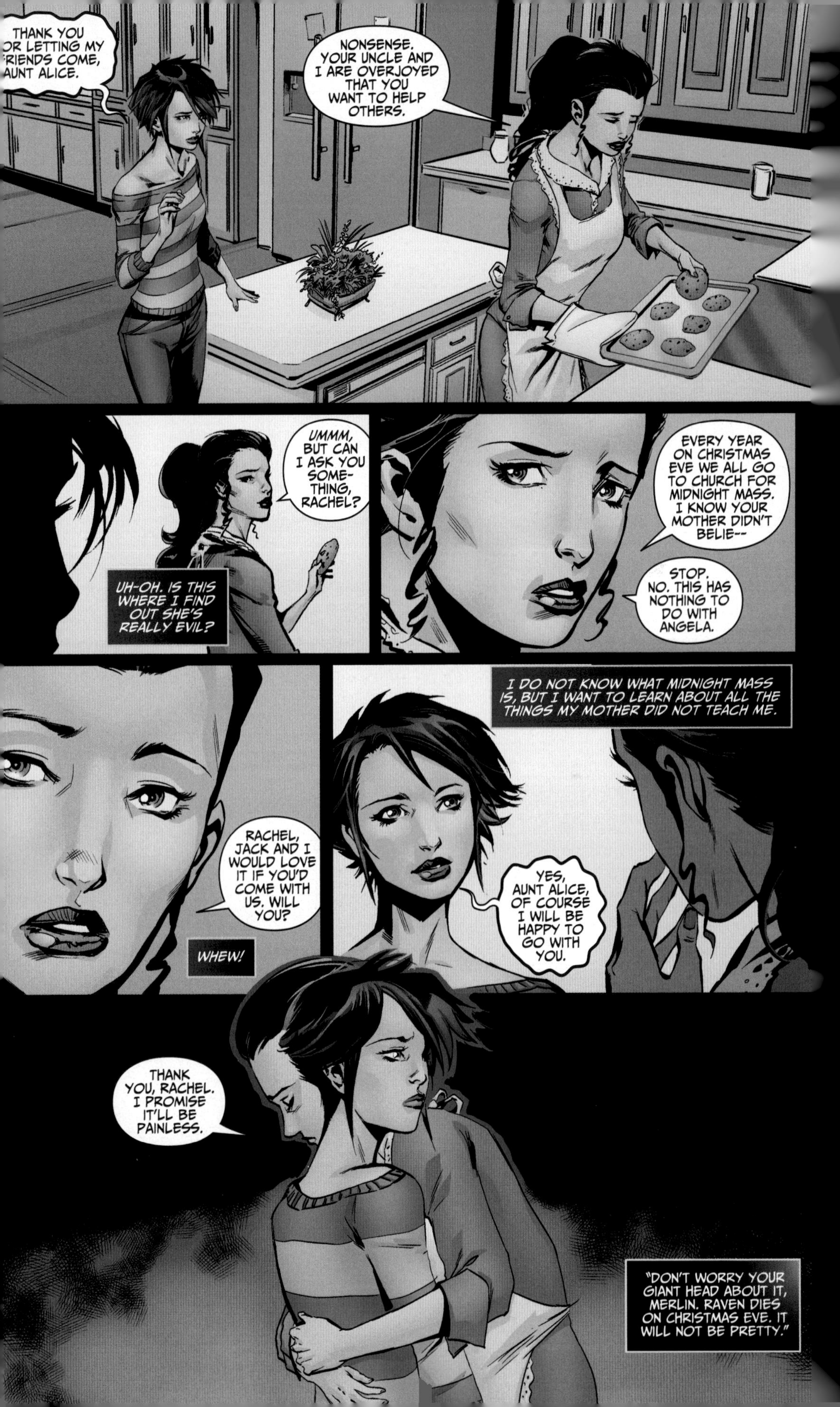
THANK YOU FOR LETTING MY FRIENDS COME, AUNT ALICE.
NONSENSE. YOUR UNCLE AND I ARE OVERJOYED THAT YOU WANT TO HELP OTHERS.
UMMM, BUT CAN I ASK YOU SOMETHING, RACHEL?
UH-OH. IS THIS WHERE I FIND OUT SHE'S REALLY EVIL?
EVERY YEAR ON CHRISTMAS EVE WE ALL GO TO CHURCH FOR MIDNIGHT MASS. I KNOW YOUR MOTHER DIDN'T BELIE--
STOP. NO. THIS HAS NOTHING TO DO WITH ANGELA.
RACHEL, JACK AND I WOULD LOVE IT IF YOU'D COME WITH US. WILL YOU?
WHEW!
I DO NOT KNOW WHAT MIDNIGHT MASS IS, BUT I WANT TO LEARN ABOUT ALL THE THINGS MY MOTHER DID NOT TEACH ME.
YES, AUNT ALICE, OF COURSE I WILL BE HAPPY TO GO WITH YOU.
THANK YOU, RACHEL. I PROMISE IT'LL BE PAINLESS.
"DON'T WORRY YOUR GIANT HEAD ABOUT IT, MERLIN. RAVEN DIES ON CHRISTMAS EVE. IT WILL NOT BE PRETTY."

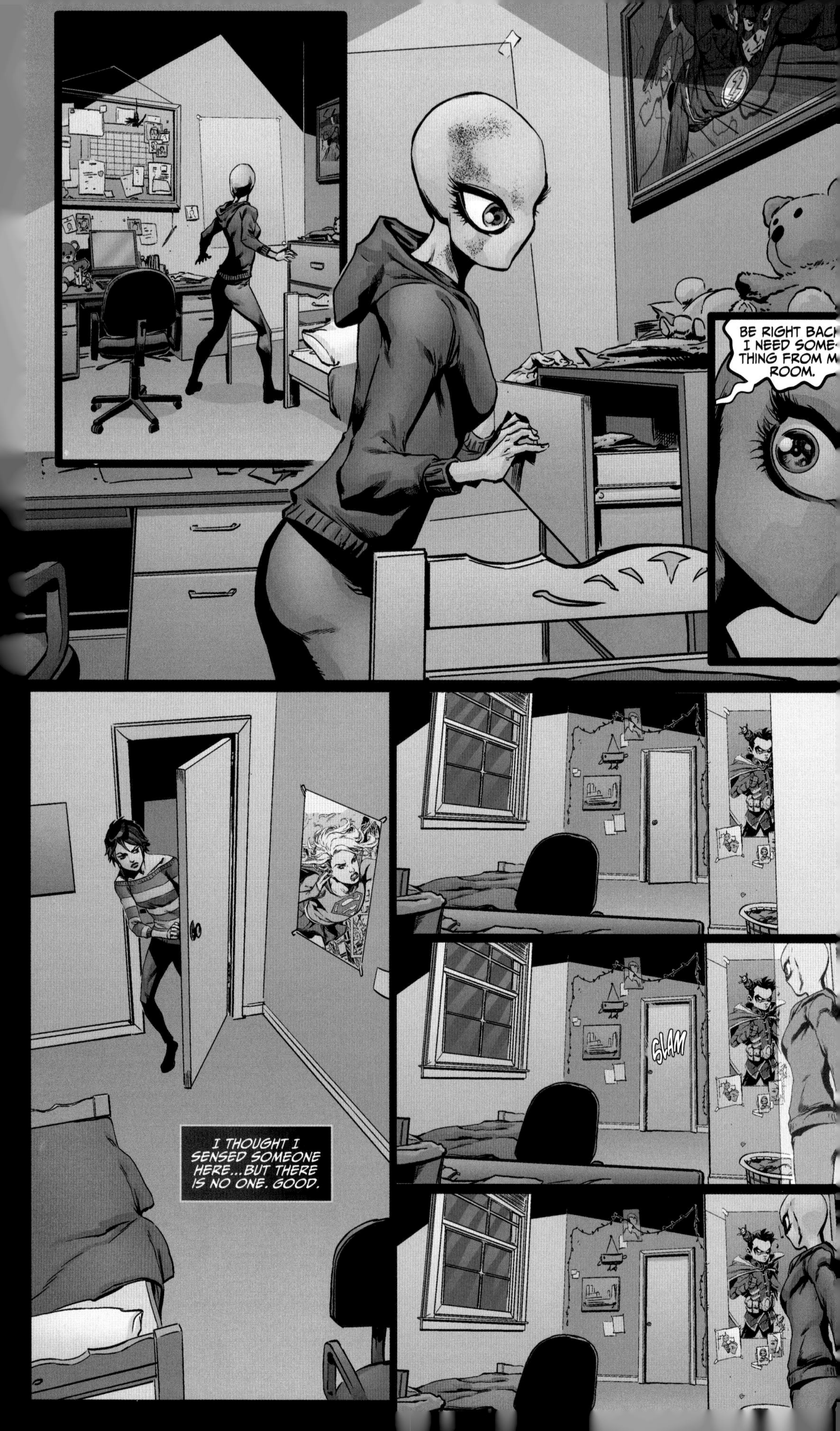

BE RIGHT BACK
I NEED SOME-
THING FROM M
ROOM.
I THOUGHT I SENSED SOMEONE HERE...BUT THERE IS NO ONE. GOOD.
SLAM

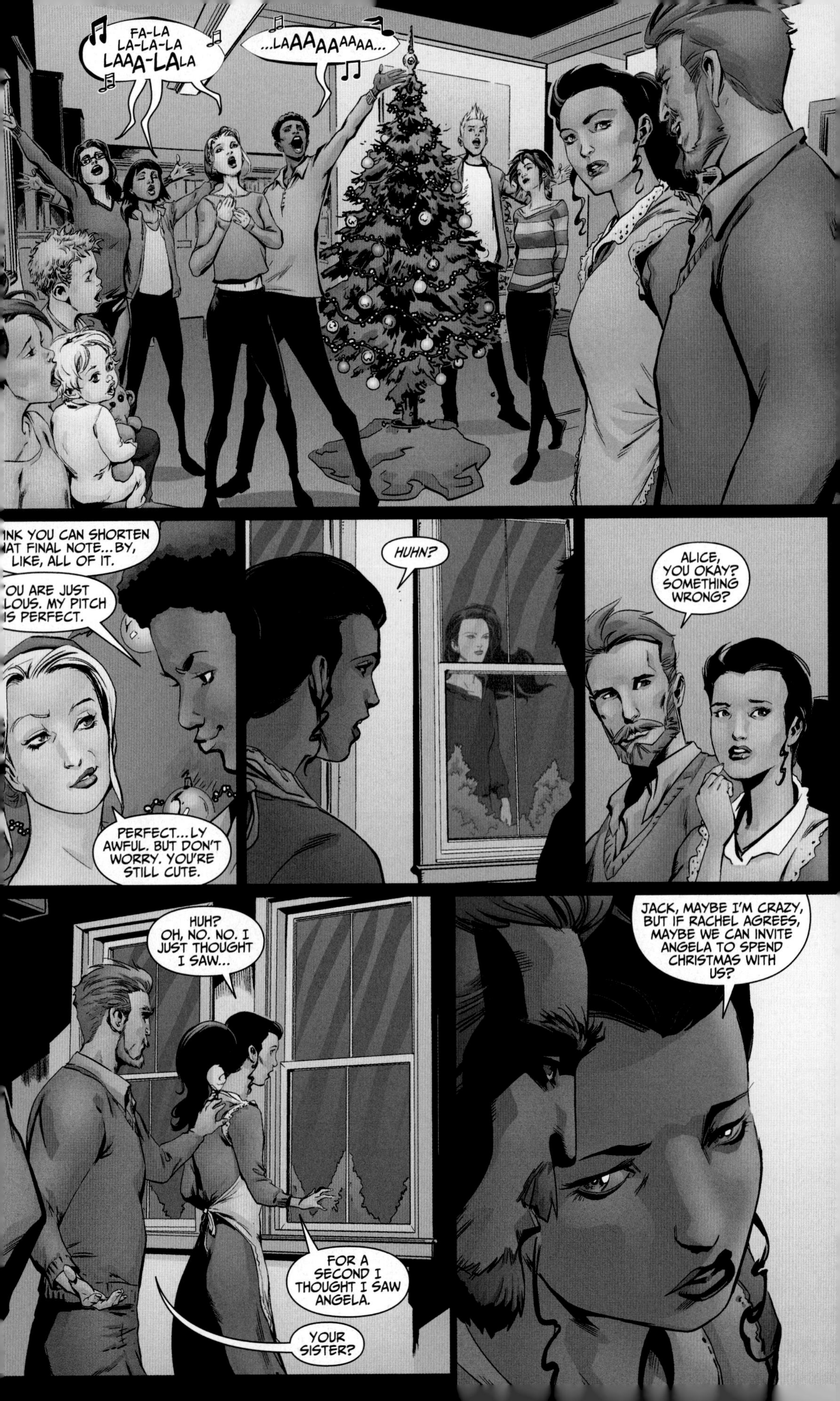

FA-LA LA-LA-LA LAAA-LALA
...LAAAAAAAA...
INK YOU CAN SHORTEN
IAT FINAL NOTE...BY, LIKE, ALL OF IT.
'OU ARE JUST LOUS. MY PITCH IS PERFECT.
PERFECT...LY AWFUL. BUT DON'T WORRY. YOU'RE STILL CUTE.
HUHN?
ALICE, YOU OKAY? SOMETHING WRONG?
HUH? OH, NO. NO. I JUST THOUGHT I SAW...
FOR A SECOND I THOUGHT I SAW ANGELA.
YOUR SISTER?
JACK, MAYBE I'M CRAZY, BUT IF RACHEL AGREES, MAYBE WE CAN INVITE ANGELA TO SPEND CHRISTMAS WITH US?

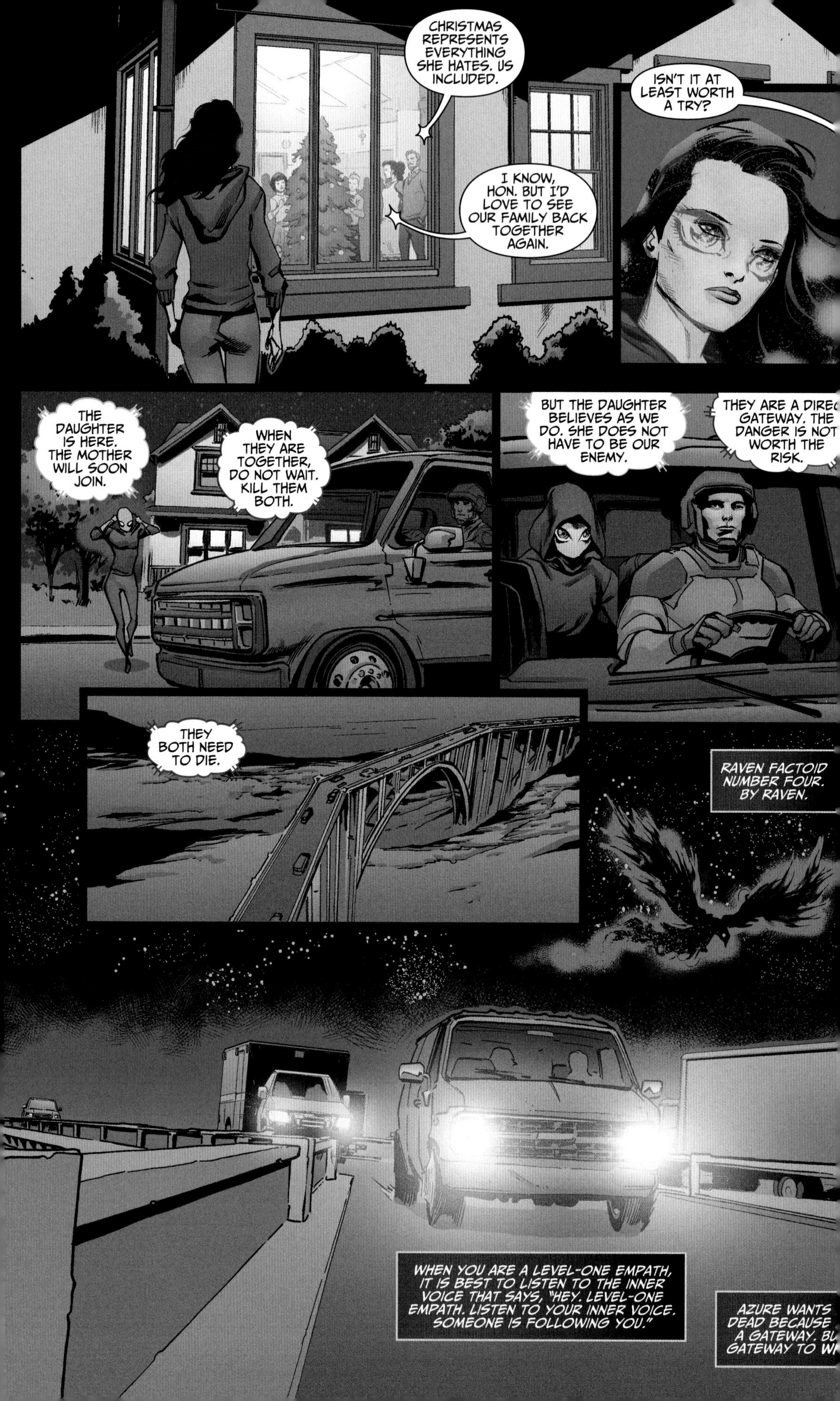
CHRISTMAS REPRESENTS EVERYTHING SHE HATES. US INCLUDED.
I KNOW, HON. BUT I'D LOVE TO SEE OUR FAMILY BACK TOGETHER AGAIN.
ISN'T IT AT LEAST WORTH A TRY?
THE DAUGHTER IS HERE. THE MOTHER WILL SOON JOIN.
WHEN THEY ARE TOGETHER, DO NOT WAIT. KILL THEM BOTH.
BUT THE DAUGHTER BELIEVES AS WE DO. SHE DOES NOT HAVE TO BE OUR ENEMY.
THEY ARE A DIREC GATEWAY. THE DANGER IS NOT WORTH THE RISK.
THEY BOTH NEED TO DIE.
RAVEN FACTOID NUMBER FOUR. BY RAVEN.
WHEN YOU ARE A LEVEL-ONE EMPATH, IT IS BEST TO LISTEN TO THE INNER VOICE THAT SAYS, "HEY, LEVEL-ONE EMPATH. LISTEN TO YOUR INNER VOICE. SOMEONE IS FOLLOWING YOU."
AZURE WANTS DEAD BECAUSE A GATEWAY. BU GATEWAY TO WH

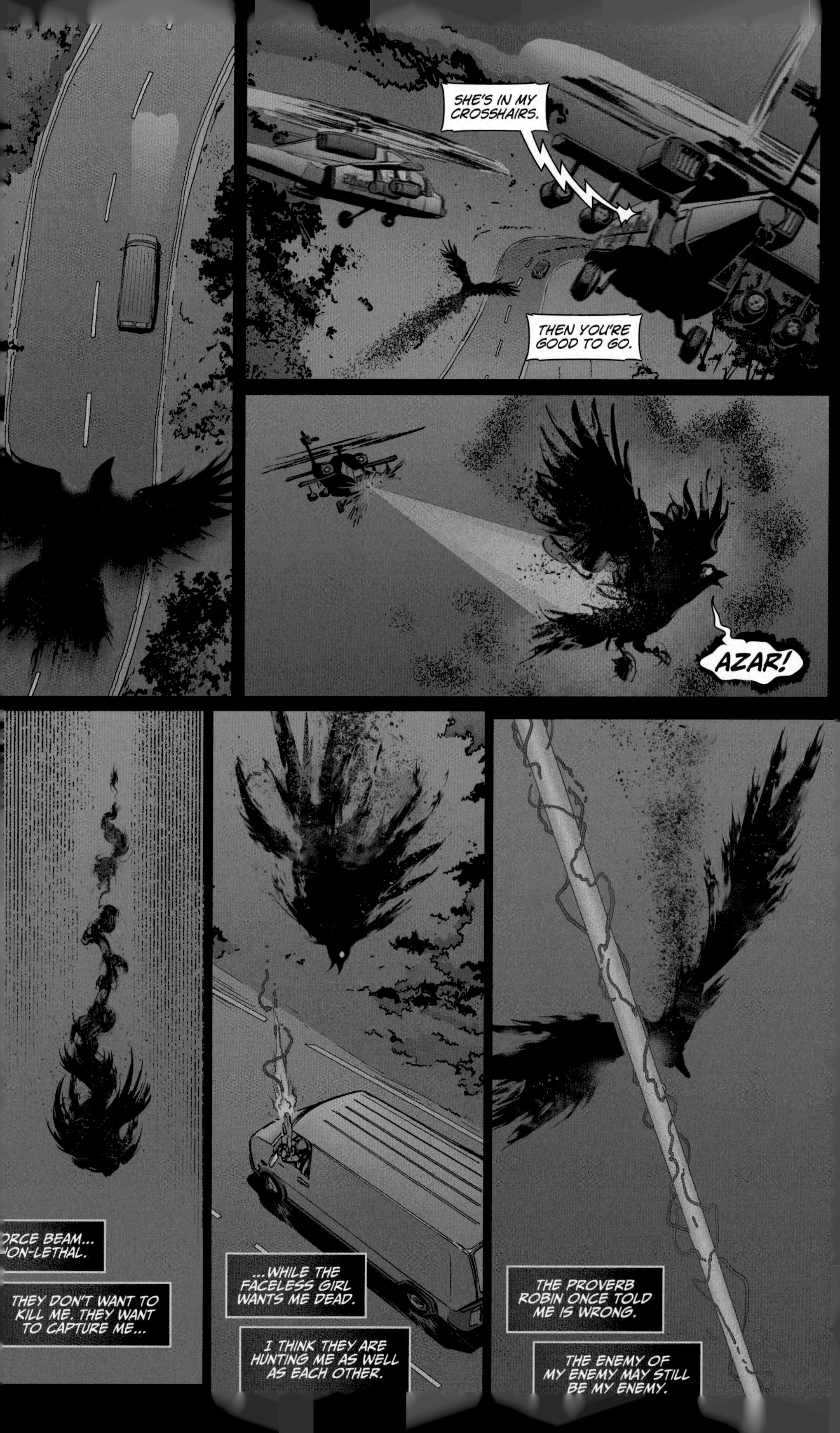
SHE'S IN MY CROSSHAIRS.
THEN YOU'RE GOOD TO GO.
AZAR!
ORCE BEAM... ON-LETHAL.
THEY DON'T WANT TO KILL ME. THEY WANT TO CAPTURE ME...
...WHILE THE FACELESS GIRL WANTS ME DEAD.
I THINK THEY ARE HUNTING ME AS WELL AS EACH OTHER.
THE PROVERB ROBIN ONCE TOLD ME IS WRONG.
THE ENEMY OF MY ENEMY MAY STILL BE MY ENEMY.

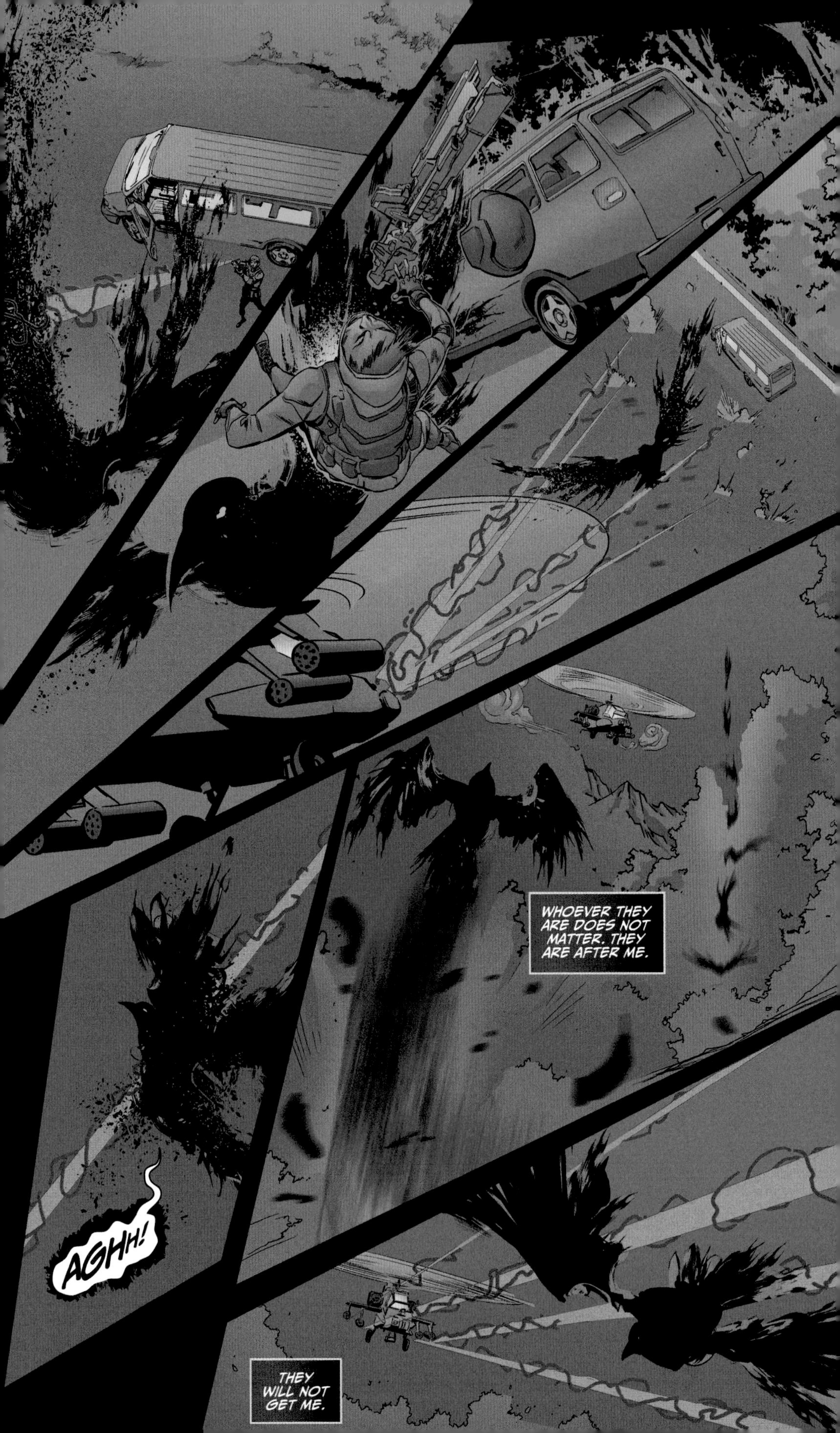
AGHH!
WHOEVER THEY ARE DOES NOT MATTER. THEY ARE AFTER ME.
THEY WILL NOT GET ME.

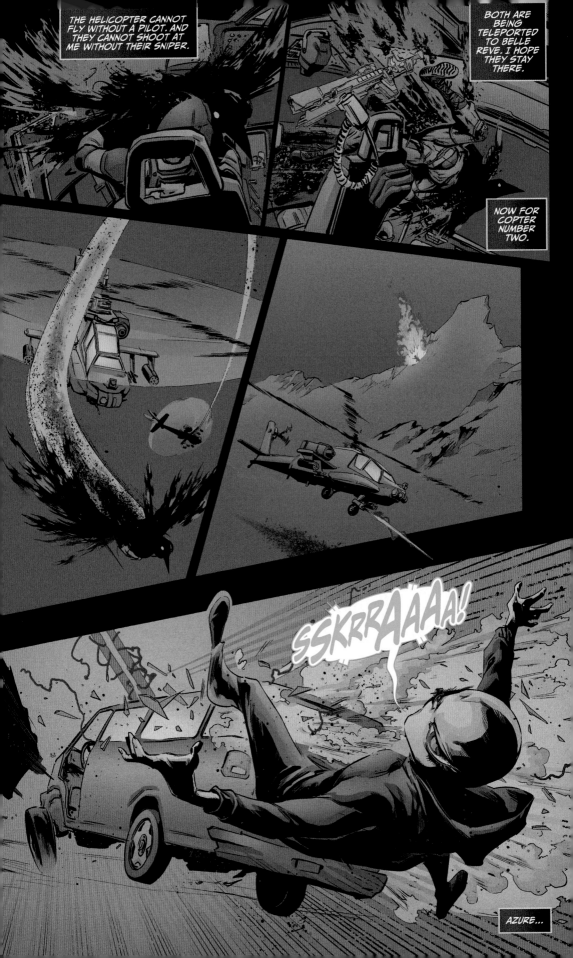

THE HELICOPTER CANNOT FLY WITHOUT A PILOT. AND THEY CANNOT SHOOT AT ME WITHOUT THEIR SNIPER.

BOTH ARE BEING TELEPORTED TO BELLE REVE. I HOPE THEY STAY THERE.

NOW FOR COPTER NUMBER TWO.

SSKRRAÄAA!

AZURE...

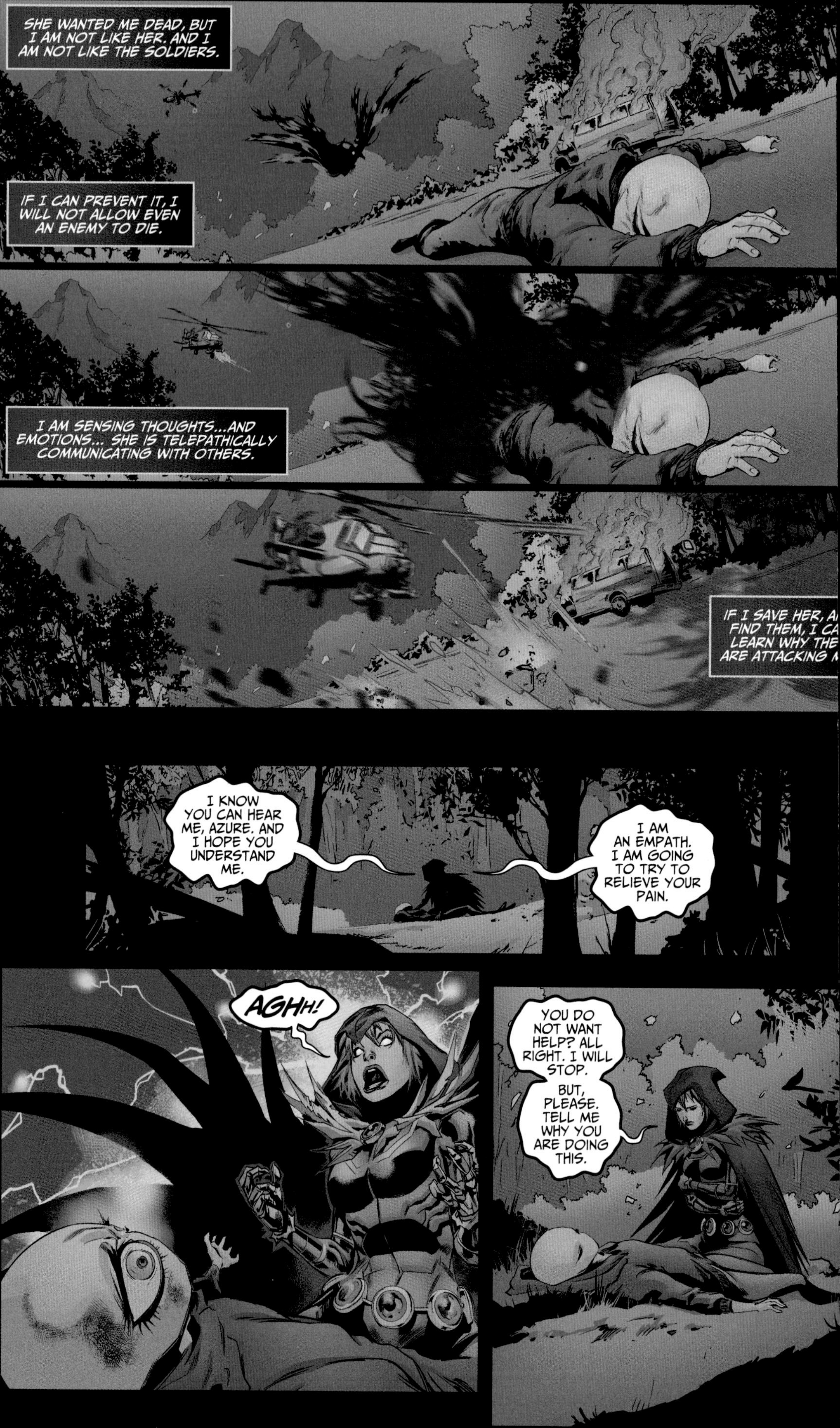
SHE WANTED ME DEAD, BUT I AM NOT LIKE HER. AND I AM NOT LIKE THE SOLDIERS.
IF I CAN PREVENT IT, I WILL NOT ALLOW EVEN AN ENEMY TO DIE.
I AM SENSING THOUGHTS...AND EMOTIONS... SHE IS TELEPATHICALLY COMMUNICATING WITH OTHERS.
IF I SAVE HER, A FIND THEM, I CA LEARN WHY THE ARE ATTACKING
I KNOW YOU CAN HEAR ME, AZURE. AND I HOPE YOU UNDERSTAND ME.
I AM AN EMPATH. I AM GOING TO TRY TO RELIEVE YOUR PAIN.
AGHH!
YOU DO NOT WANT HELP? ALL RIGHT. I WILL STOP.
BUT, PLEASE. TELL ME WHY YOU ARE DOING THIS.

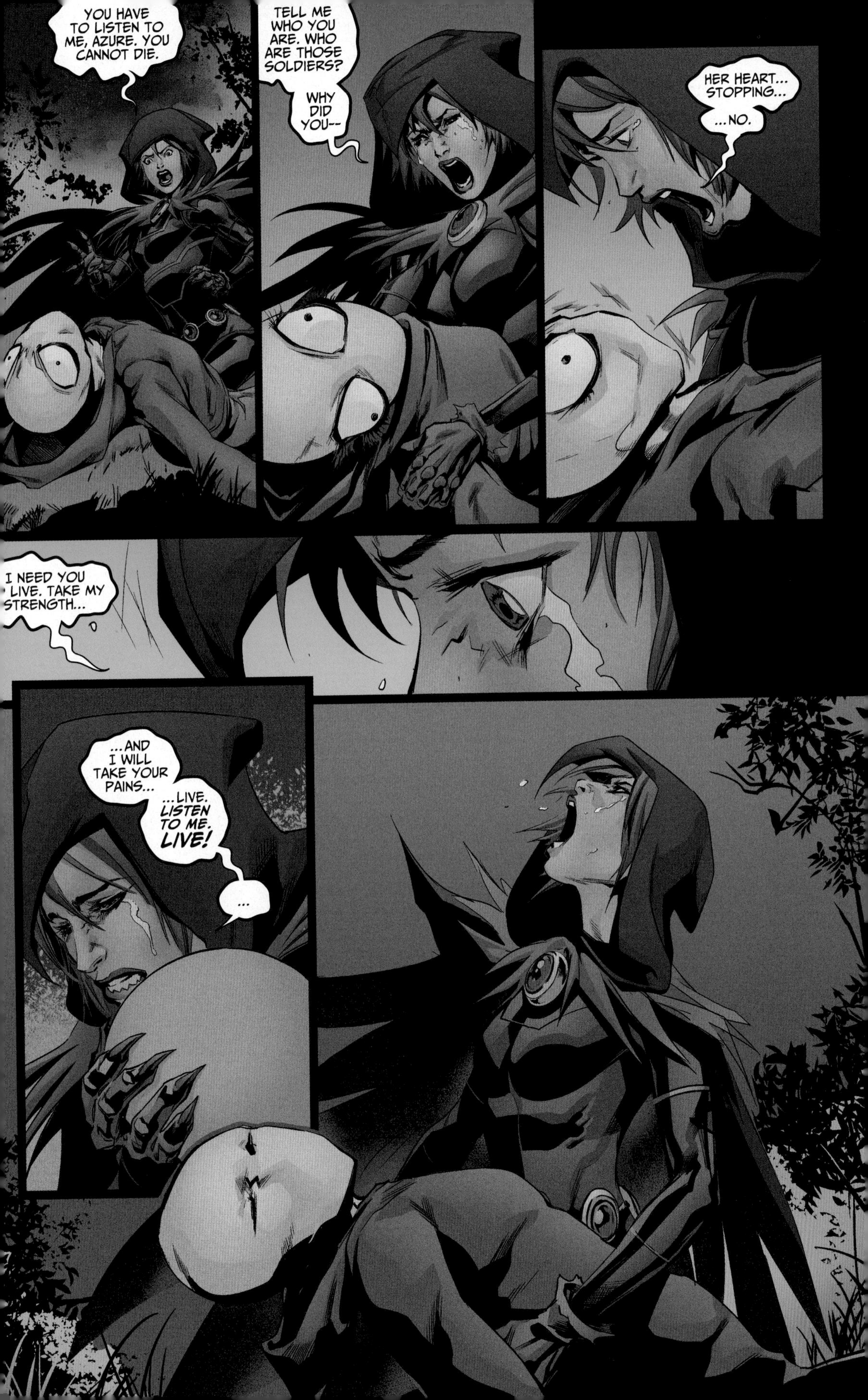
YOU HAVE TO LISTEN TO ME, AZURE. YOU CANNOT DIE.
TELL ME WHO YOU ARE. WHO ARE THOSE SOLDIERS?
WHY DID YOU--
HER HEART... STOPPING...
...NO.
I NEED YOU LIVE. TAKE MY STRENGTH...
...AND I WILL TAKE YOUR PAINS...
...LIVE. LISTEN TO ME. LIVE!
...

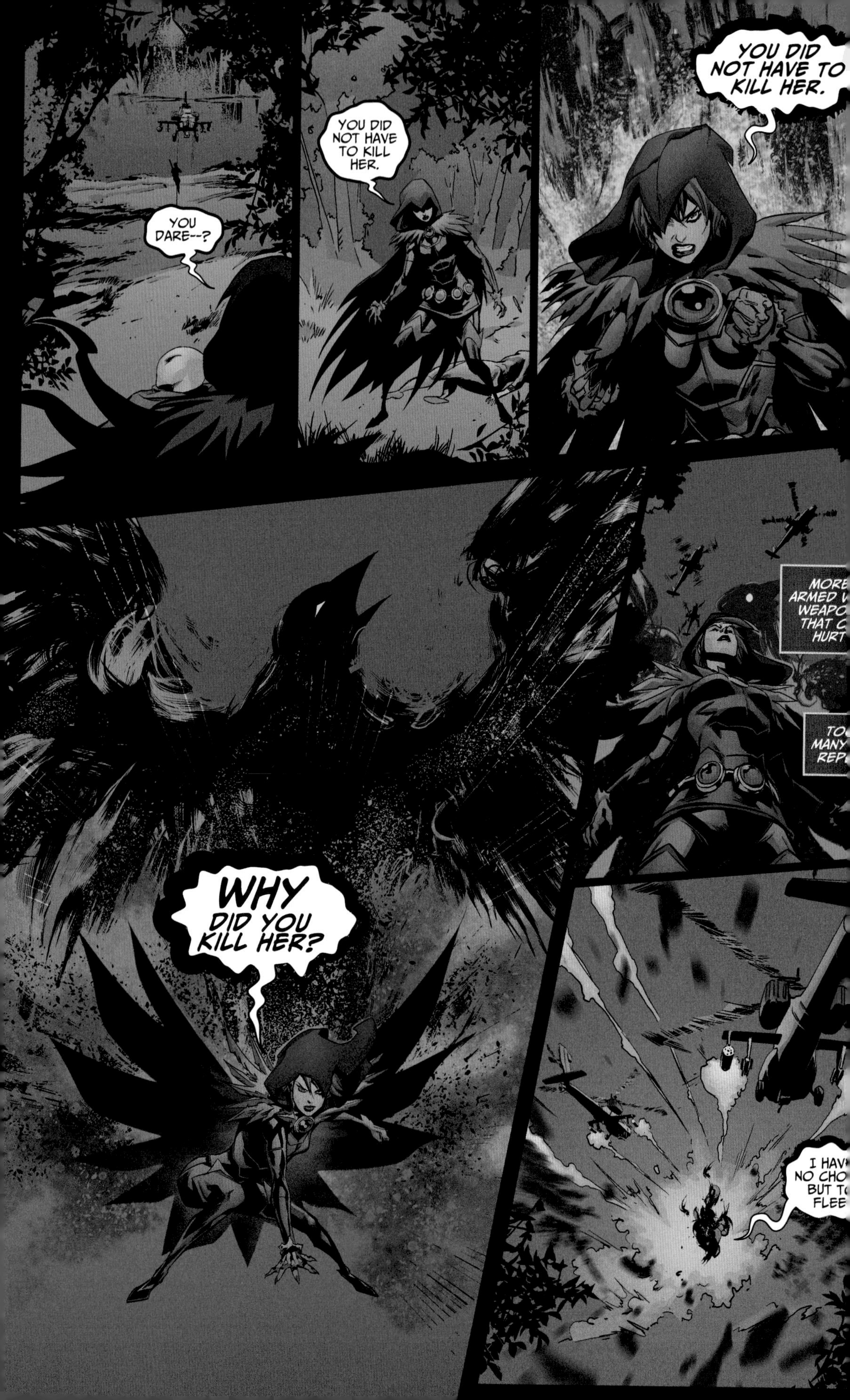
YOU DARE--?
YOU DID NOT HAVE TO KILL HER.
YOU DID NOT HAVE TO KILL HER.
WHY DID YOU KILL HER?
MORE ARMED W WEAPO THAT C HURT
TOO MANY REP
I HAV NO CHO BUT T FLEE

ξUHHHNN...ξ

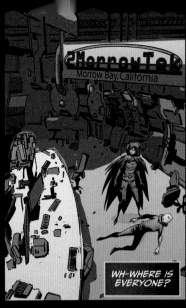

MorrowTek
Morrow Bay, California

WH-WHERE IS
EVERYONE?

HELLO?
CAN ANYONE
HEAR ME?
IS ANYONE
HERE?

EVERYONE...
EVERYTHING...HAS
BEEN REMOVED.

HUH?
YOU AGAIN?
WHO ARE
YOU?

CAN YOU
SEE ME?
WHO ARE
YOU?

-- MERLIN...
-- SHE IS...--
-- ---IT DOWN...
SHUT IT--

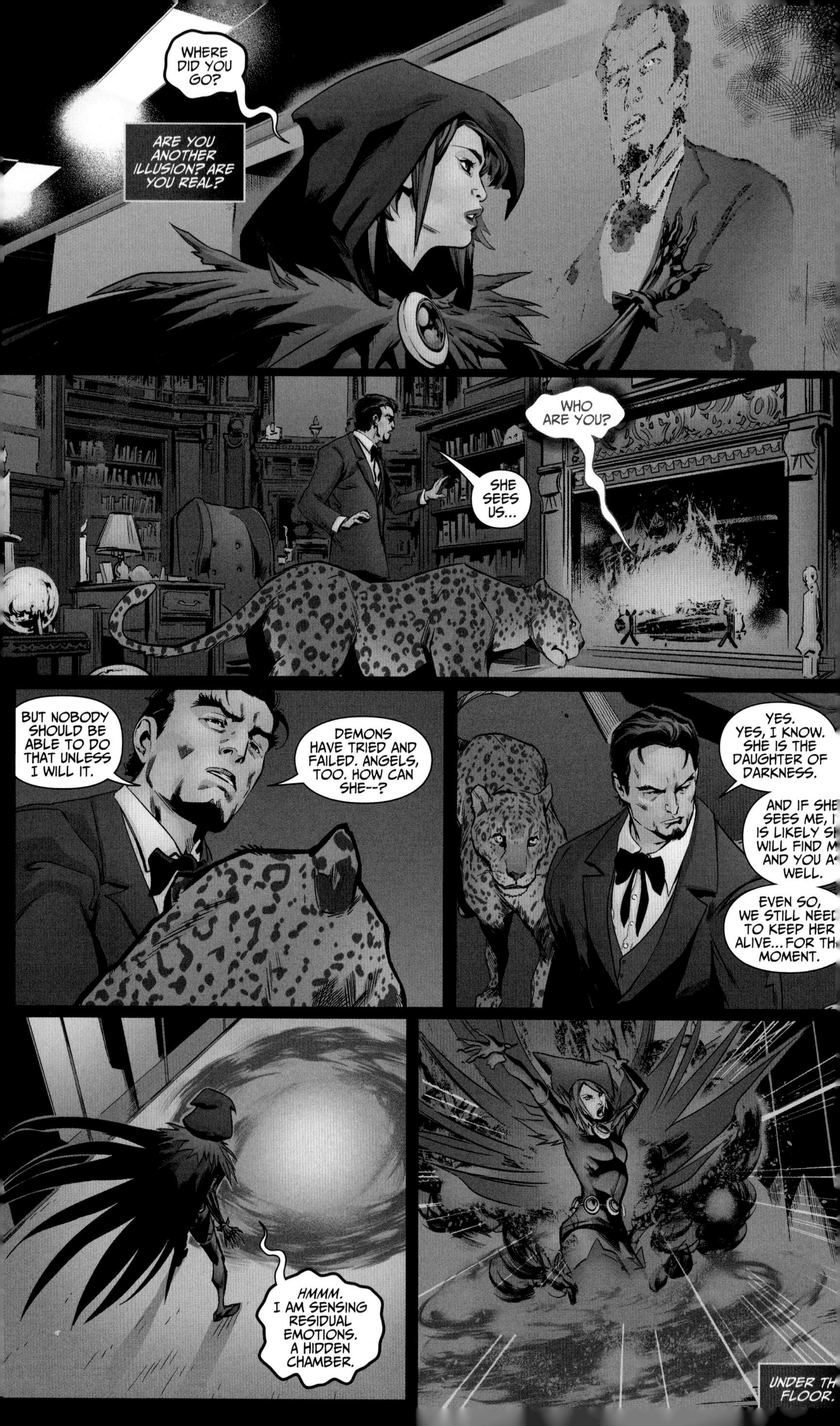
WHERE DID YOU GO?
ARE YOU ANOTHER ILLUSION? ARE YOU REAL?
WHO ARE YOU?
SHE SEES US...
BUT NOBODY SHOULD BE ABLE TO DO THAT UNLESS I WILL IT.
DEMONS HAVE TRIED AND FAILED. ANGELS, TOO. HOW CAN SHE--?
YES. YES, I KNOW. SHE IS THE DAUGHTER OF DARKNESS.
AND IF SHE SEES ME, I IS LIKELY S WILL FIND M AND YOU A WELL.
EVEN SO, WE STILL NEED TO KEEP HER ALIVE...FOR TH MOMENT.
HMMM. I AM SENSING RESIDUAL EMOTIONS. A HIDDEN CHAMBER.
UNDER TH FLOOR.

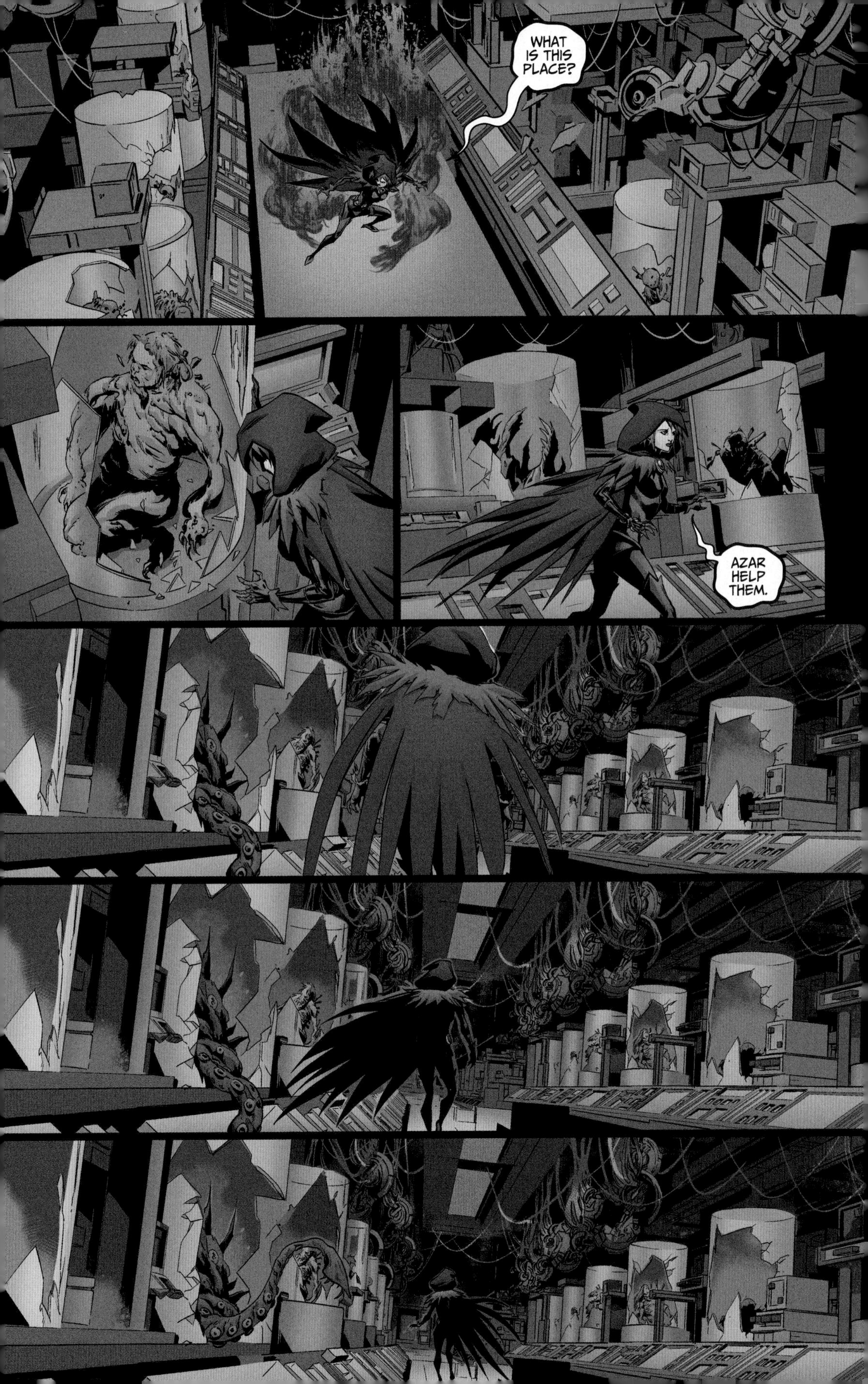
WHAT IS THIS PLACE?
AZAR HELP THEM.

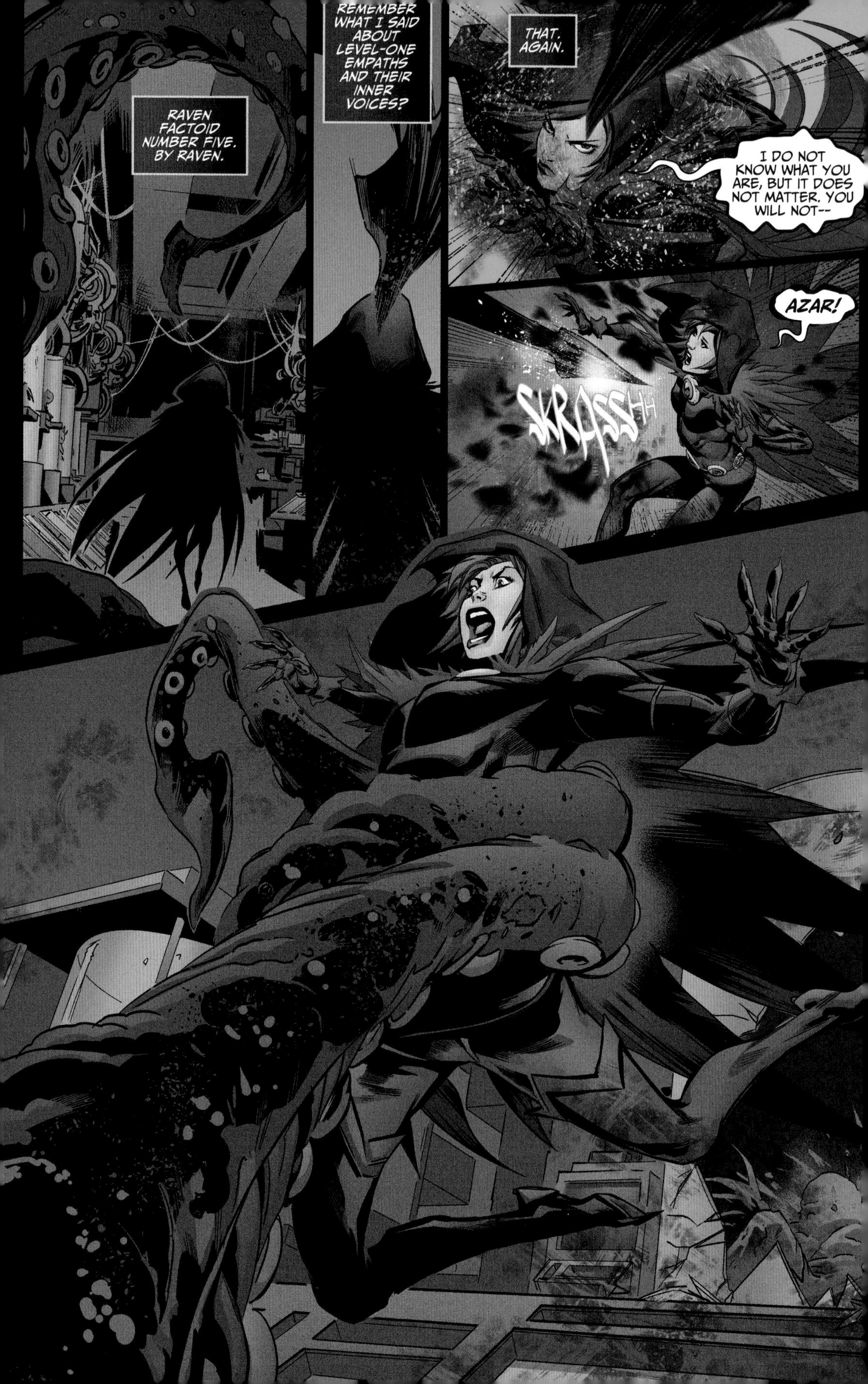
RAVEN FACTOID NUMBER FIVE. BY RAVEN.
REMEMBER WHAT I SAID ABOUT LEVEL-ONE EMPATHS AND THEIR INNER VOICES?
THAT. AGAIN.
I DO NOT KNOW WHAT YOU ARE, BUT IT DOES NOT MATTER. YOU WILL NOT--
AZAR!
SKRASSHH

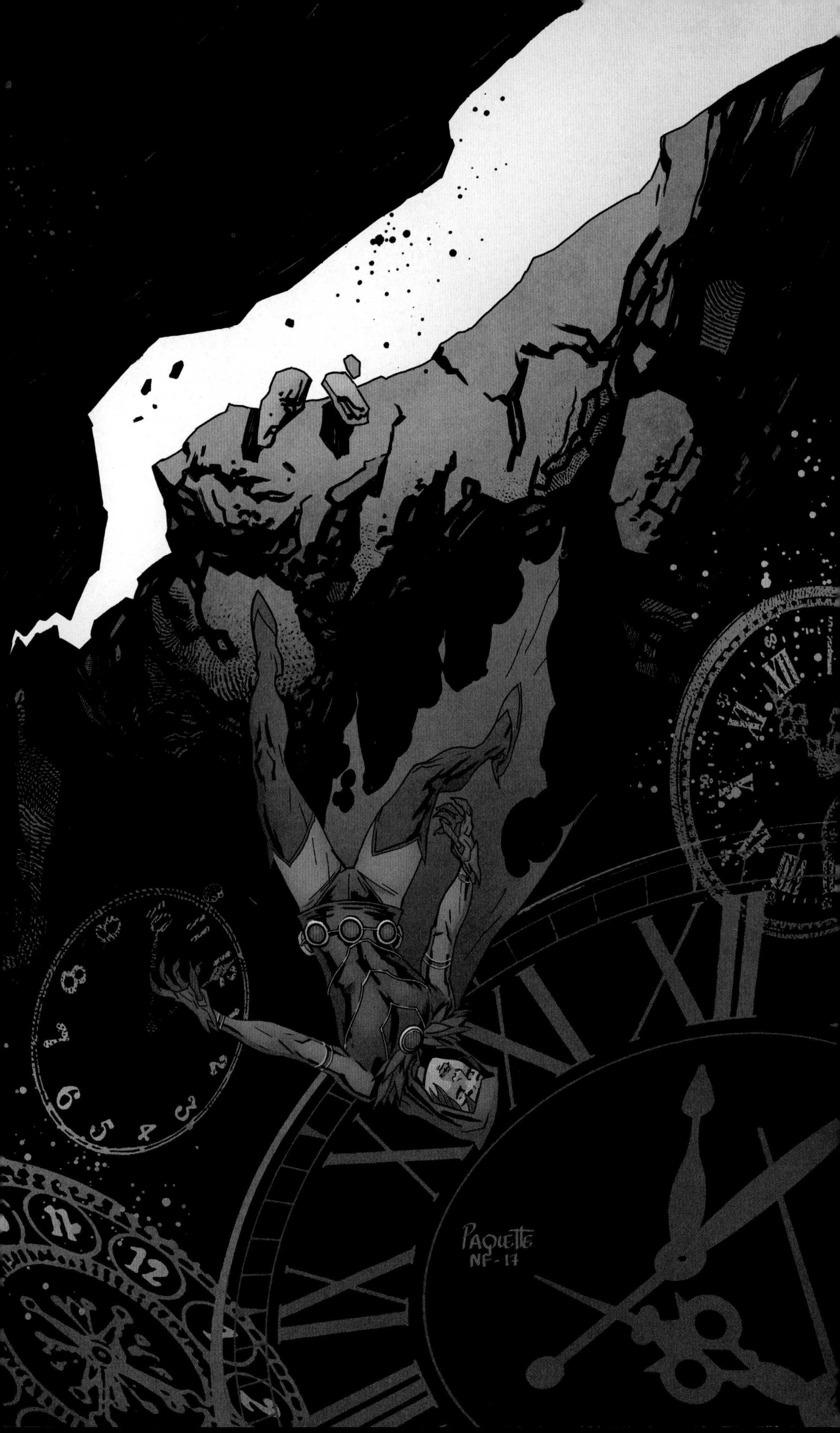
PAQUETTE
NF-17

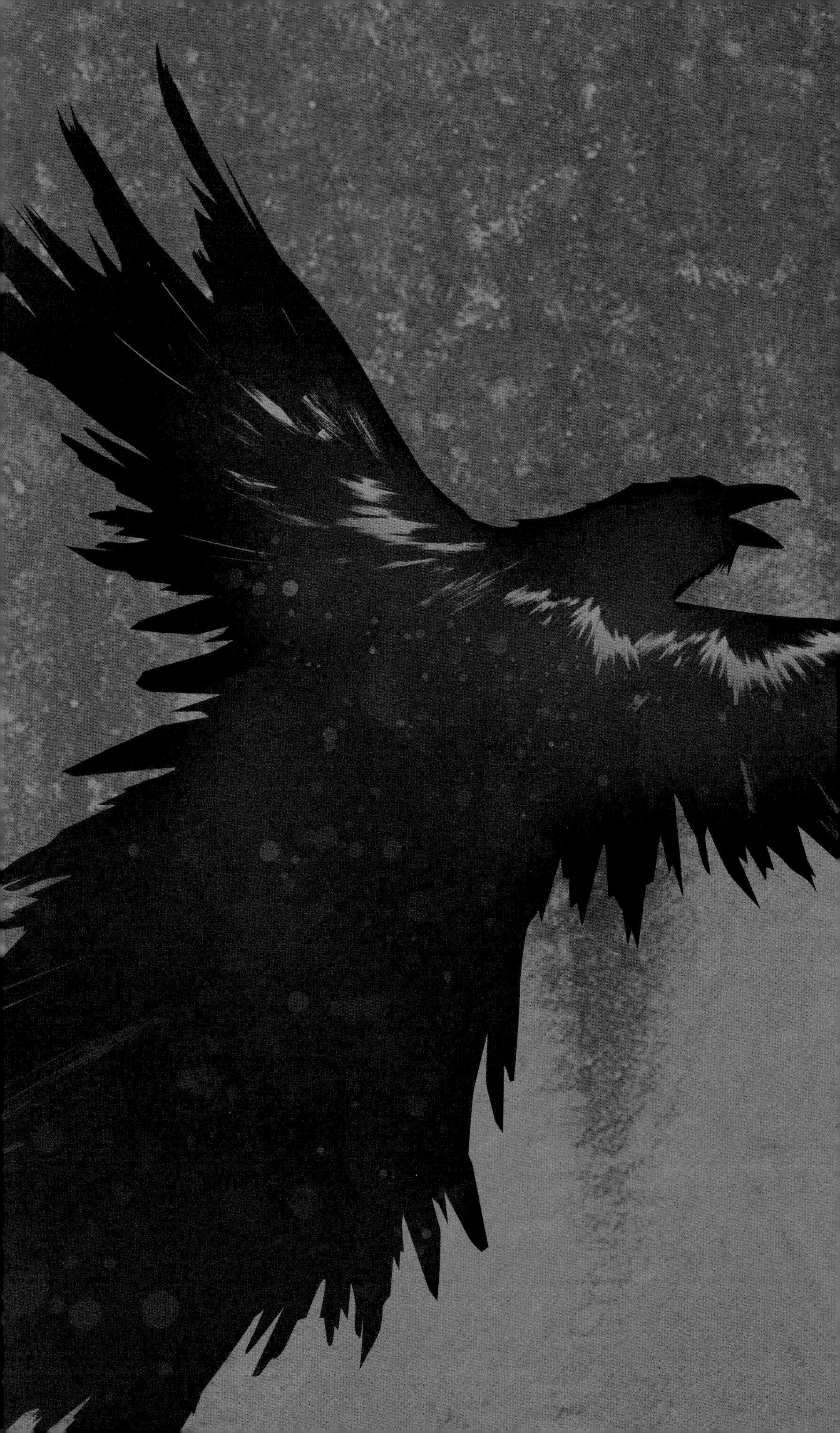

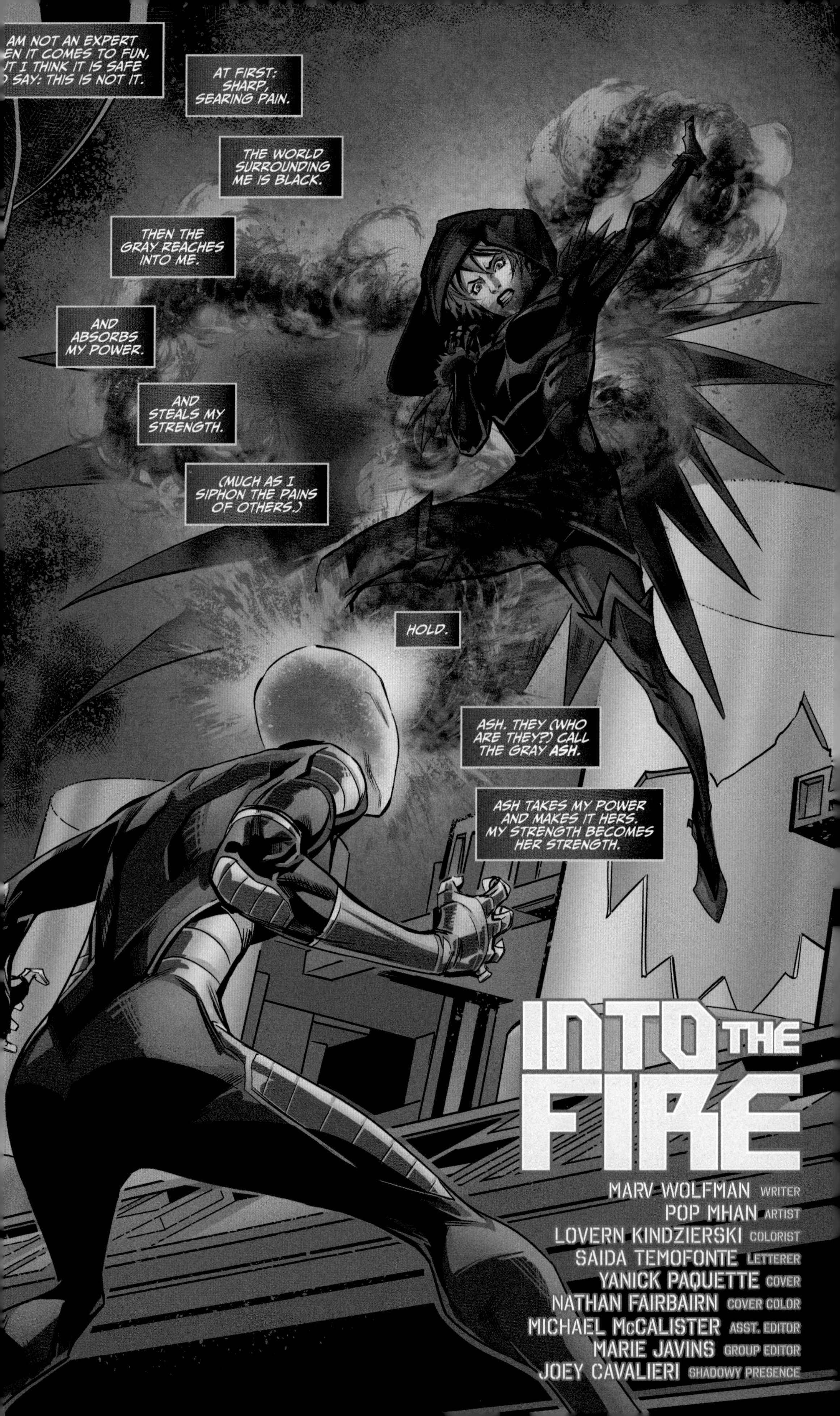
AM NOT AN EXPERT EN IT COMES TO FUN, T I THINK IT IS SAFE SAY: THIS IS NOT IT.
AT FIRST: SHARP, SEARING PAIN.
THE WORLD SURROUNDING ME IS BLACK.
THEN THE GRAY REACHES INTO ME.
AND ABSORBS MY POWER.
AND STEALS MY STRENGTH.
(MUCH AS I SIPHON THE PAINS OF OTHERS.)
HOLD.
ASH. THEY (WHO ARE THEY?) CALL THE GRAY ASH.
ASH TAKES MY POWER AND MAKES IT HERS. MY STRENGTH BECOMES HER STRENGTH.
INTO THE FIRE
MARV WOLFMAN WRITER
POP MHAN ARTIST
LOVERN KINDZIERSKI COLORIST
SAIDA TEMOFONTE LETTERER
YANICK PAQUETTE COVER
NATHAN FAIRBAIRN COVER COLOR
MICHAEL McCALISTER ASST. EDITOR
MARIE JAVINS GROUP EDITOR
JOEY CAVALIERI SHADOWY PRESENCE

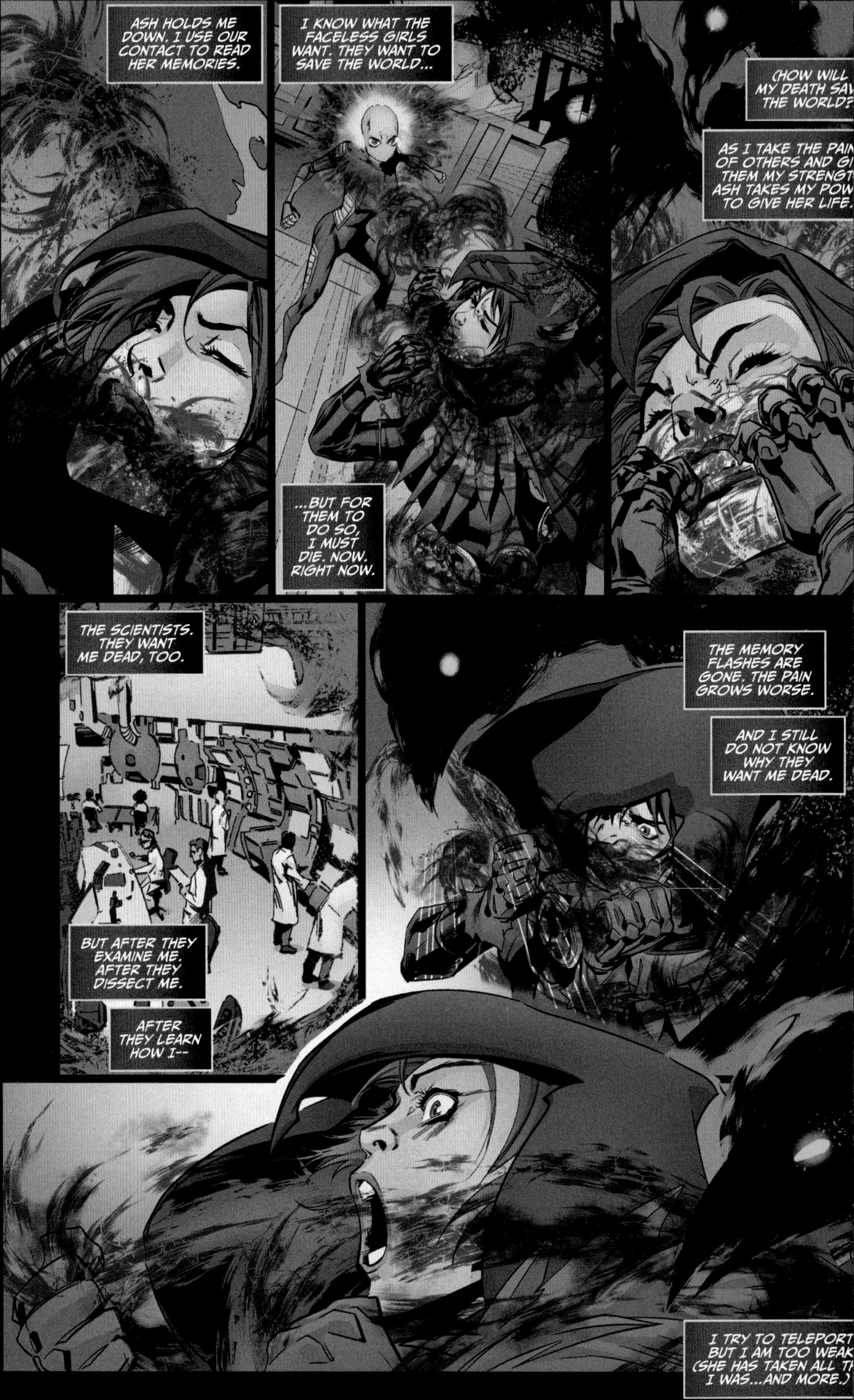

ASH HOLDS ME DOWN. I USE OUR CONTACT TO READ HER MEMORIES.
I KNOW WHAT THE FACELESS GIRLS WANT. THEY WANT TO SAVE THE WORLD...
...BUT FOR THEM TO DO SO, I MUST DIE. NOW. RIGHT NOW.
(HOW WILL MY DEATH SAV THE WORLD?
AS I TAKE THE PAIN OF OTHERS AND GI THEM MY STRENGT ASH TAKES MY POW TO GIVE HER LIFE.
THE SCIENTISTS. THEY WANT ME DEAD, TOO.
BUT AFTER THEY EXAMINE ME. AFTER THEY DISSECT ME.
AFTER THEY LEARN HOW I--
THE MEMORY FLASHES ARE GONE. THE PAIN GROWS WORSE.
AND I STILL DO NOT KNOW WHY THEY WANT ME DEAD.
I TRY TO TELEPORT BUT I AM TOO WEAK (SHE HAS TAKEN ALL TH I WAS...AND MORE.)

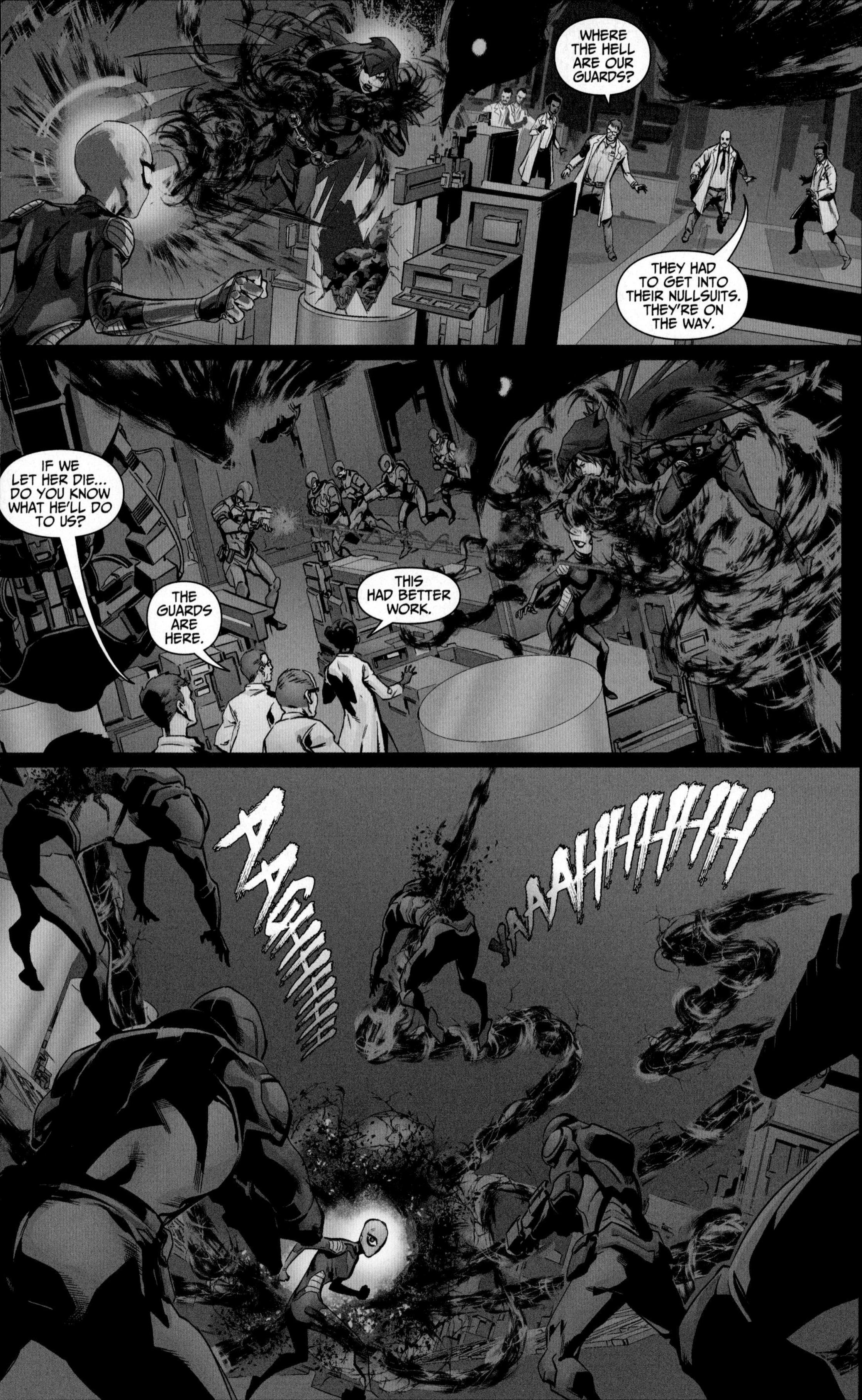
WHERE THE HELL ARE OUR GUARDS?
THEY HAD TO GET INTO THEIR NULLSUITS. THEY'RE ON THE WAY.
IF WE LET HER DIE... DO YOU KNOW WHAT HE'LL DO TO US?
THE GUARDS ARE HERE.
THIS HAD BETTER WORK.
AAGHHHHHHH
YAAAAHHHHHHH

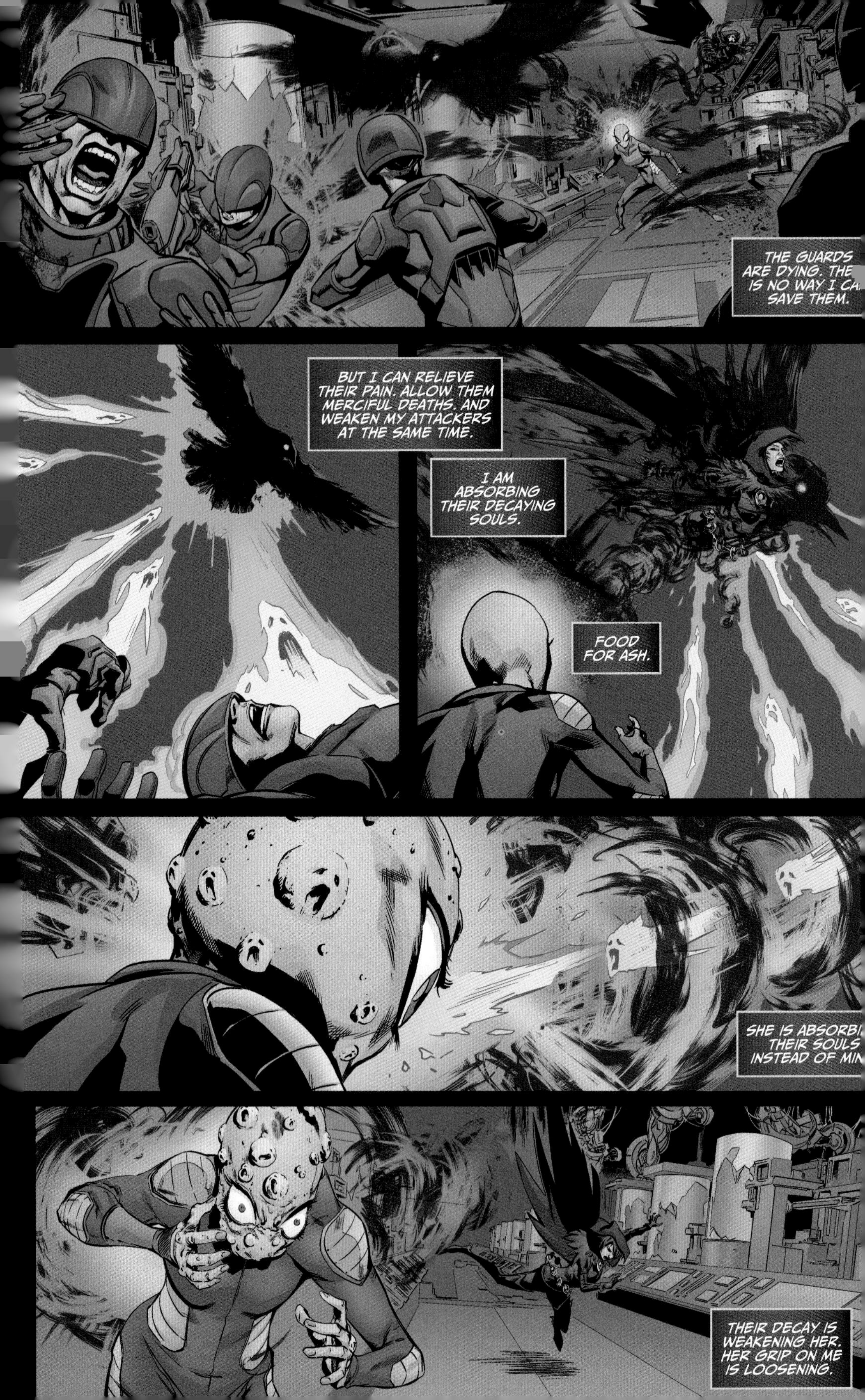
THE GUARDS ARE DYING. THE IS NO WAY I CA SAVE THEM.
BUT I CAN RELIEVE THEIR PAIN. ALLOW THEM MERCIFUL DEATHS. AND WEAKEN MY ATTACKERS AT THE SAME TIME.
I AM ABSORBING THEIR DECAYING SOULS.
FOOD FOR ASH.
SHE IS ABSORBI THEIR SOULS INSTEAD OF MIN
THEIR DECAY IS WEAKENING HER. HER GRIP ON ME IS LOOSENING.

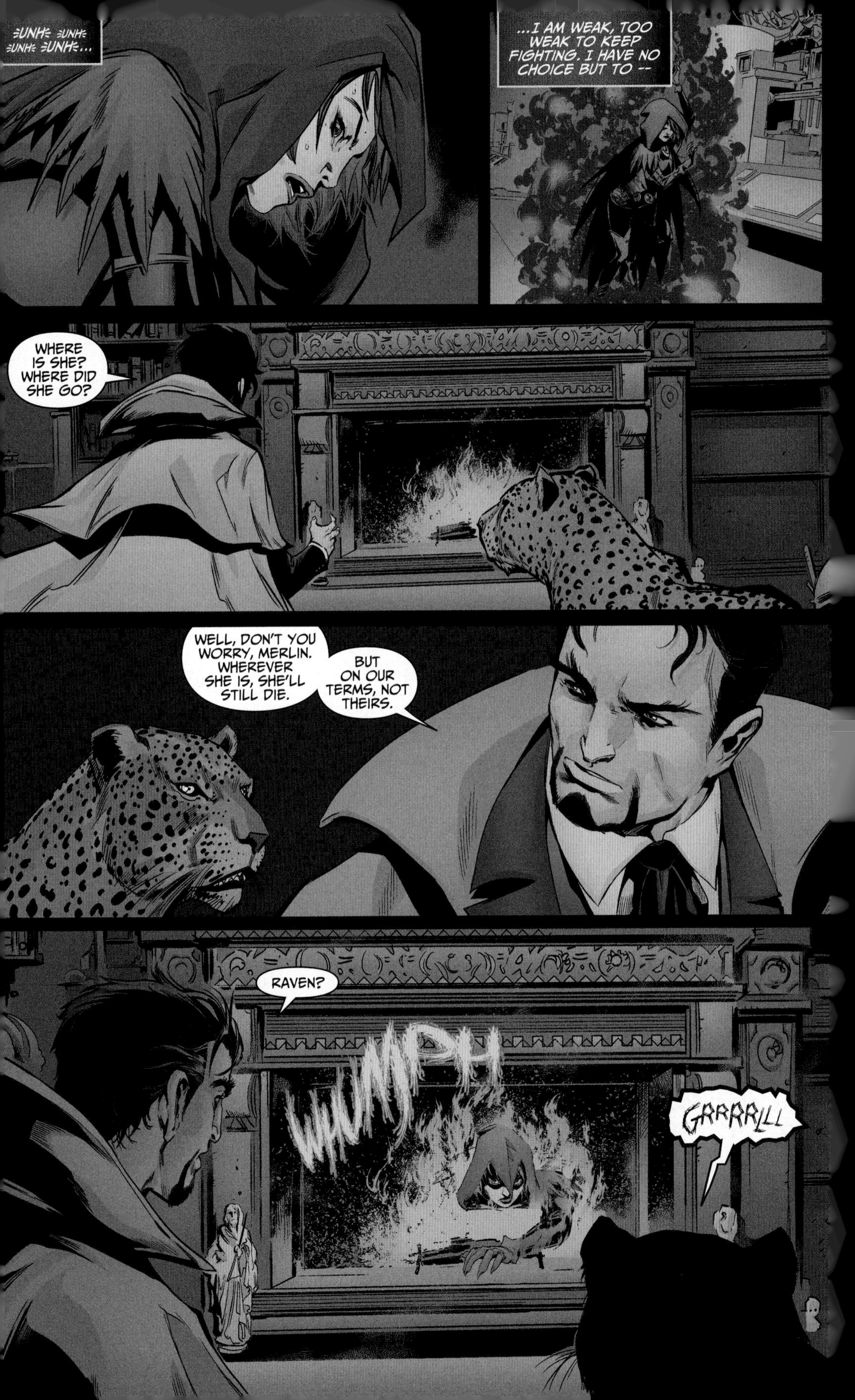

UNH UNH UNH UNH...
...I AM WEAK, TOO WEAK TO KEEP FIGHTING. I HAVE NO CHOICE BUT TO --
WHERE IS SHE? WHERE DID SHE GO?
WELL, DON'T YOU WORRY, MERLIN. WHEREVER SHE IS, SHE'LL STILL DIE.
BUT ON OUR TERMS, NOT THEIRS.
RAVEN?
WHUMPH
GRRRRLLL

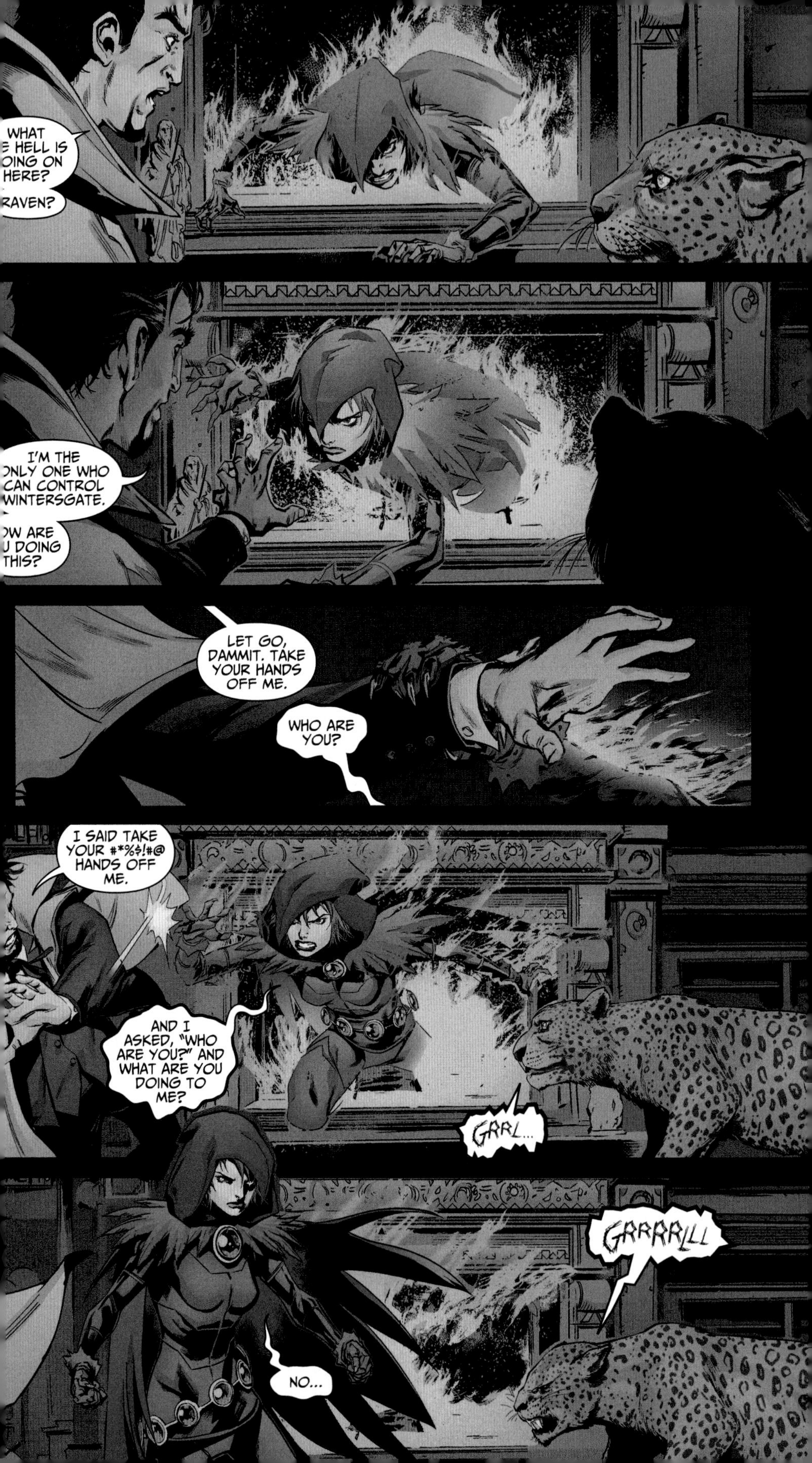
WHAT
E HELL IS
OING ON
HERE?
RAVEN?
I'M THE
ONLY ONE WHO
CAN CONTROL
WINTERSGATE.
OW ARE
U DOING
THIS?
LET GO, DAMMIT. TAKE YOUR HANDS OFF ME.
WHO ARE YOU?
I SAID TAKE YOUR #*%$!#@ HANDS OFF ME.
AND I ASKED, "WHO ARE YOU?" AND WHAT ARE YOU DOING TO ME?
GRRL...
GRRRRLLL
NO...

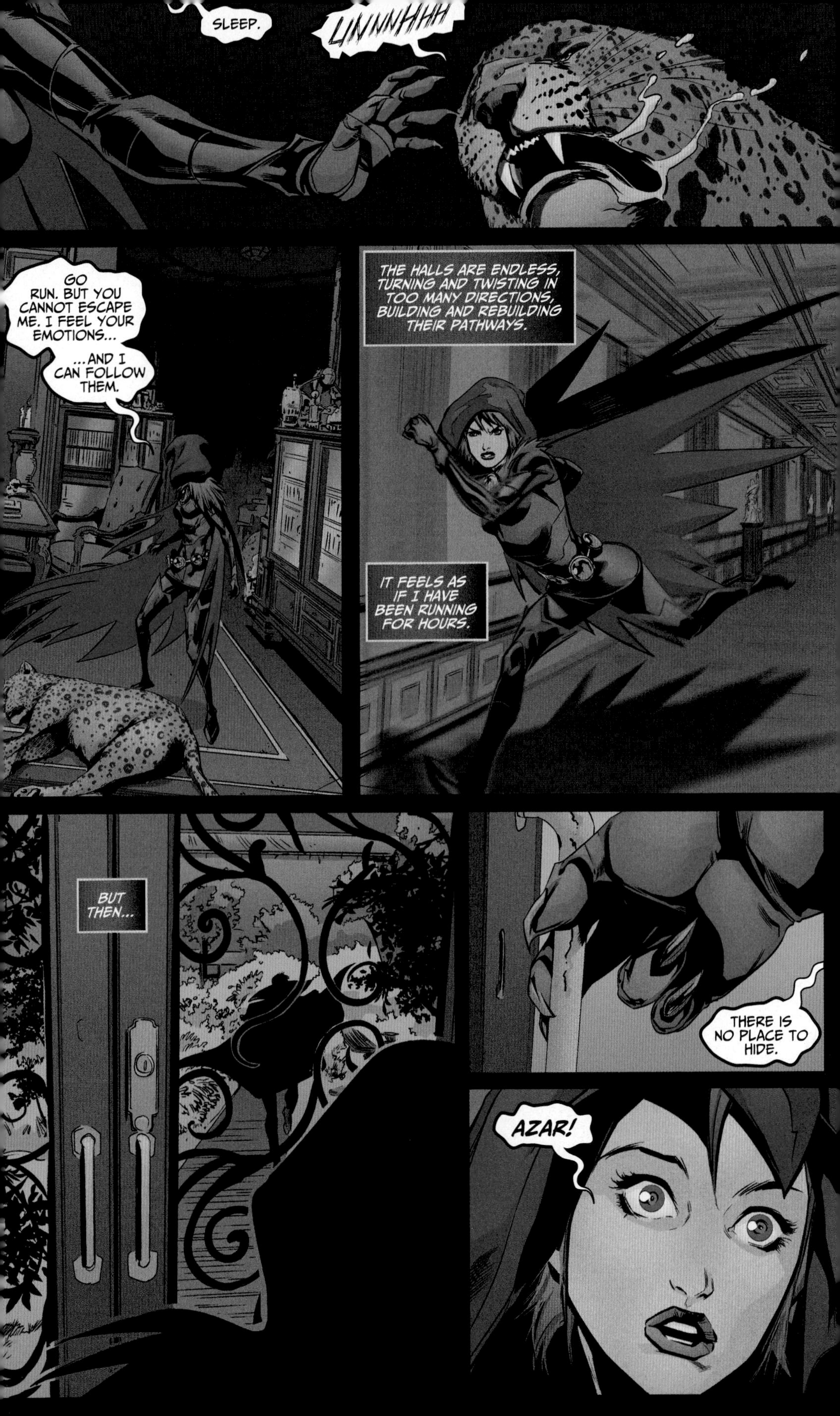
SLEEP.
UNNNHHH
GO RUN. BUT YOU CANNOT ESCAPE ME. I FEEL YOUR EMOTIONS...
...AND I CAN FOLLOW THEM.
THE HALLS ARE ENDLESS, TURNING AND TWISTING IN TOO MANY DIRECTIONS, BUILDING AND REBUILDING THEIR PATHWAYS.
IT FEELS AS IF I HAVE BEEN RUNNING FOR HOURS.
BUT THEN...
THERE IS NO PLACE TO HIDE.
AZAR!

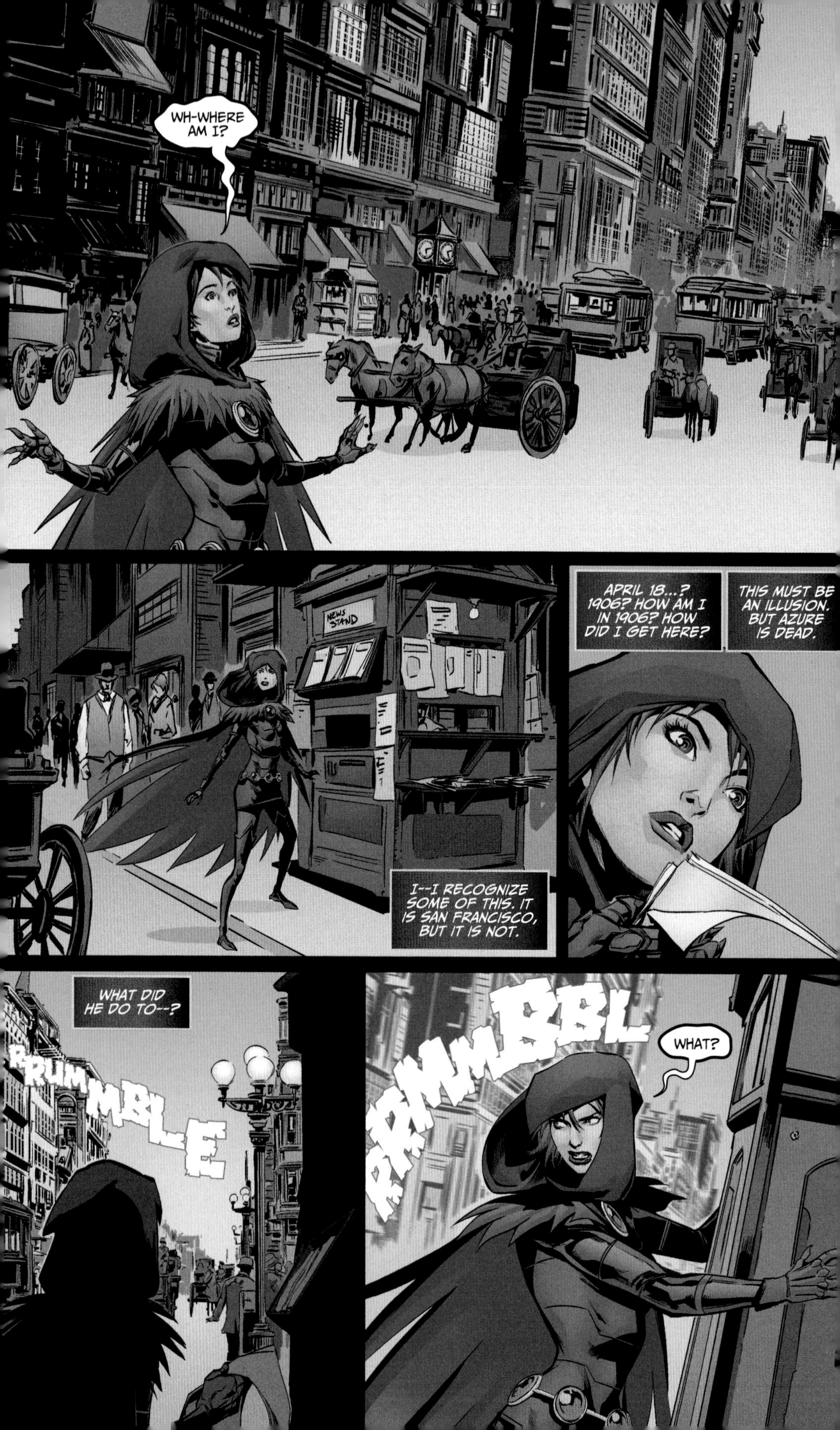
WH-WHERE AM I?
NEWS STAND
APRIL 18...? 1906? HOW AM I IN 1906? HOW DID I GET HERE?
THIS MUST BE AN ILLUSION. BUT AZURE IS DEAD.
I--I RECOGNIZE SOME OF THIS. IT IS SAN FRANCISCO, BUT IT IS NOT.
WHAT DID HE DO TO--?
RRUMMBLE
RRMMBBL
WHAT?

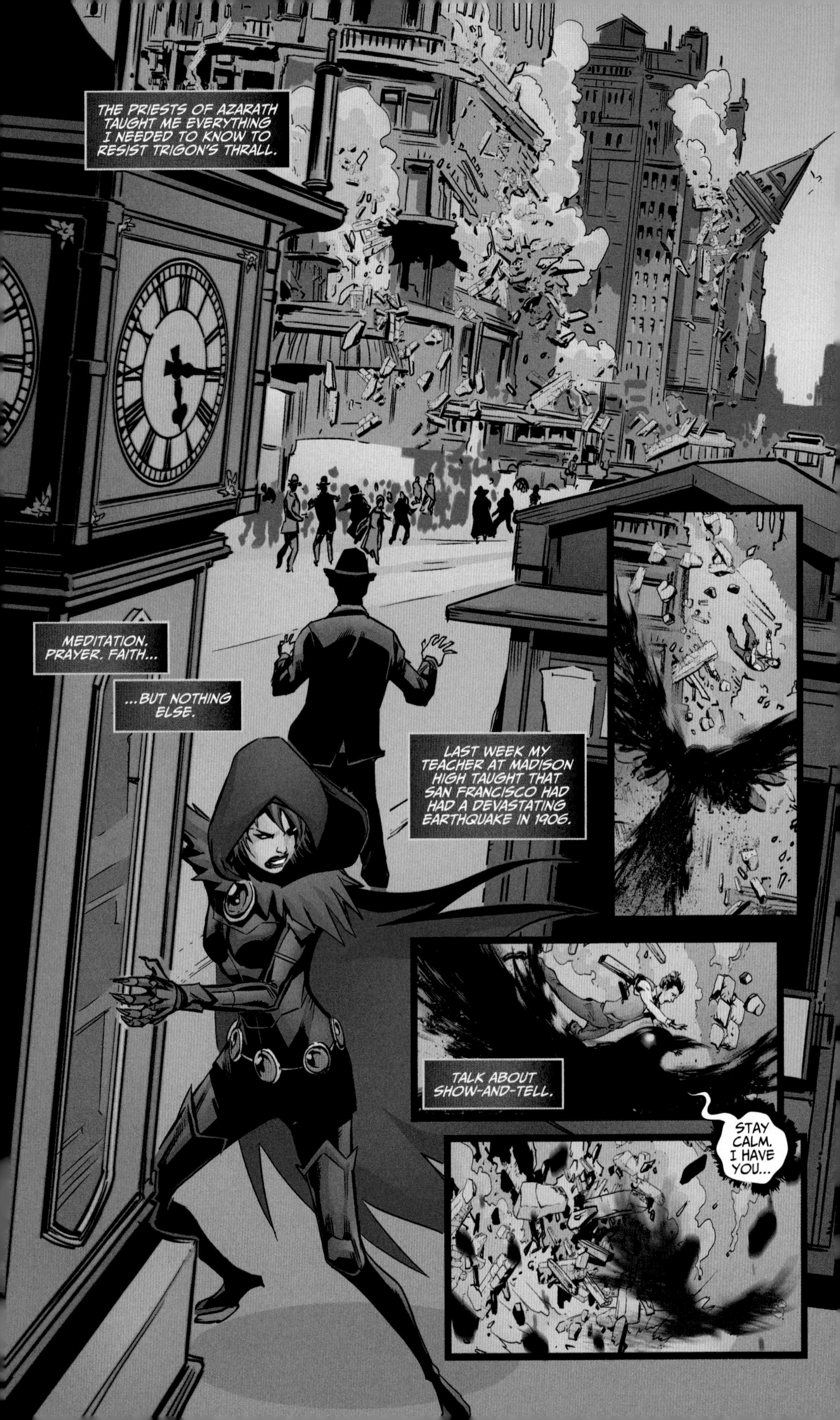
THE PRIESTS OF AZARATH TAUGHT ME EVERYTHING I NEEDED TO KNOW TO RESIST TRIGON'S THRALL.
MEDITATION. PRAYER. FAITH...
...BUT NOTHING ELSE.
LAST WEEK MY TEACHER AT MADISON HIGH TAUGHT THAT SAN FRANCISCO HAD HAD A DEVASTATING EARTHQUAKE IN 1906.
TALK ABOUT SHOW-AND-TELL.
STAY CALM. I HAVE YOU...

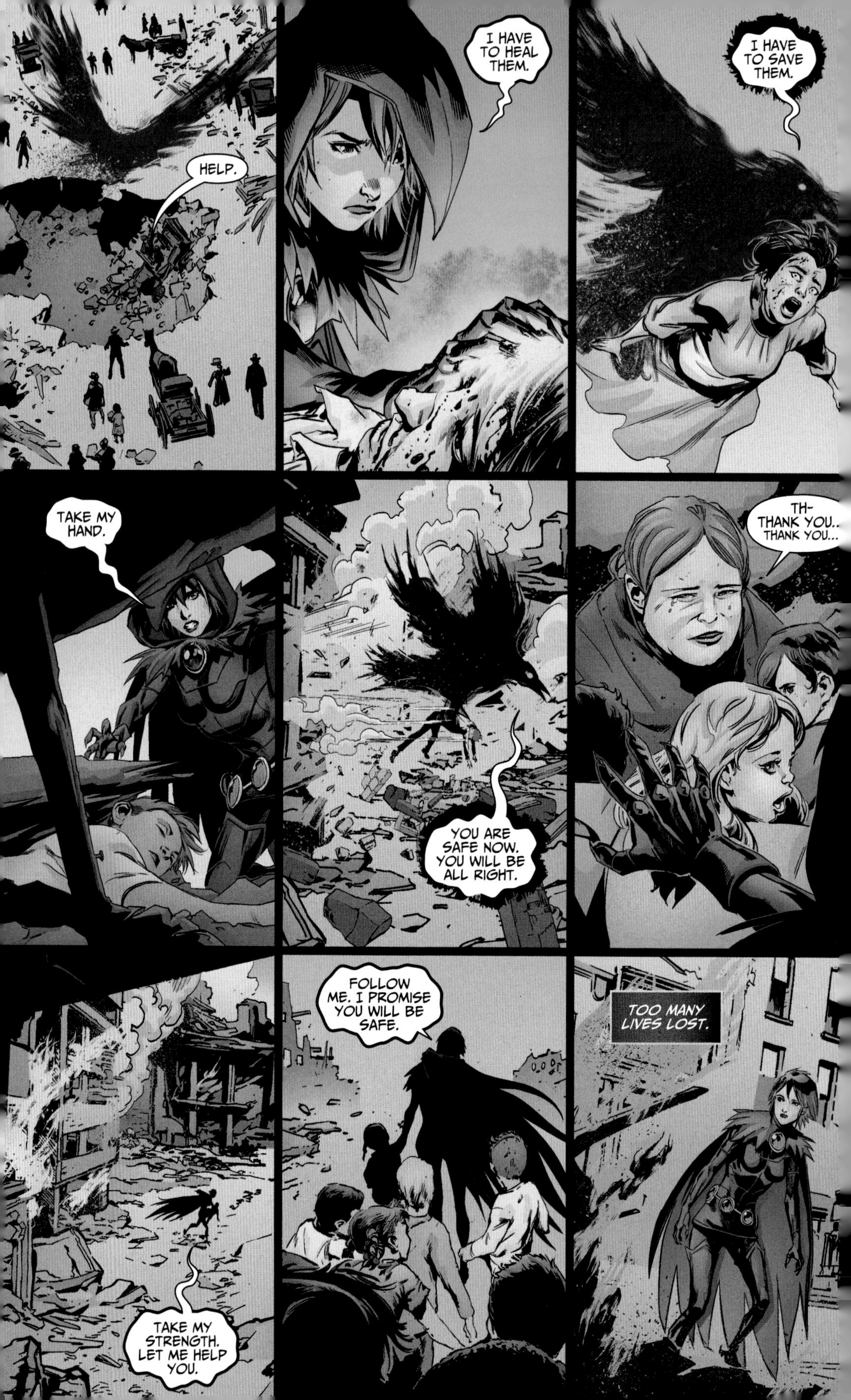
HELP.
I HAVE TO HEAL THEM.
I HAVE TO SAVE THEM.
TAKE MY HAND.
YOU ARE SAFE NOW. YOU WILL BE ALL RIGHT.
TH- THANK YOU... THANK YOU...
TAKE MY STRENGTH. LET ME HELP YOU.
FOLLOW ME. I PROMISE YOU WILL BE SAFE.
TOO MANY LIVES LOST.

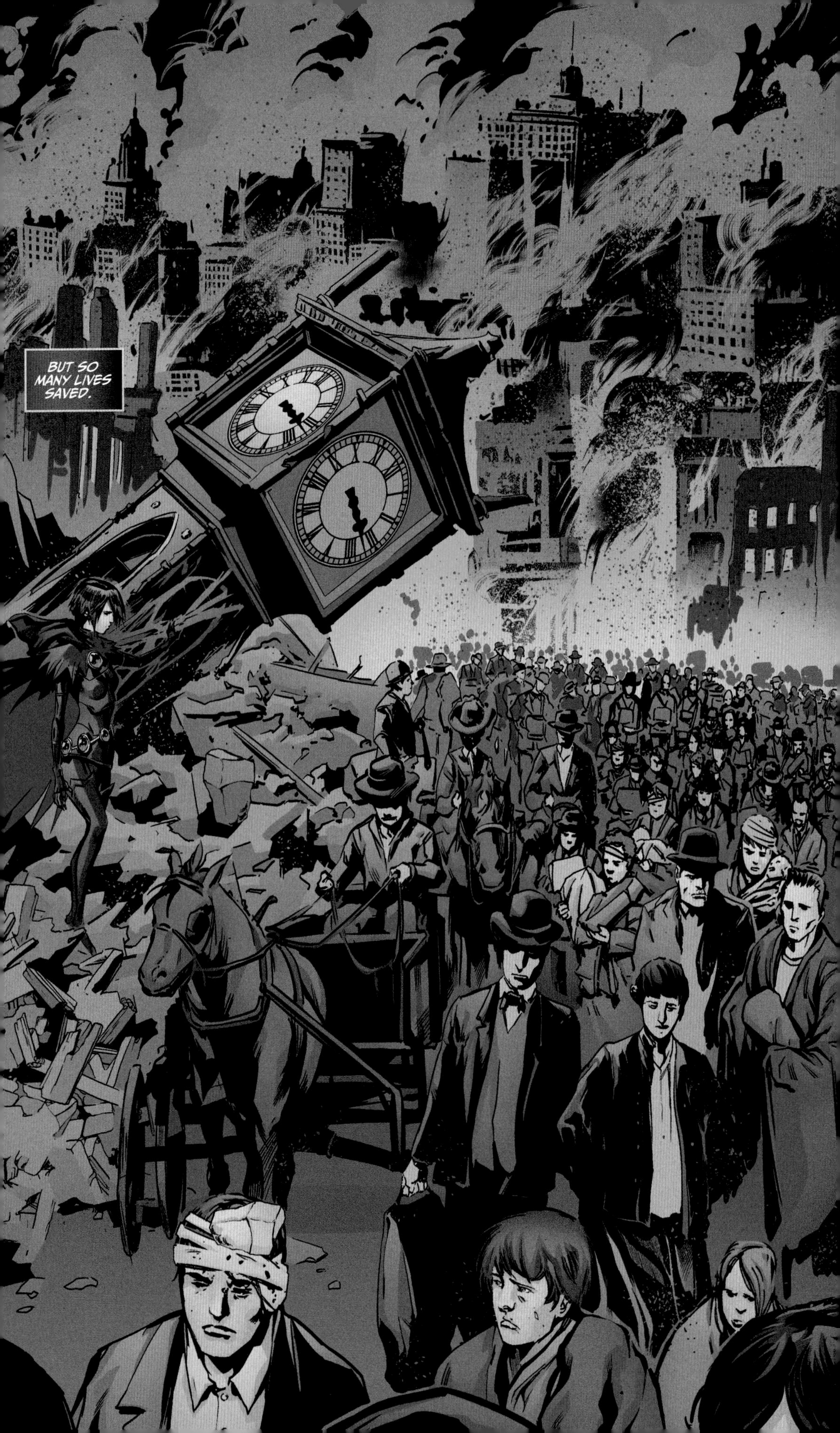
BUT SO MANY LIVES SAVED.

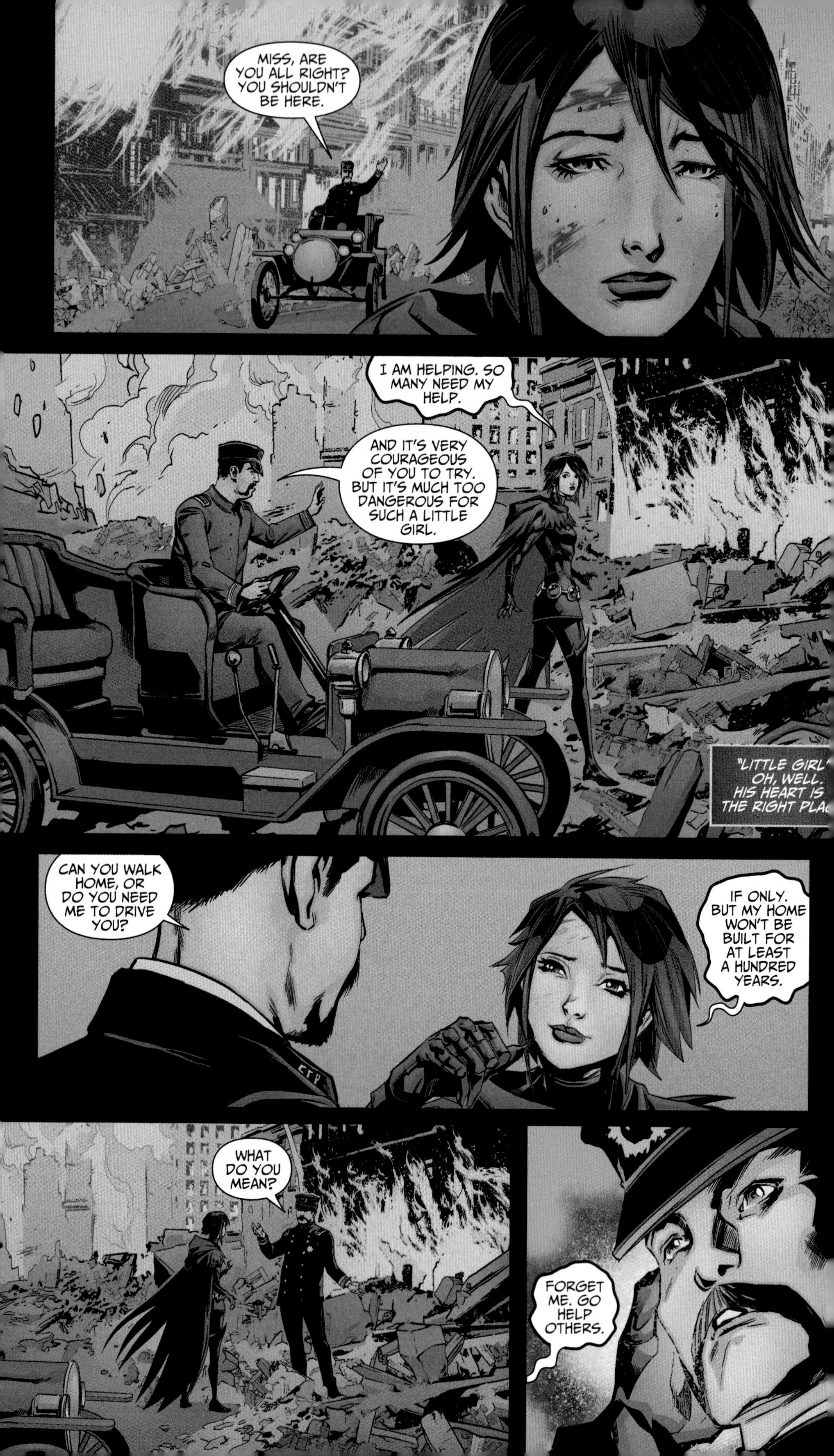
MISS, ARE YOU ALL RIGHT? YOU SHOULDN'T BE HERE.
I AM HELPING. SO MANY NEED MY HELP.
AND IT'S VERY COURAGEOUS OF YOU TO TRY. BUT IT'S MUCH TOO DANGEROUS FOR SUCH A LITTLE GIRL.
"LITTLE GIRL" OH, WELL. HIS HEART IS THE RIGHT PLA
CAN YOU WALK HOME, OR DO YOU NEED ME TO DRIVE YOU?
IF ONLY. BUT MY HOME WON'T BE BUILT FOR AT LEAST A HUNDRED YEARS.
WHAT DO YOU MEAN?
FORGET ME. GO HELP OTHERS.

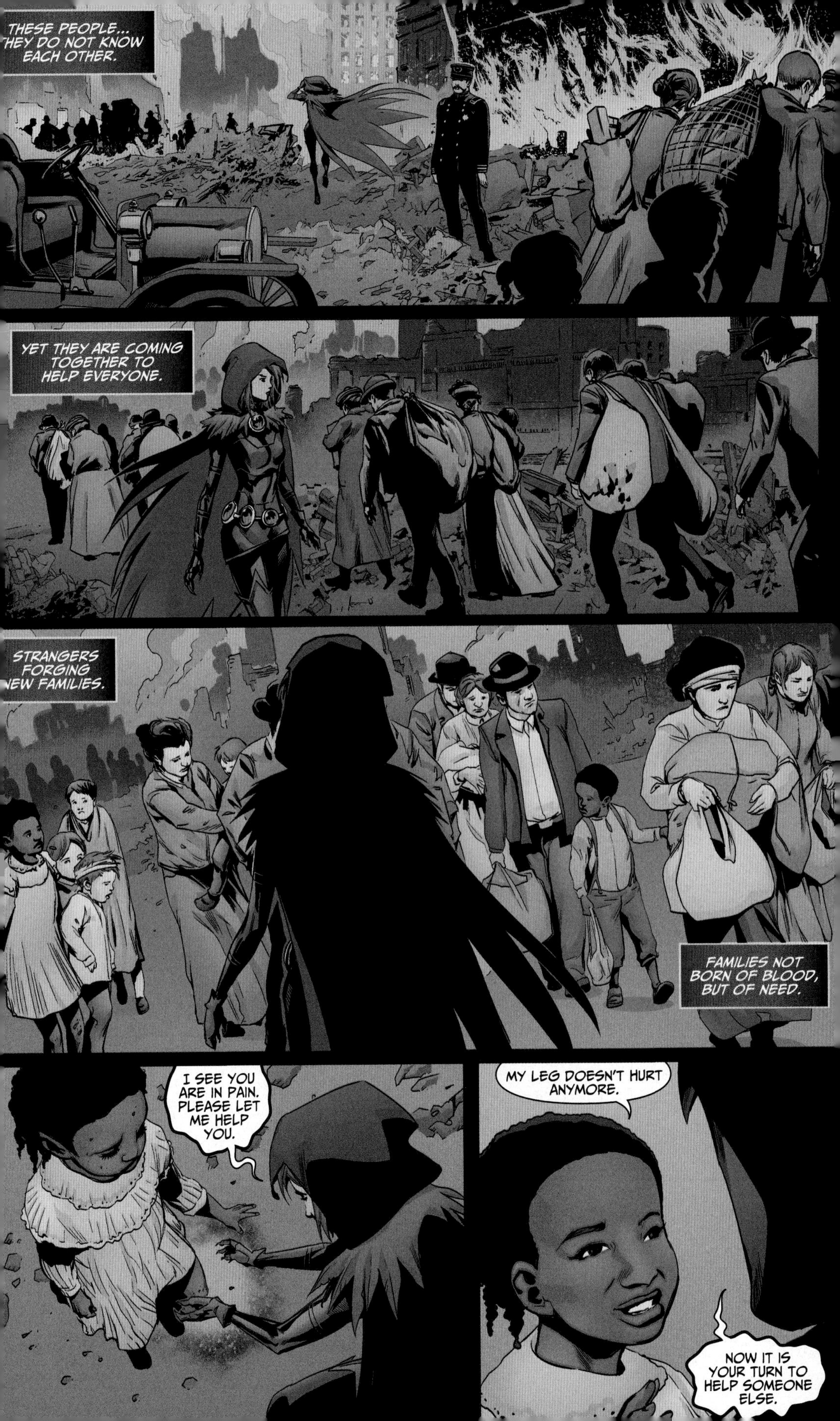
THESE PEOPLE... THEY DO NOT KNOW EACH OTHER.
YET THEY ARE COMING TOGETHER TO HELP EVERYONE.
STRANGERS FORGING NEW FAMILIES.
FAMILIES NOT BORN OF BLOOD, BUT OF NEED.
I SEE YOU ARE IN PAIN. PLEASE LET ME HELP YOU.
MY LEG DOESN'T HURT ANYMORE.
NOW IT IS YOUR TURN TO HELP SOMEONE ELSE.

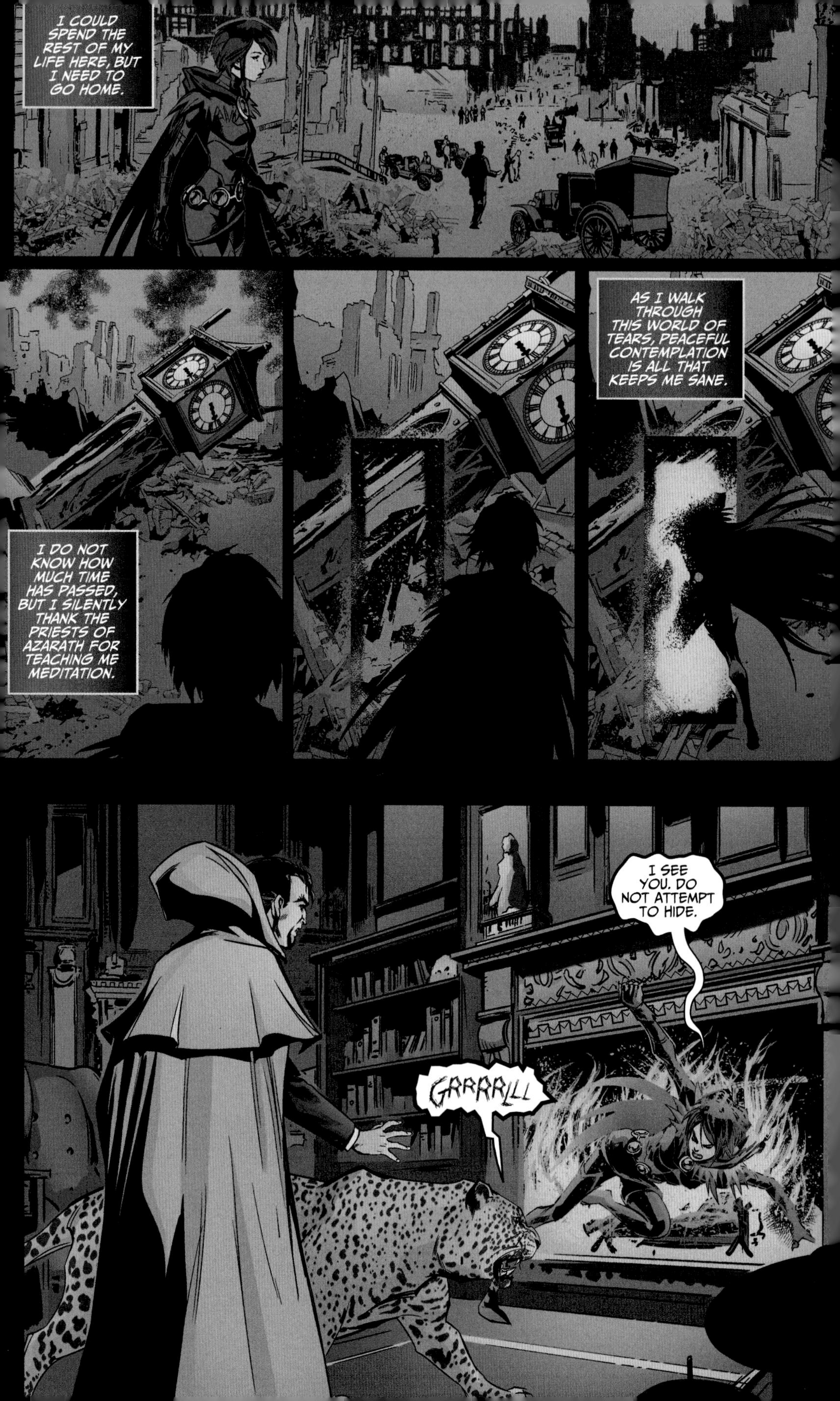
I COULD SPEND THE REST OF MY LIFE HERE, BUT I NEED TO GO HOME.
I DO NOT KNOW HOW MUCH TIME HAS PASSED, BUT I SILENTLY THANK THE PRIESTS OF AZARATH FOR TEACHING ME MEDITATION.
AS I WALK THROUGH THIS WORLD OF TEARS, PEACEFUL CONTEMPLATION IS ALL THAT KEEPS ME SANE.
I SEE YOU. DO NOT ATTEMPT TO HIDE.
GRRRRLLL

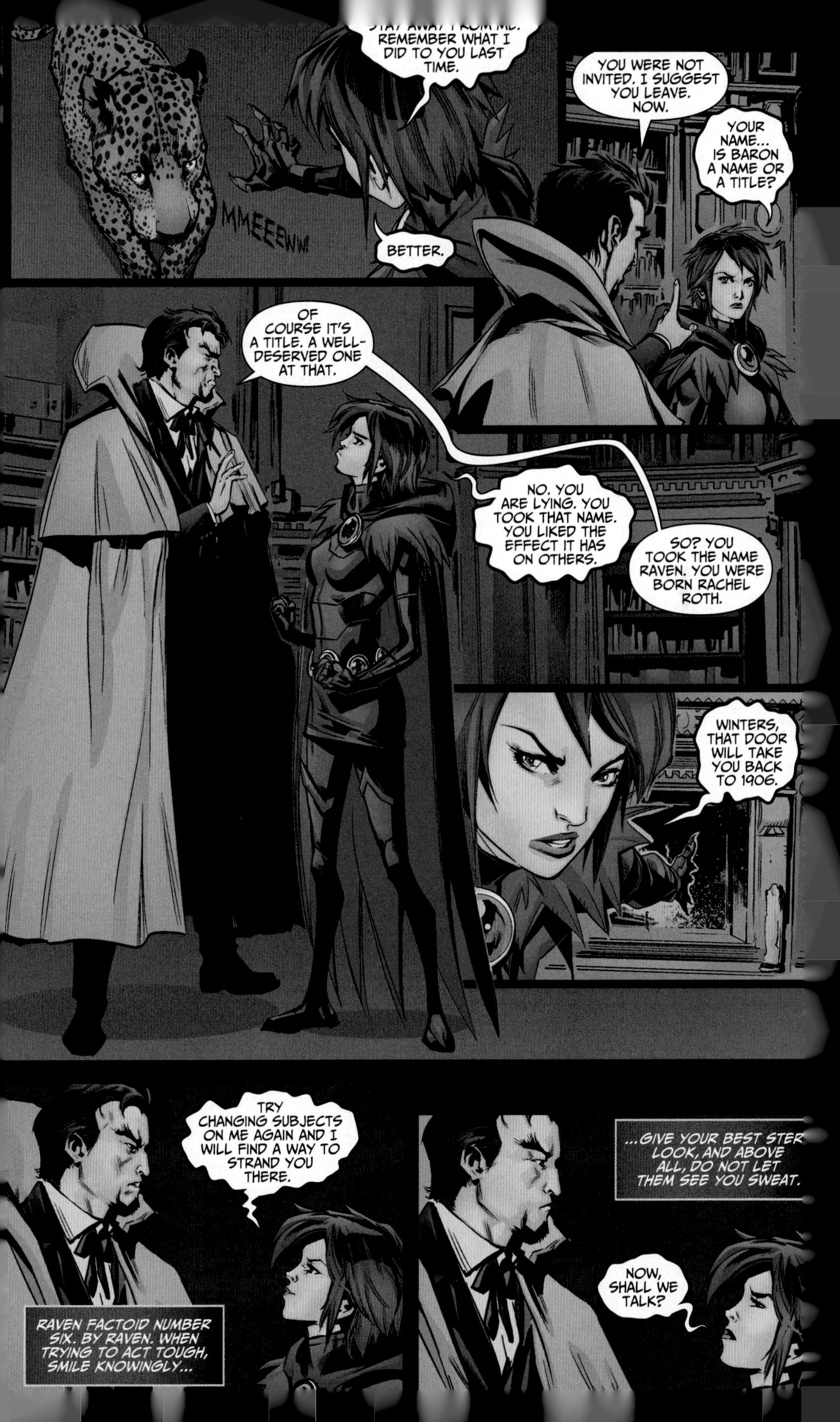
REMEMBER WHAT I DID TO YOU LAST TIME.
BETTER.
YOU WERE NOT INVITED. I SUGGEST YOU LEAVE. NOW.
YOUR NAME... IS BARON A NAME OR A TITLE?
OF COURSE IT'S A TITLE. A WELL-DESERVED ONE AT THAT.
NO. YOU ARE LYING. YOU TOOK THAT NAME. YOU LIKED THE EFFECT IT HAS ON OTHERS.
SO? YOU TOOK THE NAME RAVEN. YOU WERE BORN RACHEL ROTH.
WINTERS, THAT DOOR WILL TAKE YOU BACK TO 1906.
TRY CHANGING SUBJECTS ON ME AGAIN AND I WILL FIND A WAY TO STRAND YOU THERE.
RAVEN FACTOID NUMBER SIX. BY RAVEN. WHEN TRYING TO ACT TOUGH, SMILE KNOWINGLY...
...GIVE YOUR BEST STER
LOOK, AND ABOVE ALL, DO NOT LET THEM SEE YOU SWEAT.
NOW, SHALL WE TALK?

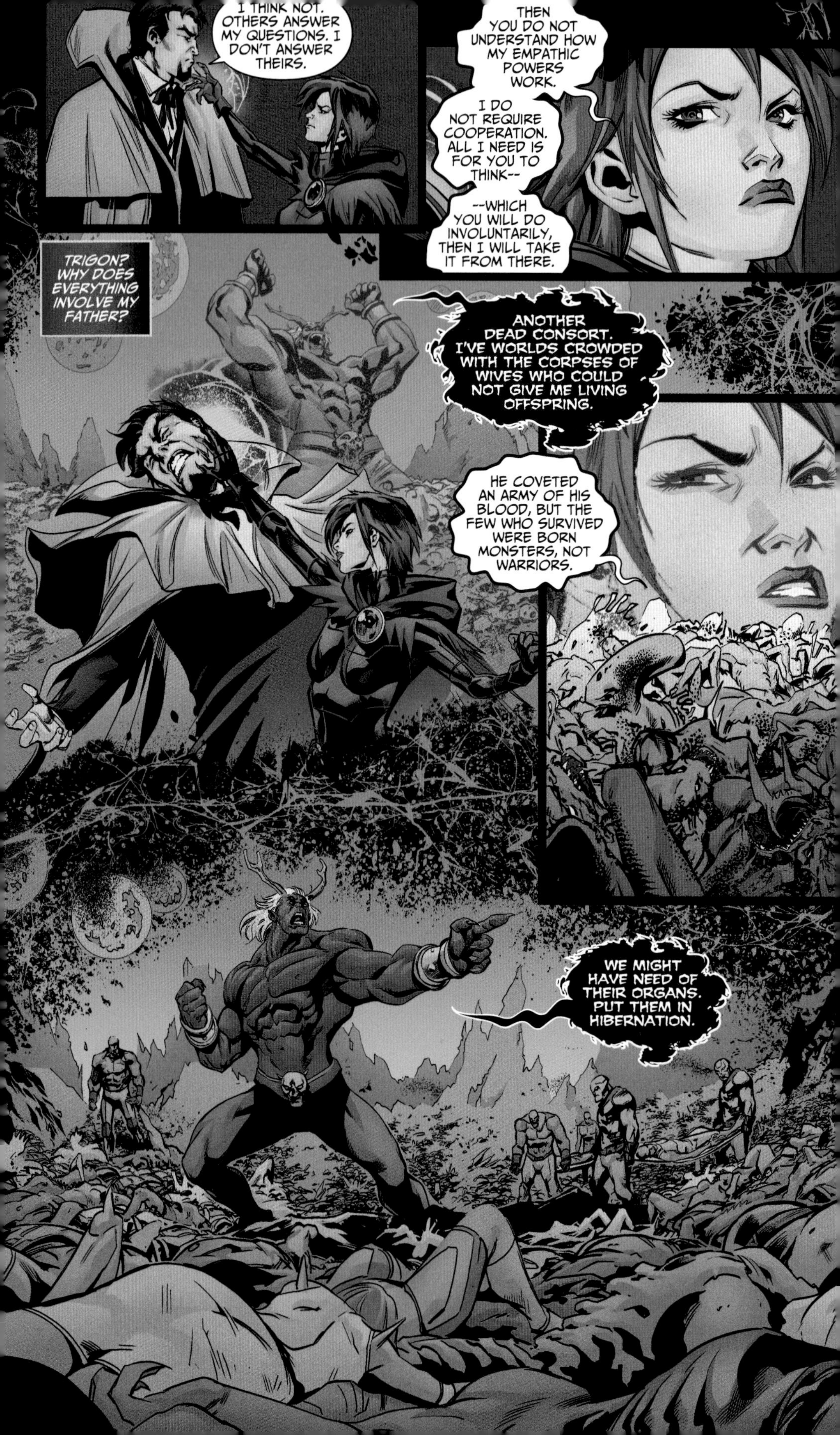
I THINK NOT. OTHERS ANSWER MY QUESTIONS. I DON'T ANSWER THEIRS.
THEN YOU DO NOT UNDERSTAND HOW MY EMPATHIC POWERS WORK.
I DO NOT REQUIRE COOPERATION. ALL I NEED IS FOR YOU TO THINK--
--WHICH YOU WILL DO INVOLUNTARILY, THEN I WILL TAKE IT FROM THERE.
TRIGON? WHY DOES EVERYTHING INVOLVE MY FATHER?
ANOTHER DEAD CONSORT. I'VE WORLDS CROWDED WITH THE CORPSES OF WIVES WHO COULD NOT GIVE ME LIVING OFFSPRING.
HE COVETED AN ARMY OF HIS BLOOD, BUT THE FEW WHO SURVIVED WERE BORN MONSTERS, NOT WARRIORS.
WE MIGHT HAVE NEED OF THEIR ORGANS. PUT THEM IN HIBERNATION.

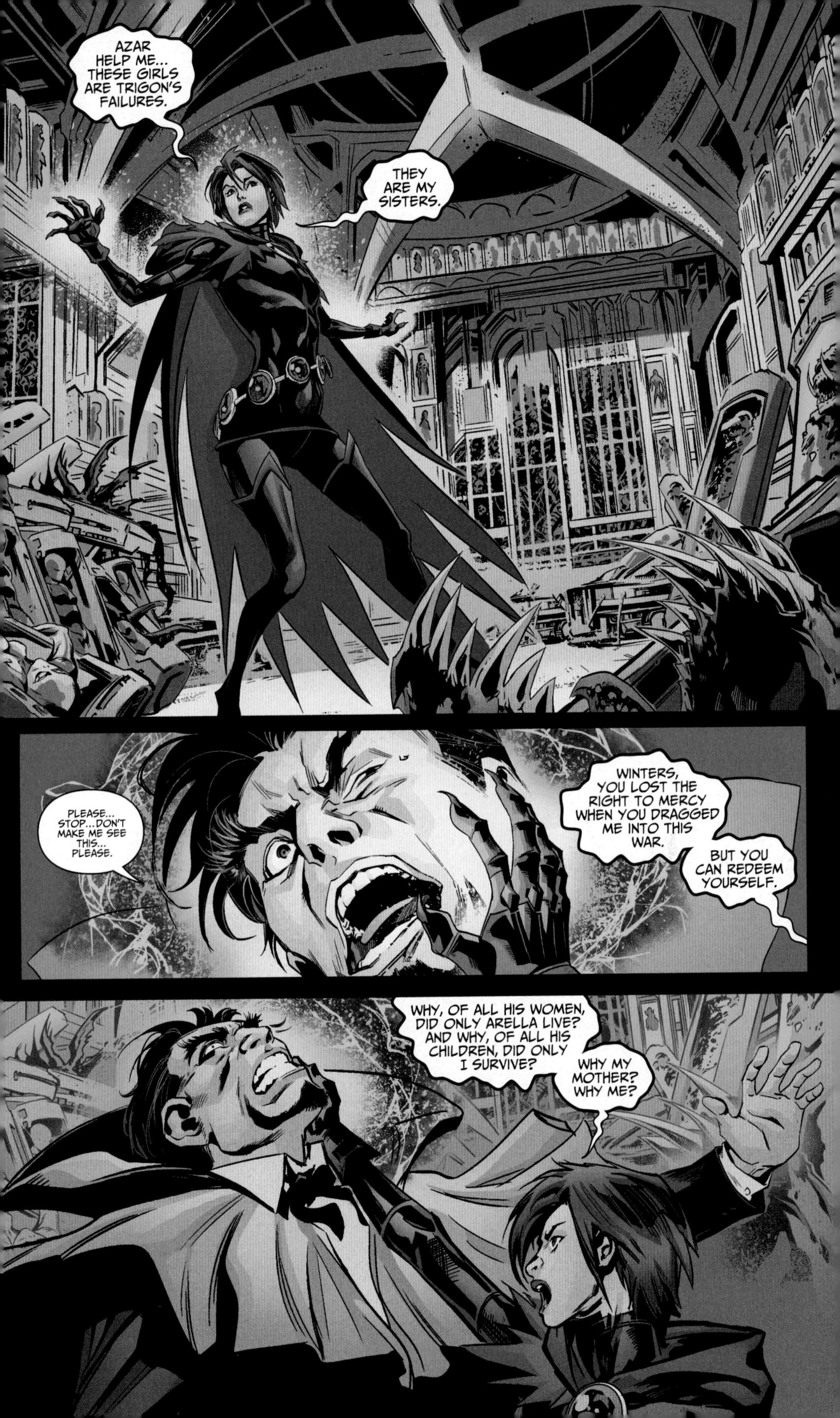
AZAR HELP ME... THESE GIRLS ARE TRIGON'S FAILURES.
THEY ARE MY SISTERS.
PLEASE... STOP...DON'T MAKE ME SEE THIS... PLEASE.
WINTERS, YOU LOST THE RIGHT TO MERCY WHEN YOU DRAGGED ME INTO THIS WAR.
BUT YOU CAN REDEEM YOURSELF.
WHY, OF ALL HIS WOMEN, DID ONLY ARELLA LIVE? AND WHY, OF ALL HIS CHILDREN, DID ONLY I SURVIVE?
WHY MY MOTHER? WHY ME?

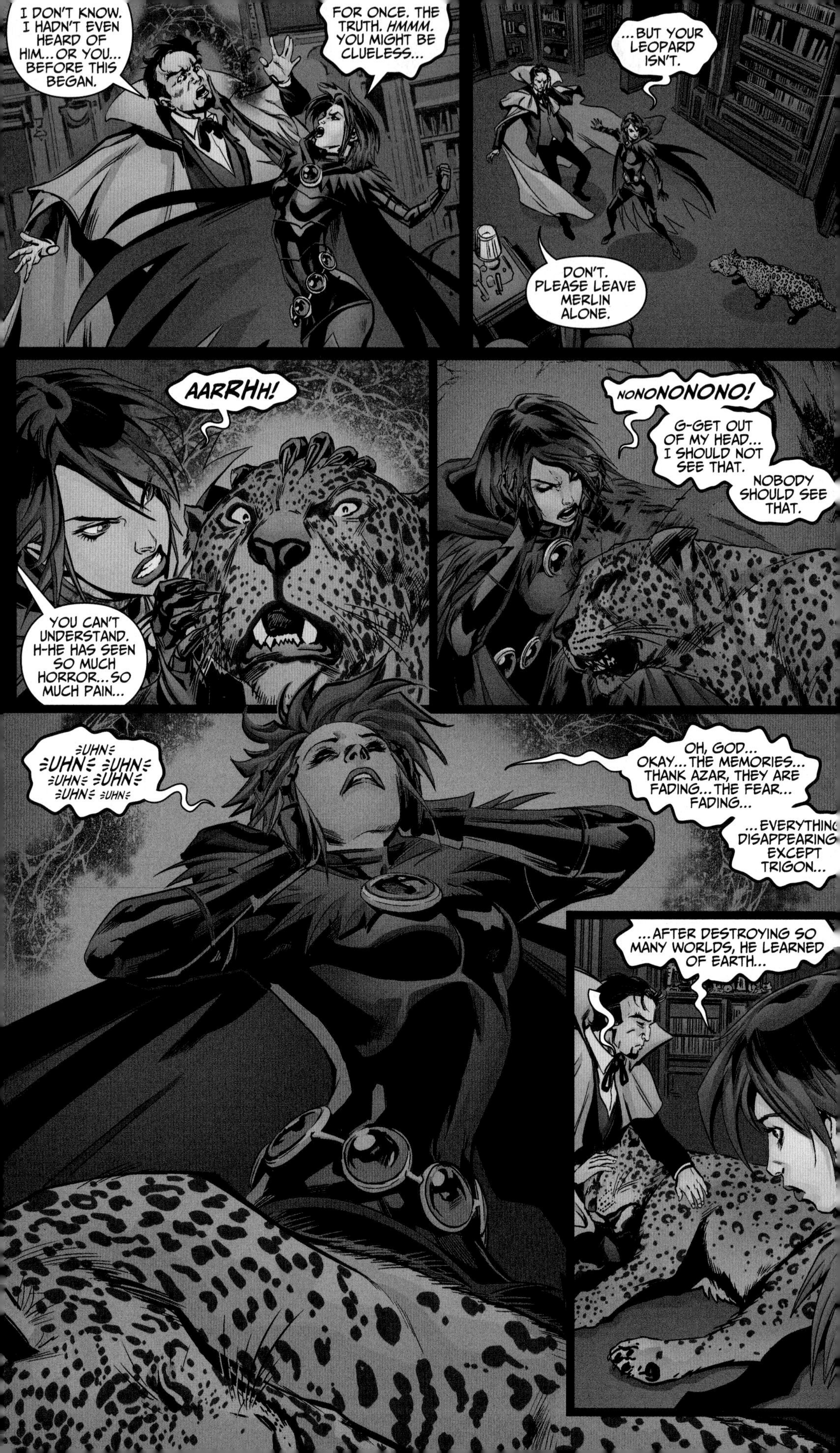
I DON'T KNOW. I HADN'T EVEN HEARD OF HIM...OR YOU... BEFORE THIS BEGAN.
FOR ONCE. THE TRUTH. HMMM. YOU MIGHT BE CLUELESS...
...BUT YOUR LEOPARD ISN'T.
DON'T. PLEASE LEAVE MERLIN ALONE.
AARRHH!
YOU CAN'T UNDERSTAND. H-HE HAS SEEN SO MUCH HORROR...SO MUCH PAIN...
NONONONONO!
G-GET OUT OF MY HEAD... I SHOULD NOT SEE THAT.
NOBODY SHOULD SEE THAT.
UHN UHN UHN UHN UHN UHN UHN UHN
OH, GOD... OKAY...THE MEMORIES... THANK AZAR, THEY ARE FADING...THE FEAR... FADING...
...EVERYTHING DISAPPEARING EXCEPT TRIGON...
...AFTER DESTROYING SO MANY WORLDS, HE LEARNED OF EARTH...

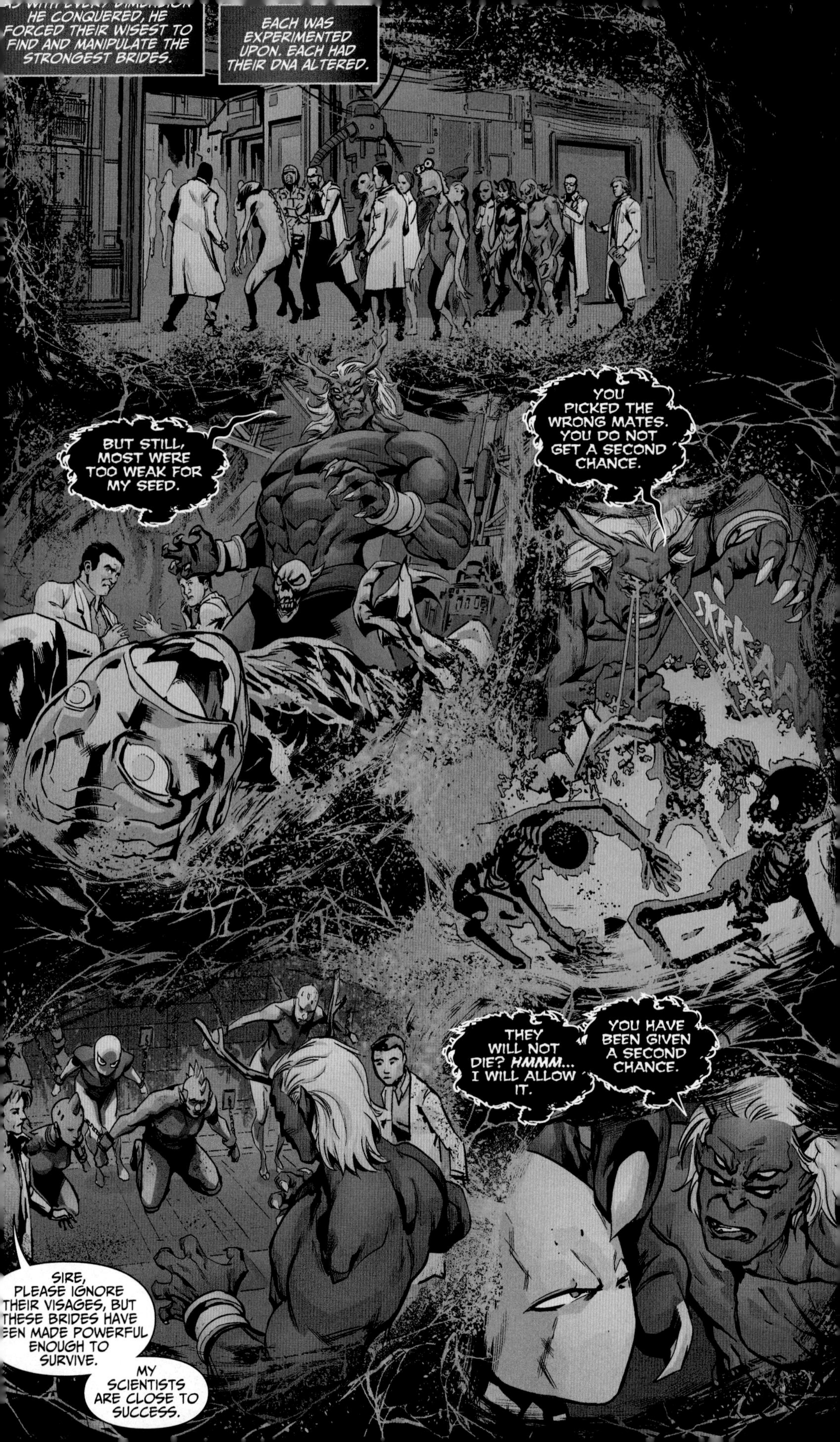
HE CONQUERED, HE FORCED THEIR WISEST TO FIND AND MANIPULATE THE STRONGEST BRIDES.
EACH WAS EXPERIMENTED UPON. EACH HAD THEIR DNA ALTERED.
BUT STILL, MOST WERE TOO WEAK FOR MY SEED.
YOU PICKED THE WRONG MATES. YOU DO NOT GET A SECOND CHANCE.
SIRE, PLEASE IGNORE THEIR VISAGES, BUT THESE BRIDES HAVE EEN MADE POWERFUL ENOUGH TO SURVIVE.
MY SCIENTISTS ARE CLOSE TO SUCCESS.
THEY WILL NOT DIE? HMMM... I WILL ALLOW IT.
YOU HAVE BEEN GIVEN A SECOND CHANCE.

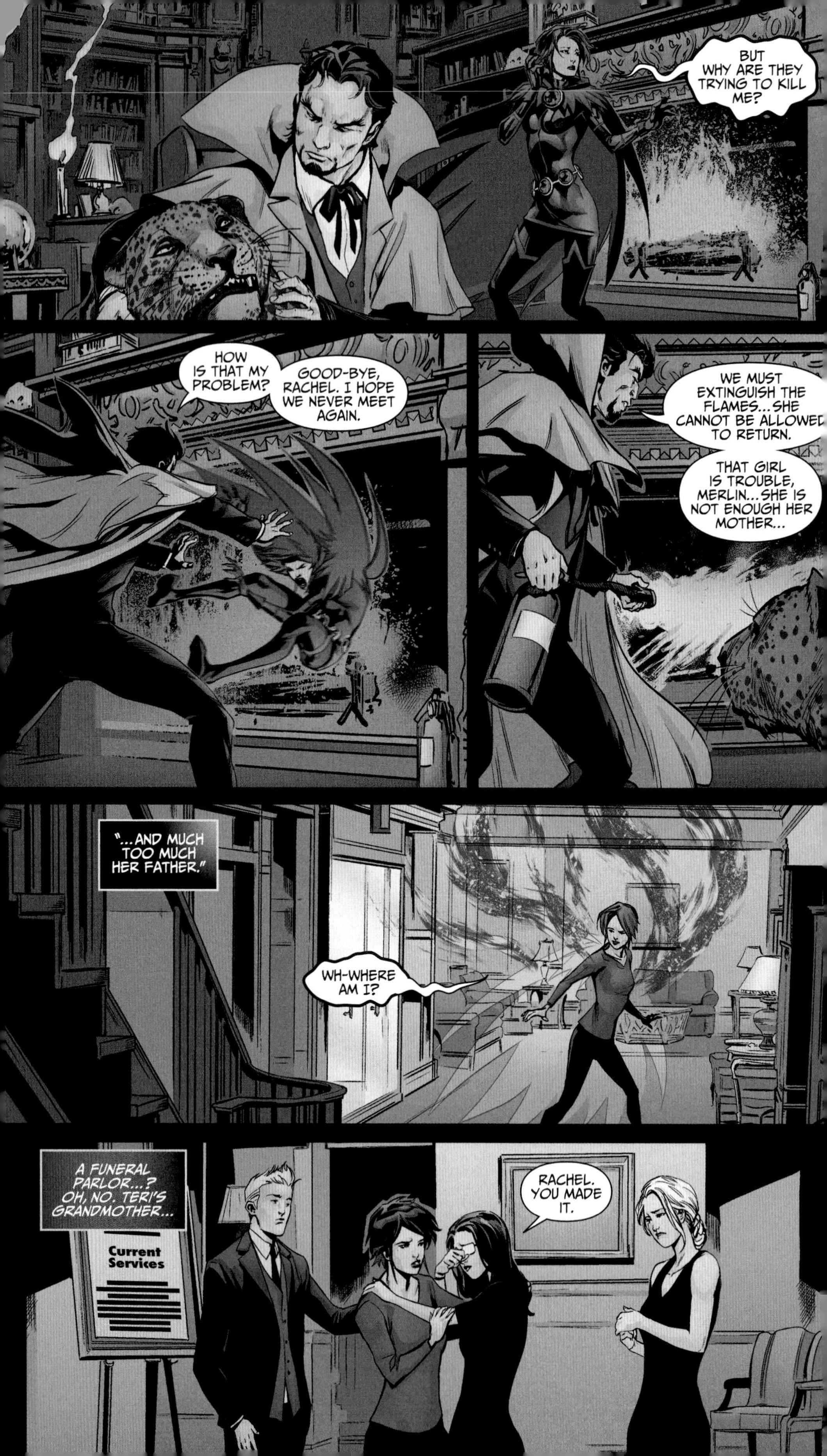
BUT WHY ARE THEY TRYING TO KILL ME?
HOW IS THAT MY PROBLEM?
GOOD-BYE, RACHEL. I HOPE WE NEVER MEET AGAIN.
WE MUST EXTINGUISH THE FLAMES...SHE CANNOT BE ALLOWED TO RETURN.
THAT GIRL IS TROUBLE, MERLIN...SHE IS NOT ENOUGH HER MOTHER...
"...AND MUCH TOO MUCH HER FATHER."
WH-WHERE AM I?
A FUNERAL PARLOR...? OH, NO. TERI'S GRANDMOTHER...
Current Services
RACHEL. YOU MADE IT.

OF COURSE... I'M SO SORRY. HOW ARE YOU?

I DON'T KNOW. AWFUL. TERRIBLE. THANK GOD FOR YOUR AUNT AND UNCLE. THEY'VE TAKEN CHARGE.

TERI'S GRANDMOTHER PREPARED EVERYTHING IN ADVANCE. SHE WAS AN AMAZING WOMAN.

I KNOW. MY PARENTS NAMED ME AFTER HER. I LOVED HER SO MUCH.

EVERYONE DID, DEAR. AND SHE LOVED YOU.

SHE WAS SO PROUD OF THE YOUNG WOMAN YOU'VE BECOME.

OH, GOD. WHAT DO I DO NOW? I HAVE NOBODY...I...I DON'T KNOW WHAT TO DO.

YOU HAVE US, TERI. YOU'LL ALWAYS HAVE US.

I SO WANT TO EASE HER PAINS, BUT ALL I CAN DO IS HOLD HER...

...AND LET HER KNOW ALL HER FRIENDS WILL BE THERE FOR HER.

RAVEN?

I MEAN.. RACHEL?

WHAT? WHO?

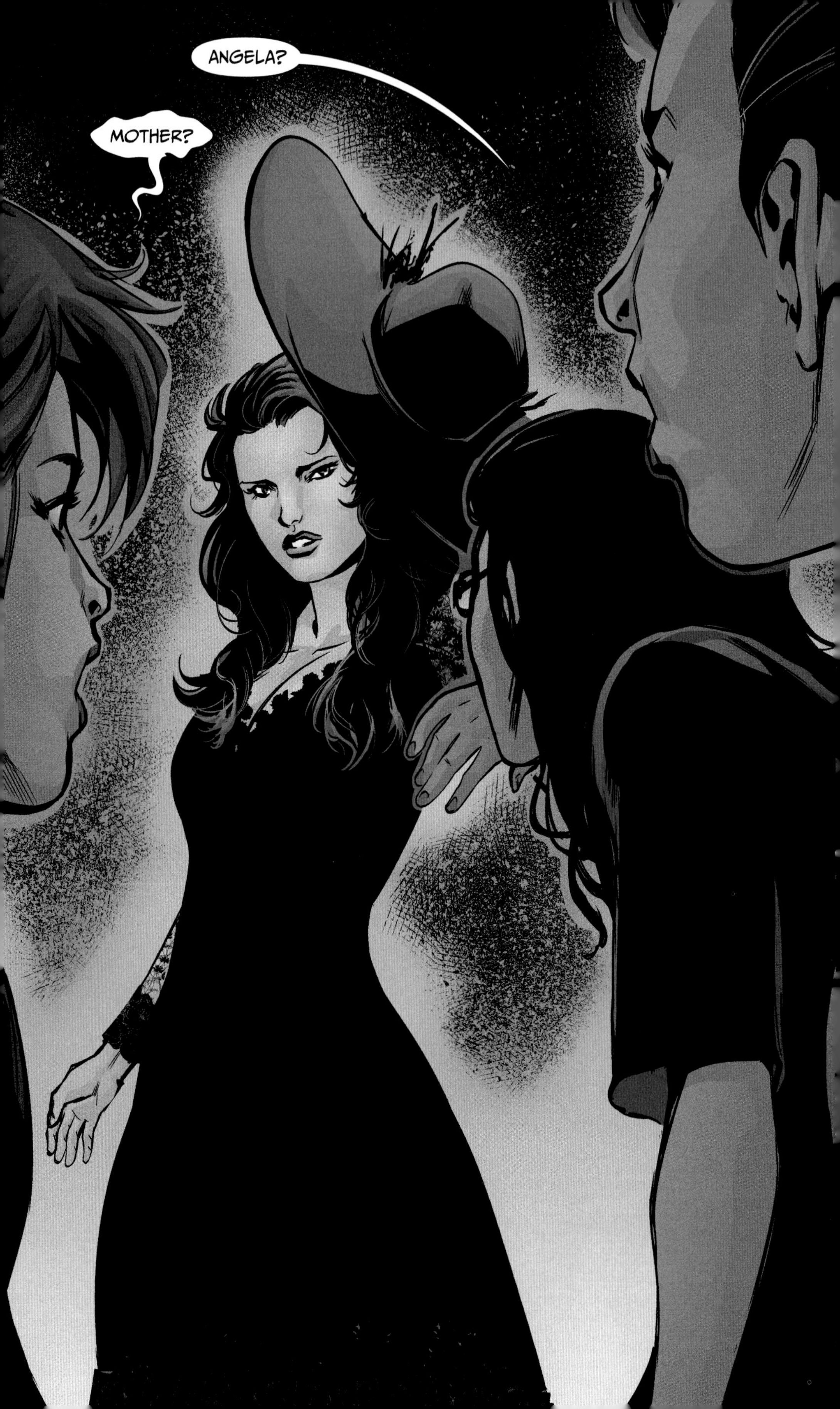
ANGELA?
MOTHER?

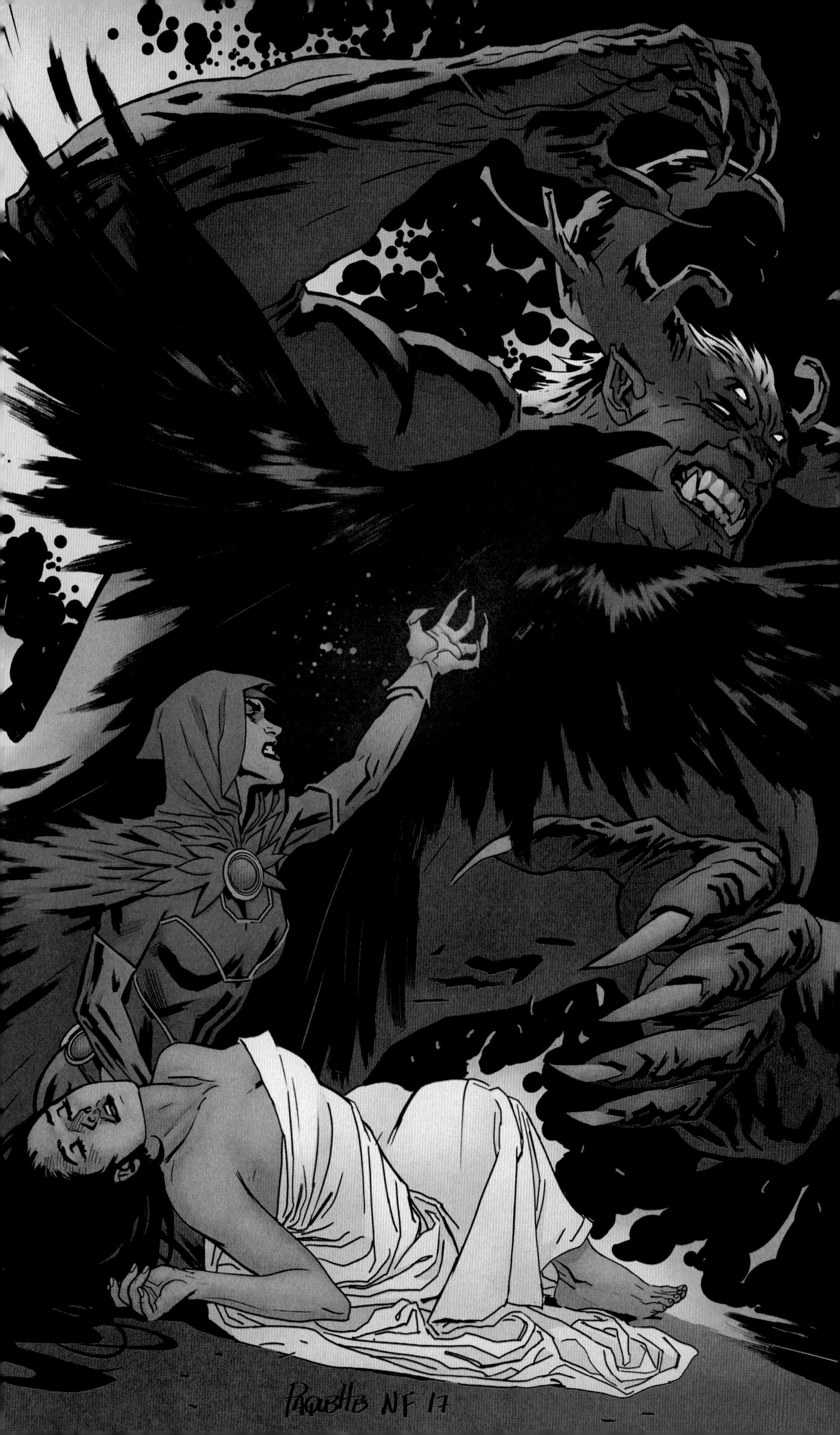

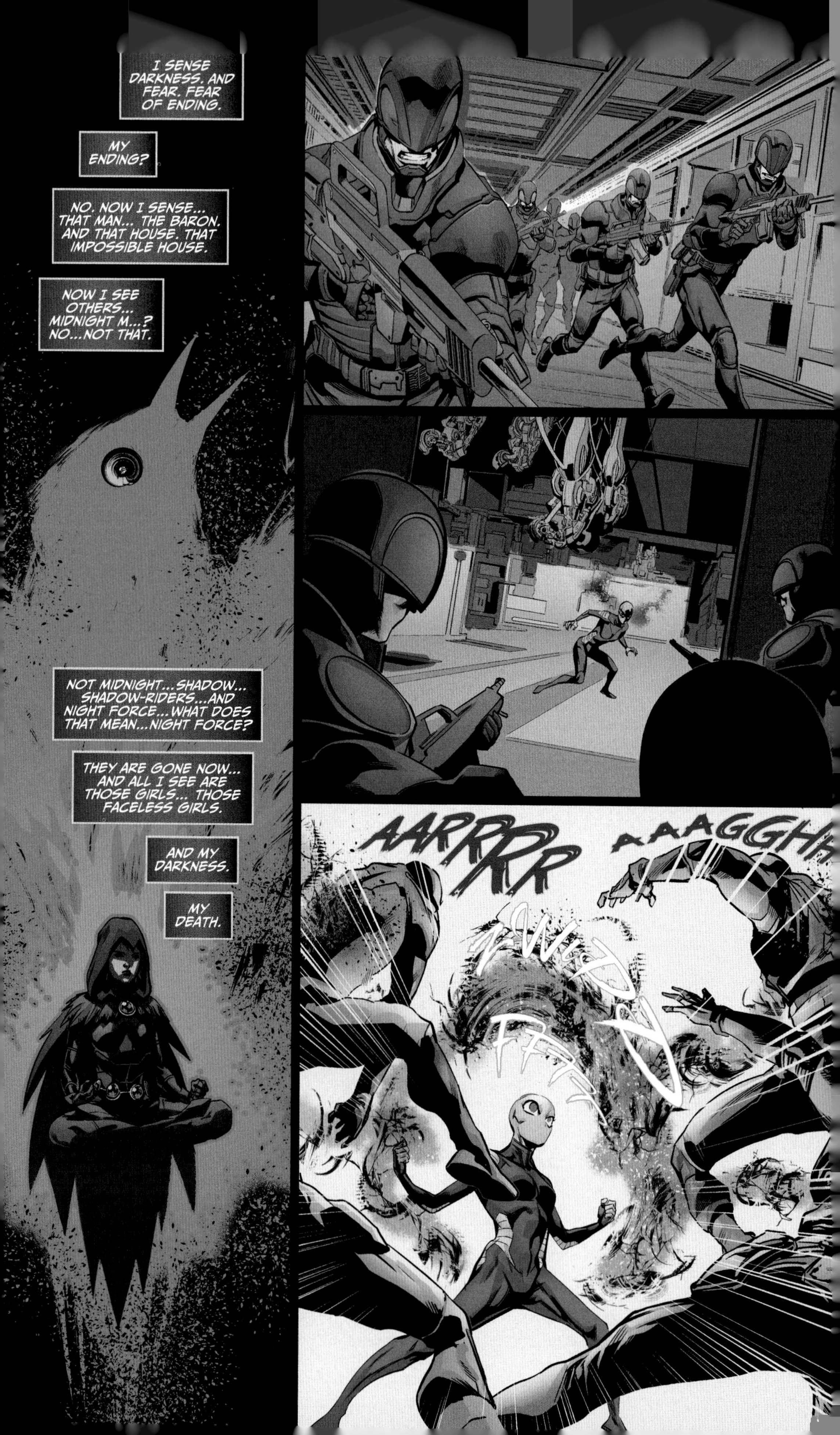
I SENSE DARKNESS. AND FEAR. FEAR OF ENDING.
MY ENDING?
NO. NOW I SENSE... THAT MAN... THE BARON. AND THAT HOUSE. THAT IMPOSSIBLE HOUSE.
NOW I SEE OTHERS... MIDNIGHT M...? NO...NOT THAT.
NOT MIDNIGHT...SHADOW... SHADOW-RIDERS...AND NIGHT FORCE...WHAT DOES THAT MEAN...NIGHT FORCE?
THEY ARE GONE NOW... AND ALL I SEE ARE THOSE GIRLS... THOSE FACELESS GIRLS.
AND MY DARKNESS.
MY DEATH.
AARRRRR
AAAAGGGHH

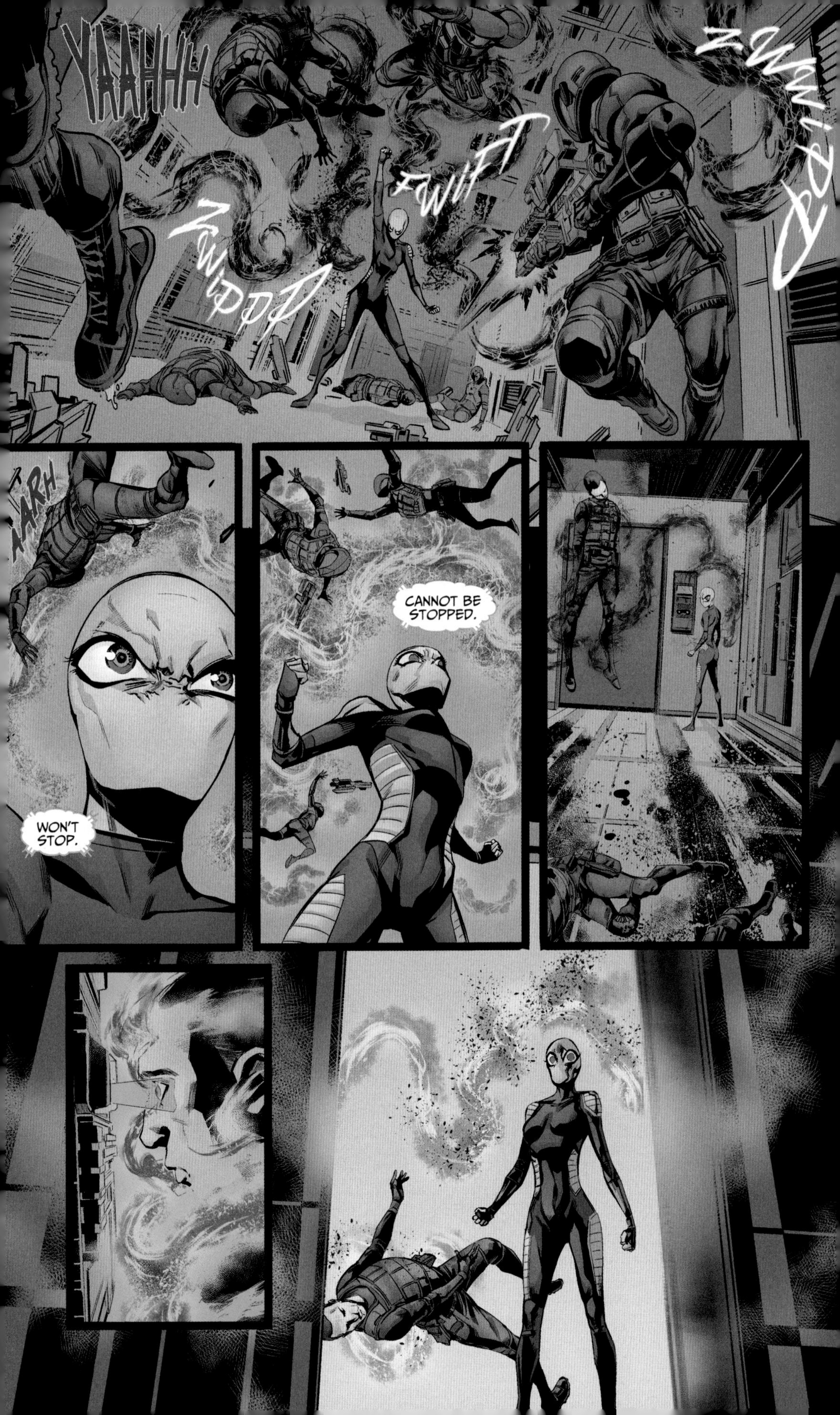
YAAHHH
ZWIPP
FWIFFT
ZWIPPP
AARH
WON'T STOP.
CANNOT BE STOPPED.

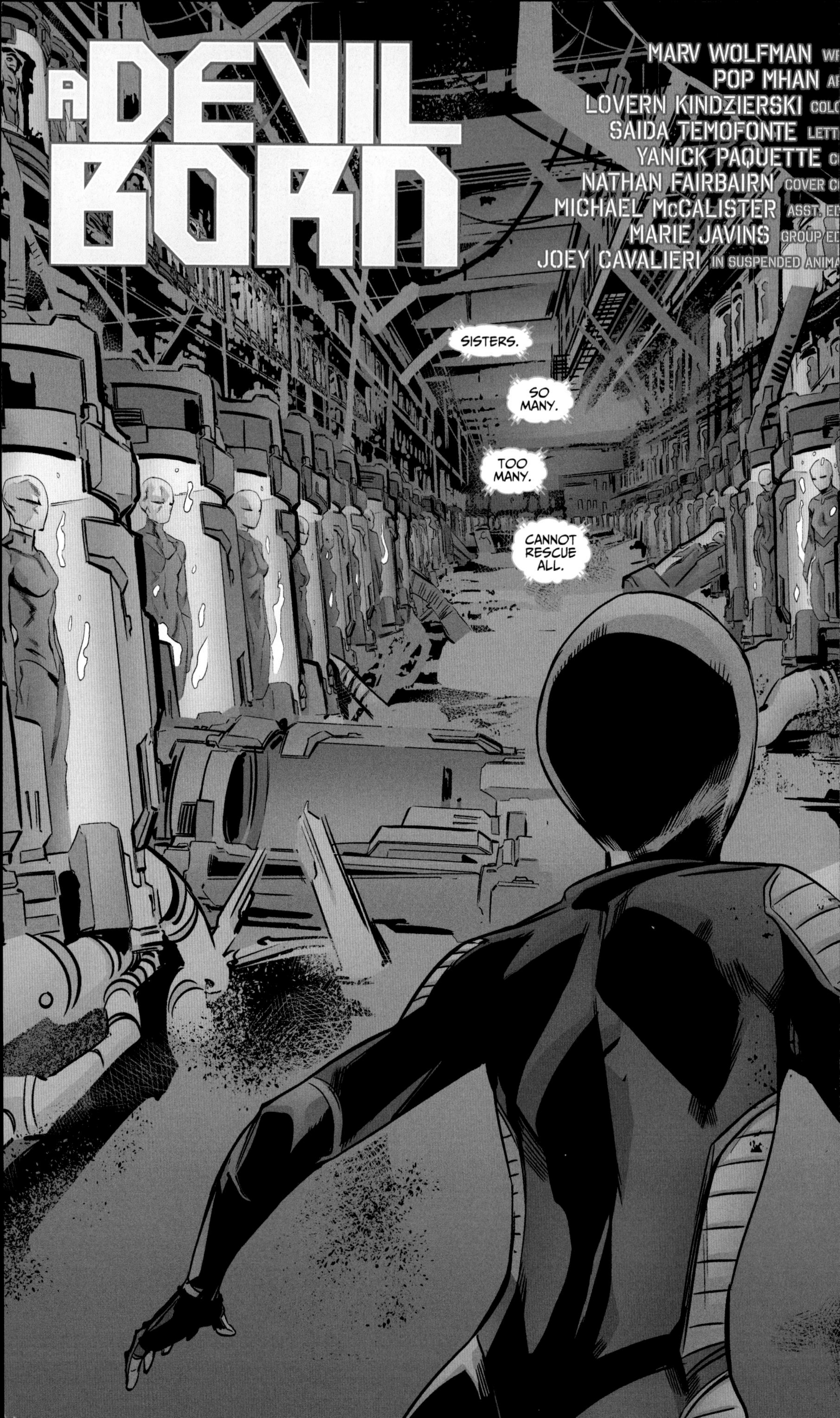
A DEVIL BORN
MARV WOLFMAN WR
POP MHAN AR
LOVERN KINDZIERSKI COLO
SAIDA TEMOFONTE LETT
YANICK PAQUETTE C
NATHAN FAIRBAIRN COVER C
MICHAEL McCALISTER ASST. ED
MARIE JAVINS GROUP ED
JOEY CAVALIERI IN SUSPENDED ANIMA
SISTERS.
SO MANY.
TOO MANY.
CANNOT RESCUE ALL.

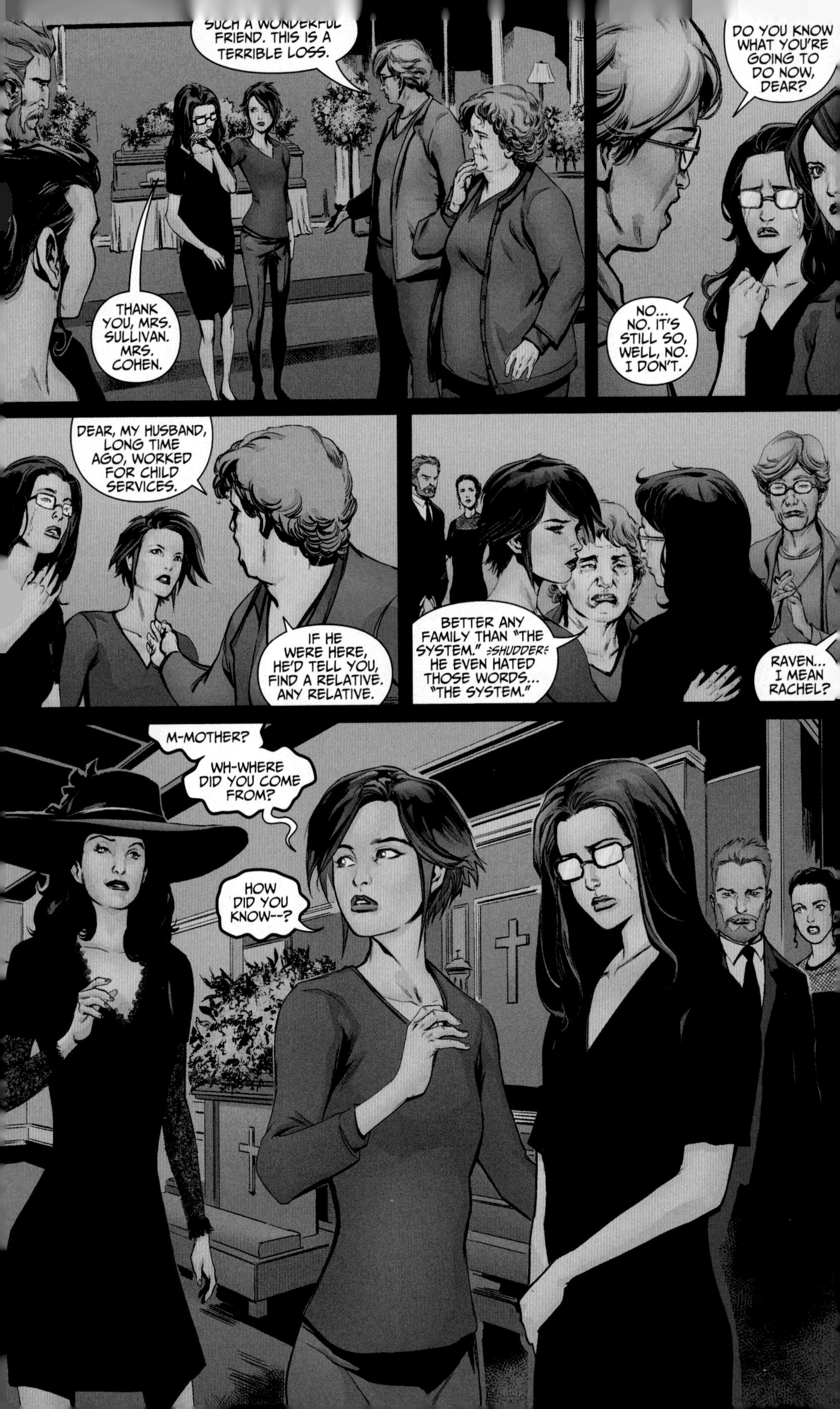
SUCH A WONDERFUL FRIEND. THIS IS A TERRIBLE LOSS.
THANK YOU, MRS. SULLIVAN. MRS. COHEN.
DO YOU KNOW WHAT YOU'RE GOING TO DO NOW, DEAR?
NO... NO. IT'S STILL SO, WELL, NO. I DON'T.
DEAR, MY HUSBAND, LONG TIME AGO, WORKED FOR CHILD SERVICES.
IF HE WERE HERE, HE'D TELL YOU, FIND A RELATIVE. ANY RELATIVE.
BETTER ANY FAMILY THAN "THE SYSTEM." SHUDDER HE EVEN HATED THOSE WORDS... "THE SYSTEM."
RAVEN... I MEAN RACHEL?
M-MOTHER?
WH-WHERE DID YOU COME FROM?
HOW DID YOU KNOW--?

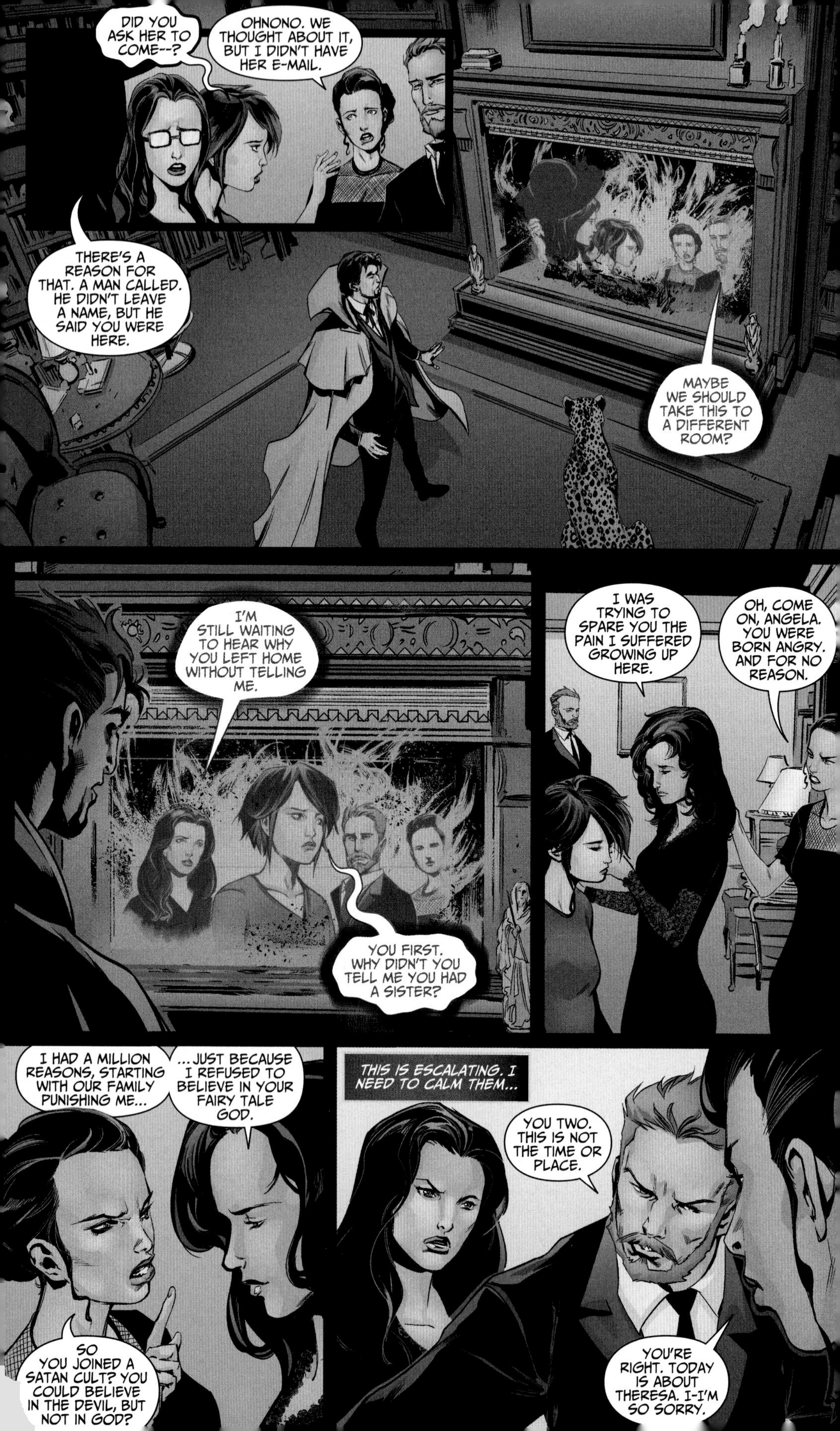
DID YOU ASK HER TO COME--?
OHNONO. WE THOUGHT ABOUT IT, BUT I DIDN'T HAVE HER E-MAIL.
THERE'S A REASON FOR THAT. A MAN CALLED. HE DIDN'T LEAVE A NAME, BUT HE SAID YOU WERE HERE.
MAYBE WE SHOULD TAKE THIS TO A DIFFERENT ROOM?
I'M STILL WAITING TO HEAR WHY YOU LEFT HOME WITHOUT TELLING ME.
YOU FIRST. WHY DIDN'T YOU TELL ME YOU HAD A SISTER?
I WAS TRYING TO SPARE YOU THE PAIN I SUFFERED GROWING UP HERE.
OH, COME ON, ANGELA. YOU WERE BORN ANGRY. AND FOR NO REASON.
I HAD A MILLION REASONS, STARTING WITH OUR FAMILY PUNISHING ME...
...JUST BECAUSE I REFUSED TO BELIEVE IN YOUR FAIRY TALE GOD.
SO YOU JOINED A SATAN CULT? YOU COULD BELIEVE IN THE DEVIL, BUT NOT IN GOD?
THIS IS ESCALATING. I NEED TO CALM THEM...
YOU TWO. THIS IS NOT THE TIME OR PLACE.
YOU'RE RIGHT. TODAY IS ABOUT THERESA. I-I'M SO SORRY.

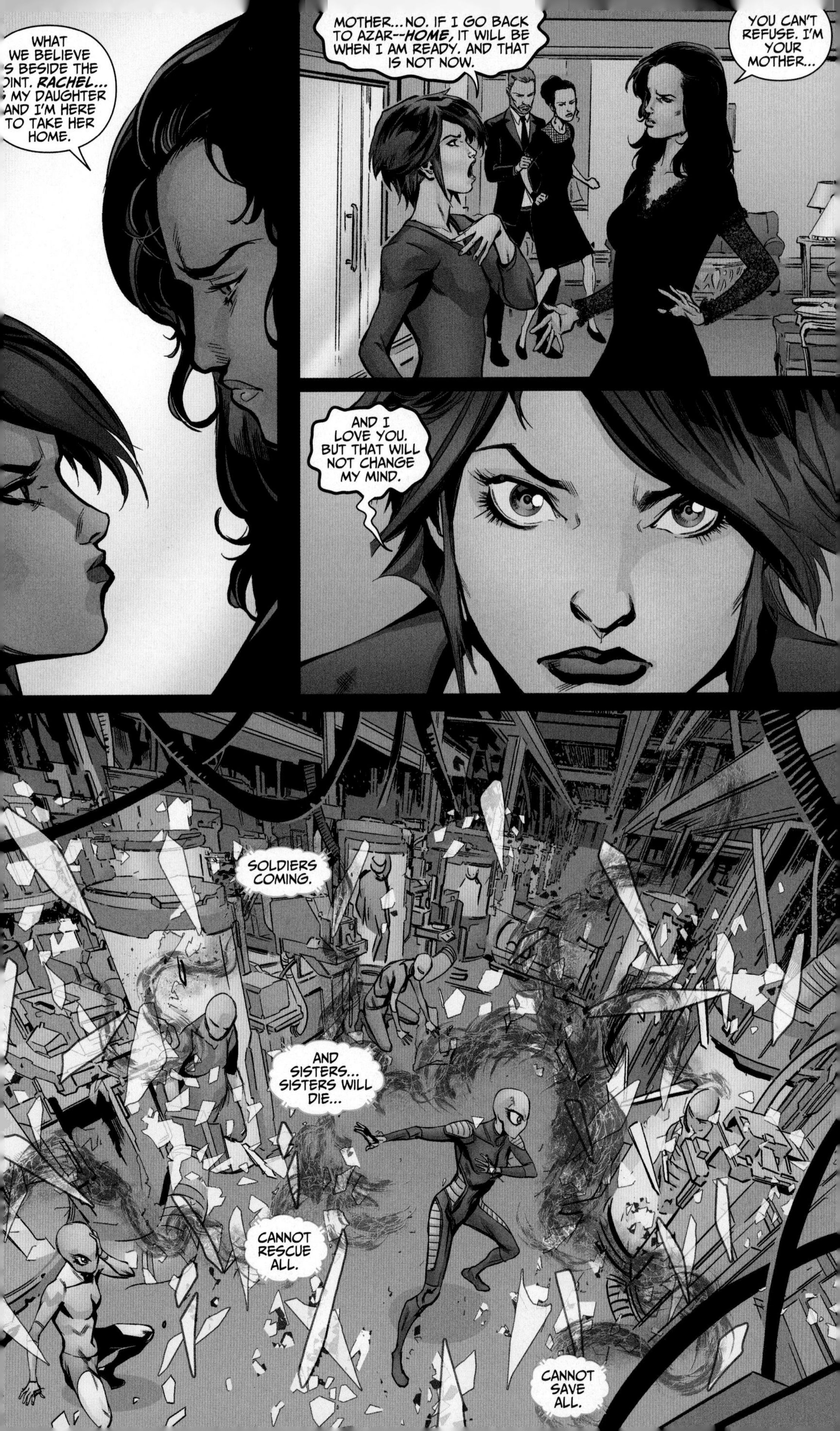
WHAT WE BELIEVE IS BESIDE THE POINT. RACHEL... IS MY DAUGHTER AND I'M HERE TO TAKE HER HOME.
MOTHER... NO. IF I GO BACK TO AZAR--HOME, IT WILL BE WHEN I AM READY. AND THAT IS NOT NOW.
YOU CAN'T REFUSE. I'M YOUR MOTHER...
AND I LOVE YOU. BUT THAT WILL NOT CHANGE MY MIND.
SOLDIERS COMING.
AND SISTERS... SISTERS WILL DIE...
CANNOT RESCUE ALL.
CANNOT SAVE ALL.

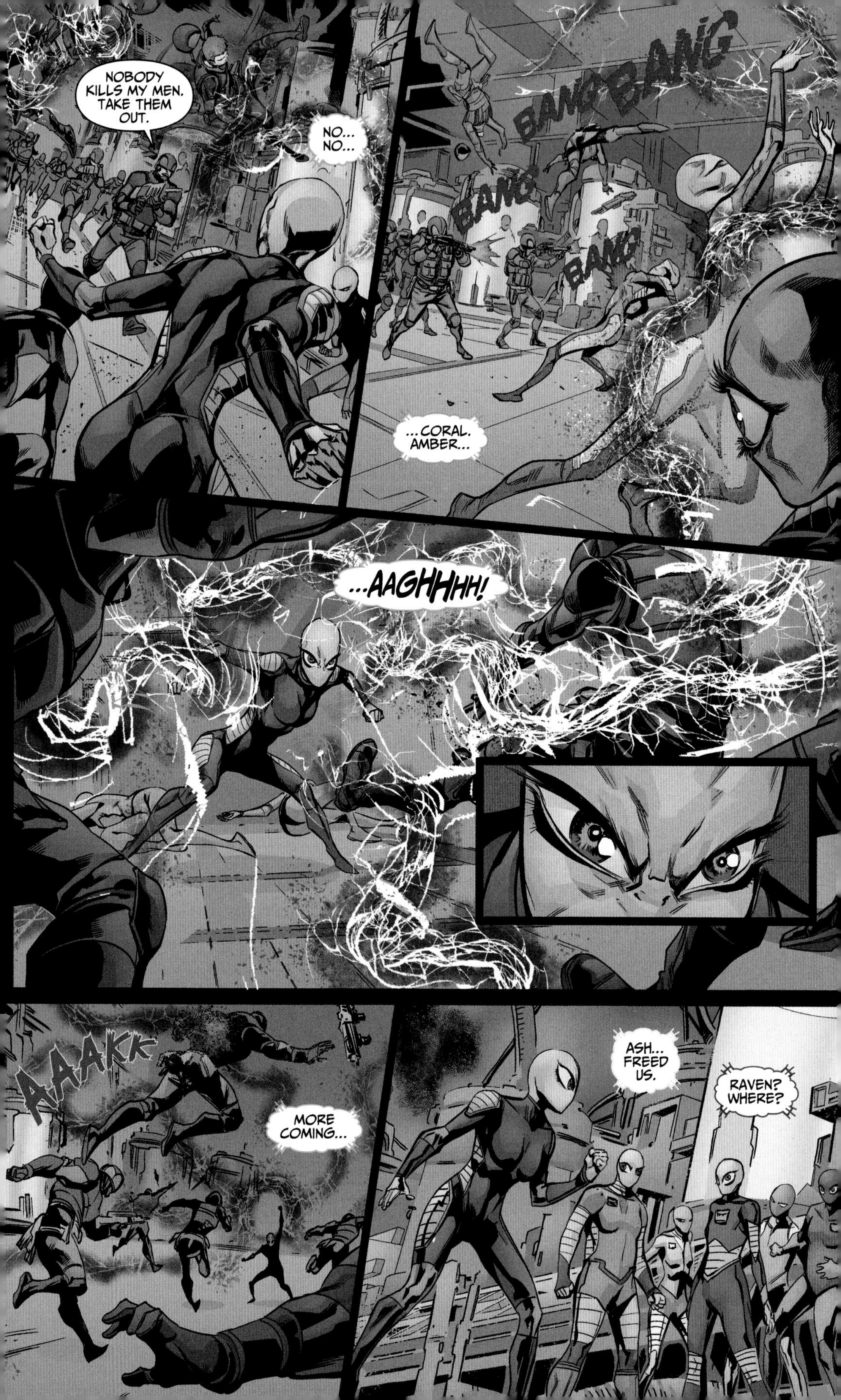
NOBODY KILLS MY MEN. TAKE THEM OUT.
NO... NO...
BANG BANG
BANG
BANG
BANG
...CORAL. AMBER...
...AAGHHHH!
AAAKK
MORE COMING...
ASH... FREED US.
RAVEN? WHERE?

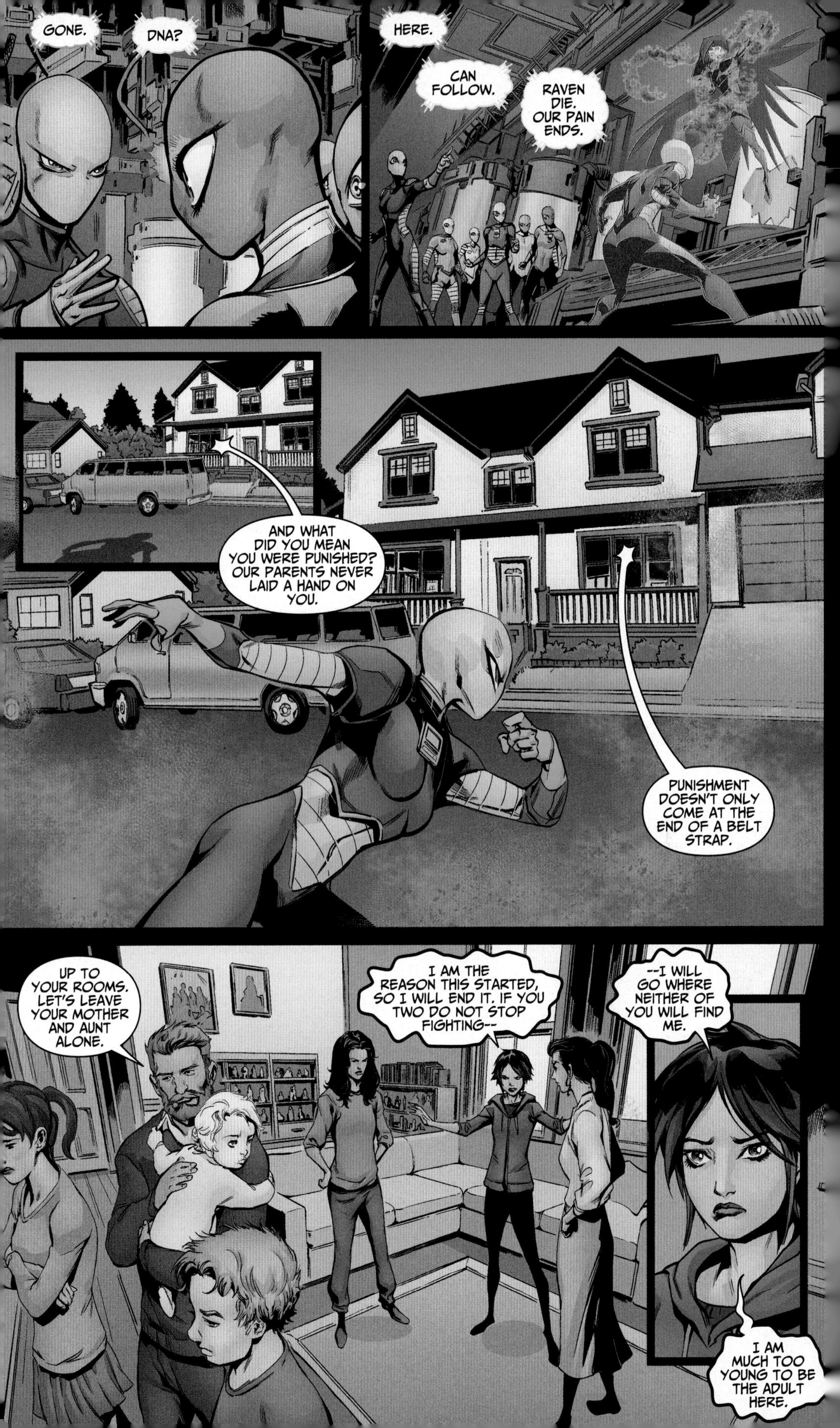
GONE.
DNA?
HERE.
CAN FOLLOW.
RAVEN DIE. OUR PAIN ENDS.
AND WHAT DID YOU MEAN YOU WERE PUNISHED? OUR PARENTS NEVER LAID A HAND ON YOU.
PUNISHMENT DOESN'T ONLY COME AT THE END OF A BELT STRAP.
UP TO YOUR ROOMS. LET'S LEAVE YOUR MOTHER AND AUNT ALONE.
I AM THE REASON THIS STARTED, SO I WILL END IT. IF YOU TWO DO NOT STOP FIGHTING--
--I WILL GO WHERE NEITHER OF YOU WILL FIND ME.
I AM MUCH TOO YOUNG TO BE THE ADULT HERE.

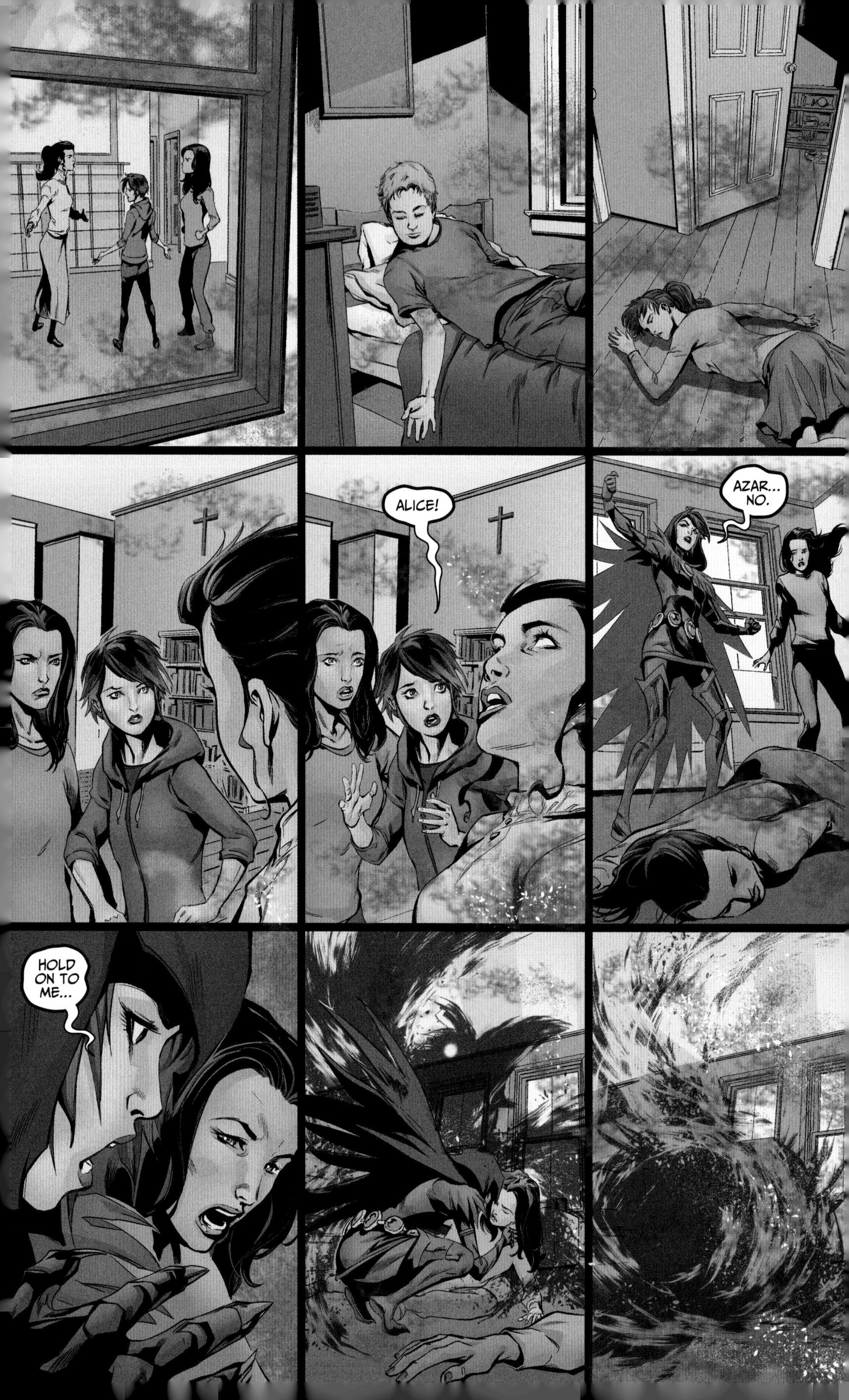
ALICE!
AZAR... NO.
HOLD ON TO ME...

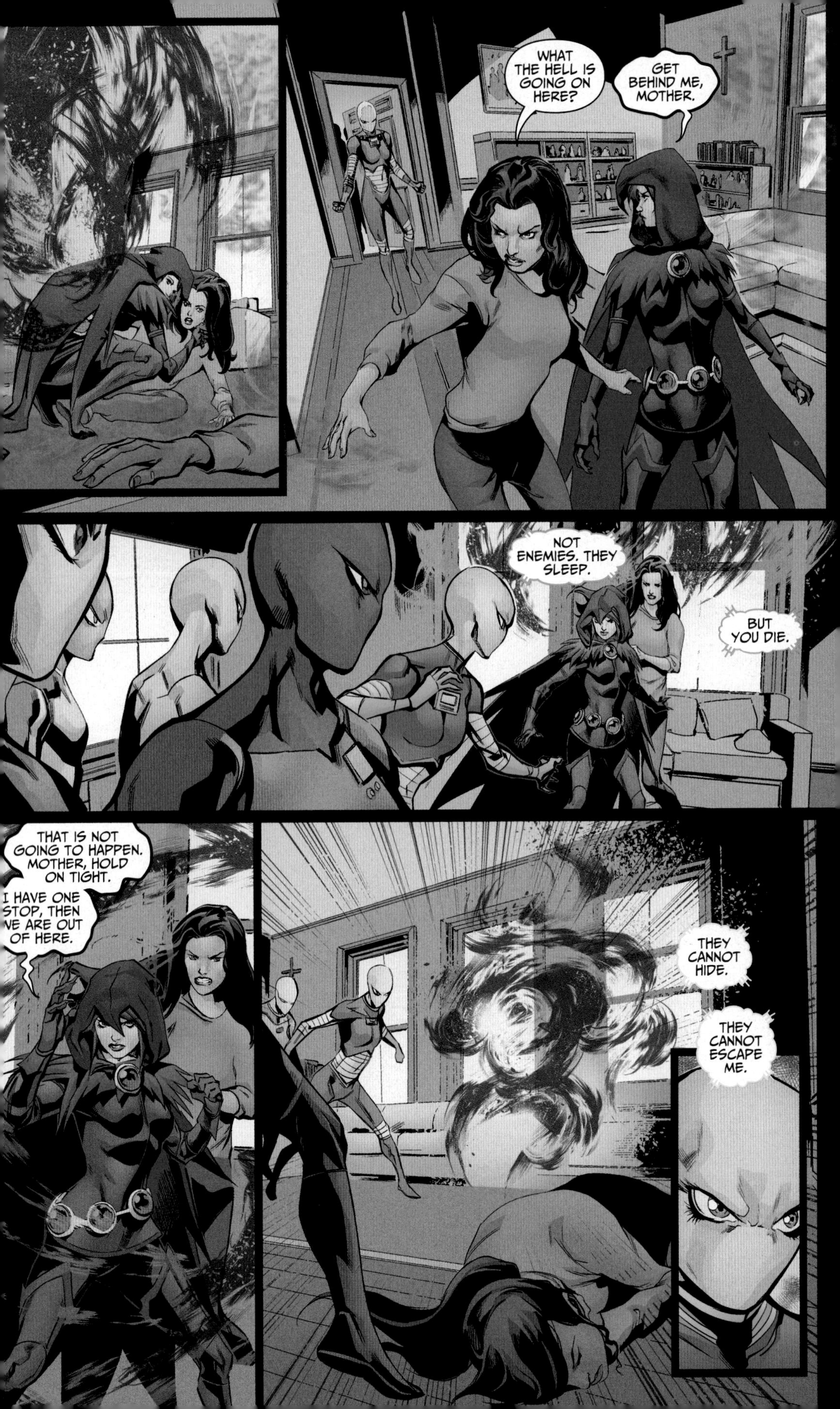
WHAT THE HELL IS GOING ON HERE?
GET BEHIND ME, MOTHER.
NOT ENEMIES. THEY SLEEP.
BUT YOU DIE.
THAT IS NOT GOING TO HAPPEN. MOTHER, HOLD ON TIGHT.
I HAVE ONE STOP, THEN VE ARE OUT OF HERE.
THEY CANNOT HIDE.
THEY CANNOT ESCAPE ME.

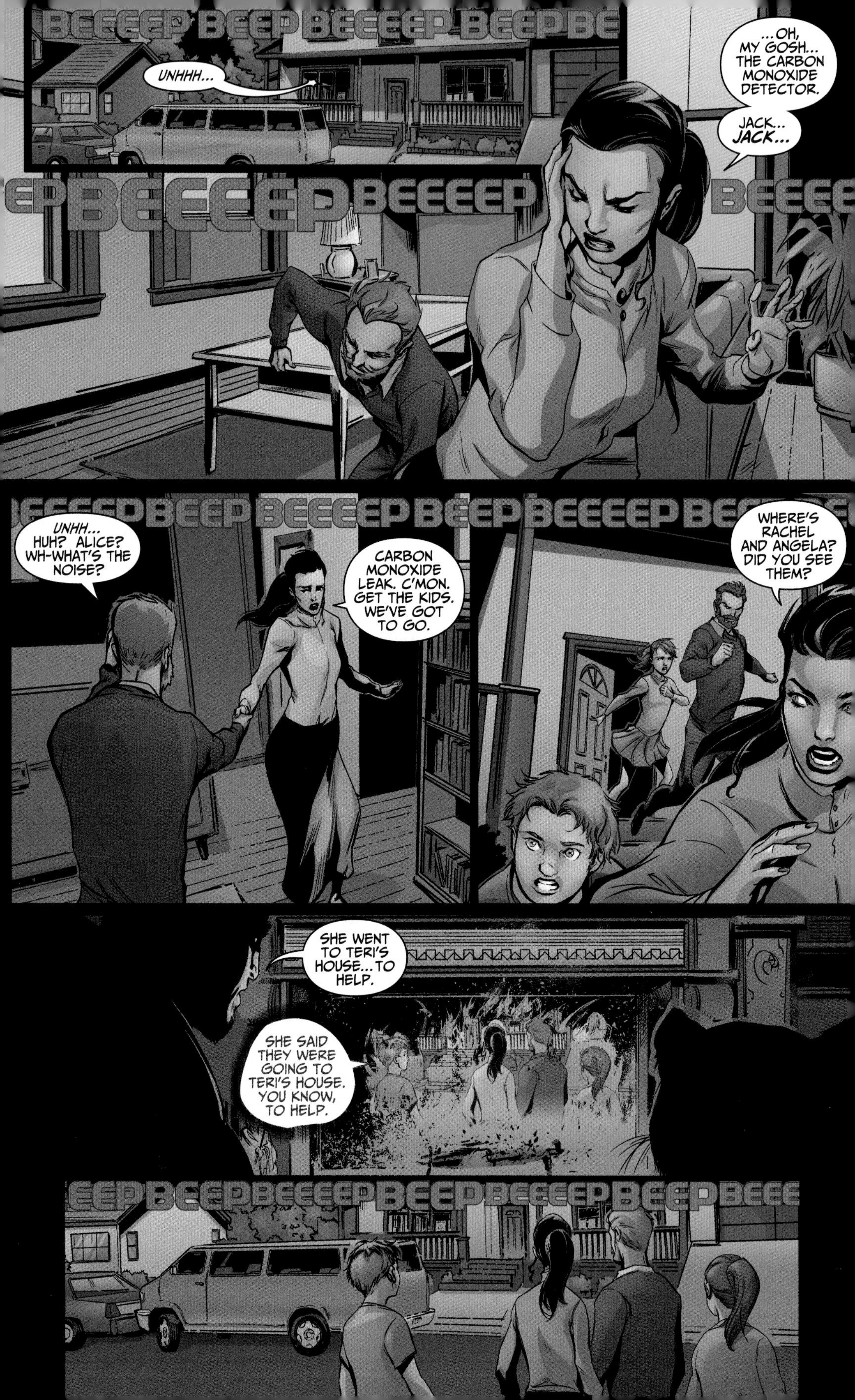

BEEEEP BEEEP BEEEEP BEEEP
UNHHH...
...OH, MY GOSH... THE CARBON MONOXIDE DETECTOR.
JACK... JACK...
BEEEEP BEEEEP
BEEEEP BEEEEP BEEEEP
UNHH... HUH? ALICE? WH-WHAT'S THE NOISE?
CARBON MONOXIDE LEAK. C'MON. GET THE KIDS. WE'VE GOT TO GO.
WHERE'S RACHEL AND ANGELA? DID YOU SEE THEM?
SHE WENT TO TERI'S HOUSE... TO HELP.
SHE SAID THEY WERE GOING TO TERI'S HOUSE. YOU KNOW, TO HELP.
BEEEP BEEEEP BEEP BEEEEP BEEP BEEEE

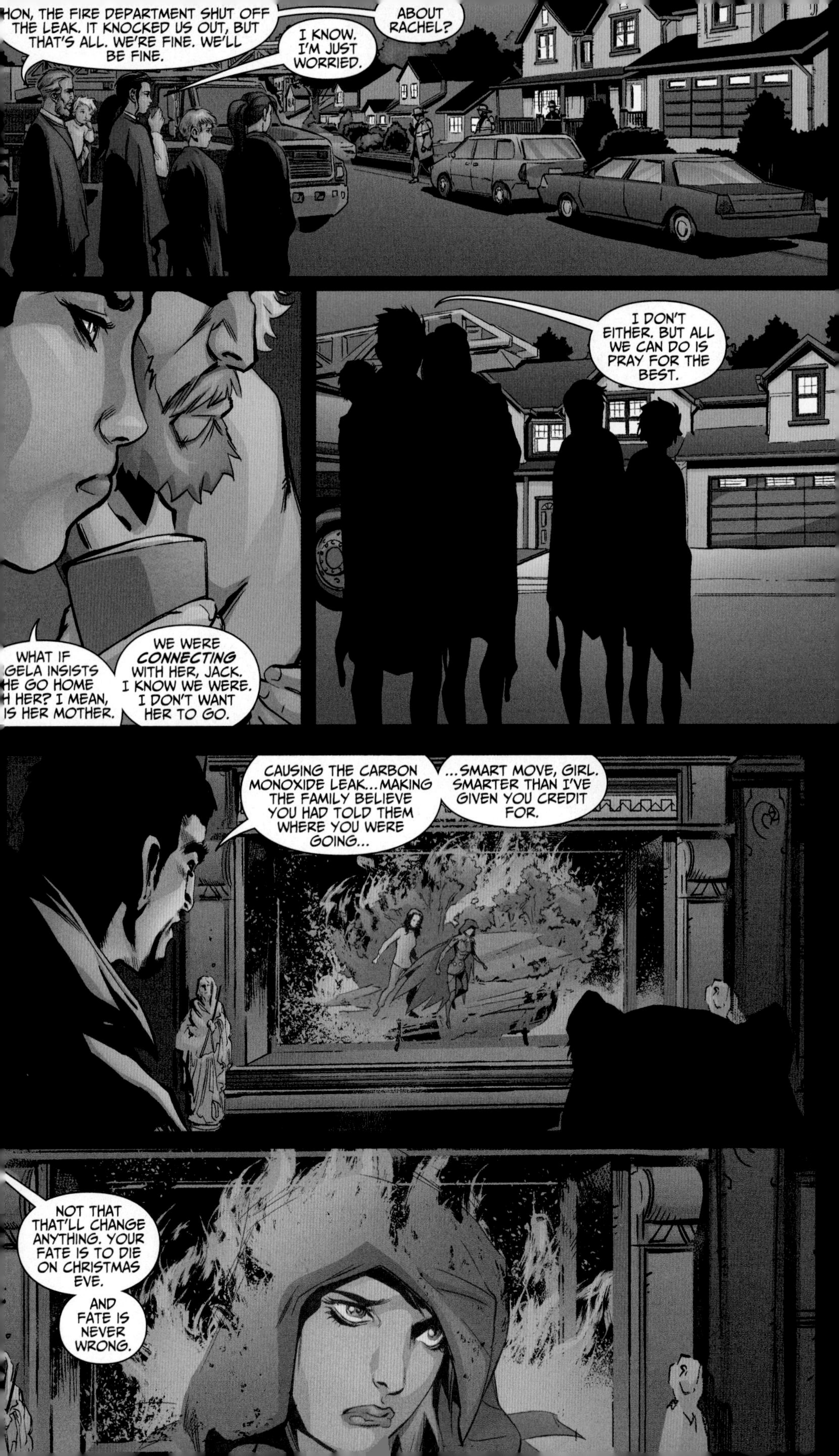
HON, THE FIRE DEPARTMENT SHUT OFF THE LEAK. IT KNOCKED US OUT, BUT THAT'S ALL. WE'RE FINE. WE'LL BE FINE.
I KNOW. I'M JUST WORRIED.
ABOUT RACHEL?
WHAT IF GELA INSISTS HE GO HOME H HER? I MEAN, IS HER MOTHER.
WE WERE *CONNECTING* WITH HER, JACK. I KNOW WE WERE. I DON'T WANT HER TO GO.
I DON'T EITHER. BUT ALL WE CAN DO IS PRAY FOR THE BEST.
CAUSING THE CARBON MONOXIDE LEAK...MAKING THE FAMILY BELIEVE YOU HAD TOLD THEM WHERE YOU WERE GOING...
...SMART MOVE, GIRL. SMARTER THAN I'VE GIVEN YOU CREDIT FOR.
NOT THAT THAT'LL CHANGE ANYTHING. YOUR FATE IS TO DIE ON CHRISTMAS EVE.
AND FATE IS NEVER WRONG.

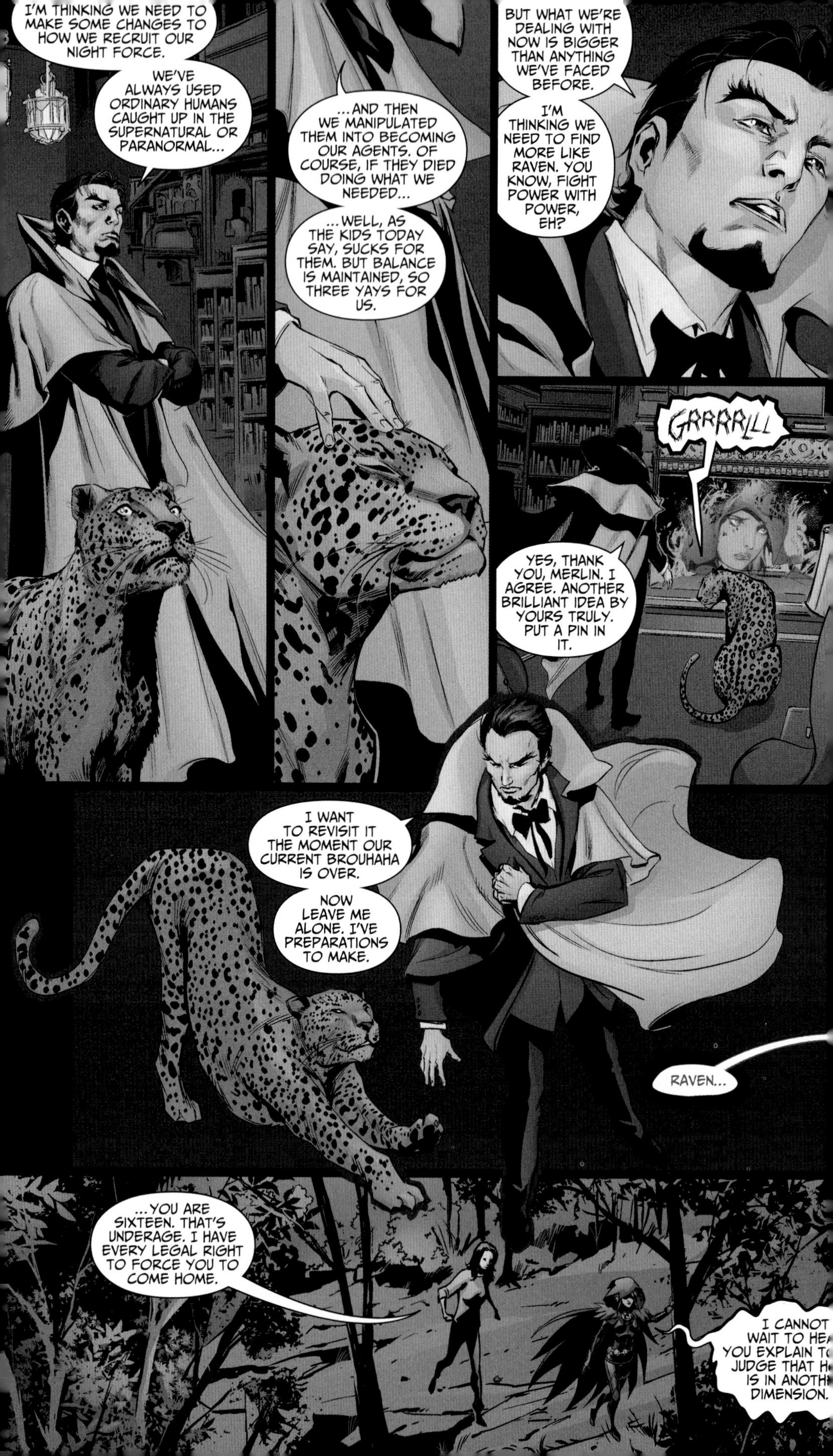
I'M THINKING WE NEED TO MAKE SOME CHANGES TO HOW WE RECRUIT OUR NIGHT FORCE.
WE'VE ALWAYS USED ORDINARY HUMANS CAUGHT UP IN THE SUPERNATURAL OR PARANORMAL...
...AND THEN WE MANIPULATED THEM INTO BECOMING OUR AGENTS. OF COURSE, IF THEY DIED DOING WHAT WE NEEDED...
...WELL, AS THE KIDS TODAY SAY, SUCKS FOR THEM. BUT BALANCE IS MAINTAINED, SO THREE YAYS FOR US.
BUT WHAT WE'RE DEALING WITH NOW IS BIGGER THAN ANYTHING WE'VE FACED BEFORE.
I'M THINKING WE NEED TO FIND MORE LIKE RAVEN. YOU KNOW, FIGHT POWER WITH POWER, EH?
GRRRRLLL
YES, THANK YOU, MERLIN. I AGREE. ANOTHER BRILLIANT IDEA BY YOURS TRULY. PUT A PIN IN IT.
I WANT TO REVISIT IT THE MOMENT OUR CURRENT BROUHAHA IS OVER.
NOW LEAVE ME ALONE. I'VE PREPARATIONS TO MAKE.
RAVEN...
...YOU ARE SIXTEEN. THAT'S UNDERAGE. I HAVE EVERY LEGAL RIGHT TO FORCE YOU TO COME HOME.

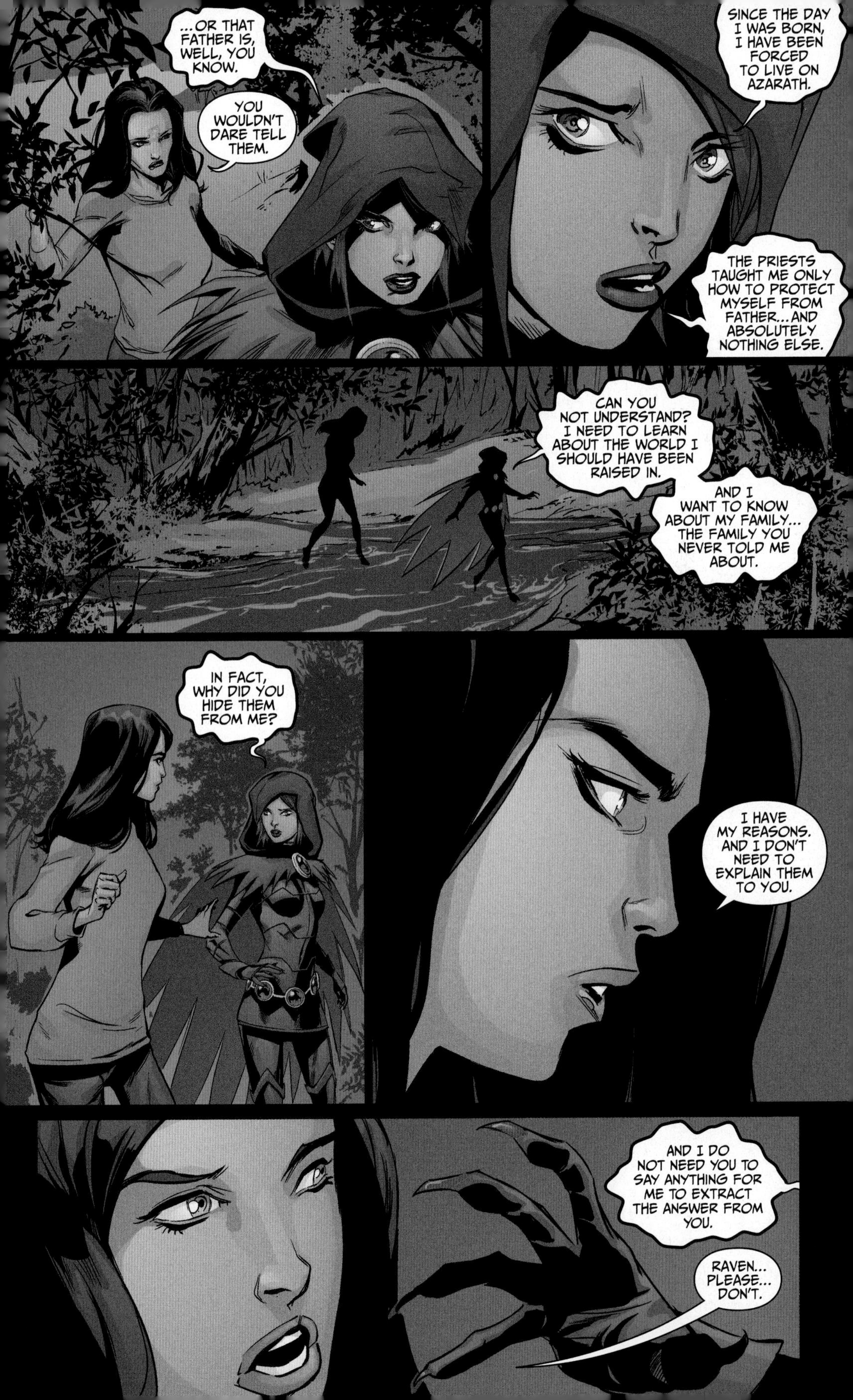
...OR THAT FATHER IS, WELL, YOU KNOW.
YOU WOULDN'T DARE TELL THEM.
SINCE THE DAY I WAS BORN, I HAVE BEEN FORCED TO LIVE ON AZARATH.
THE PRIESTS TAUGHT ME ONLY HOW TO PROTECT MYSELF FROM FATHER...AND ABSOLUTELY NOTHING ELSE.
CAN YOU NOT UNDERSTAND? I NEED TO LEARN ABOUT THE WORLD I SHOULD HAVE BEEN RAISED IN.
AND I WANT TO KNOW ABOUT MY FAMILY... THE FAMILY YOU NEVER TOLD ME ABOUT.
IN FACT, WHY DID YOU HIDE THEM FROM ME?
I HAVE MY REASONS. AND I DON'T NEED TO EXPLAIN THEM TO YOU.
AND I DO NOT NEED YOU TO SAY ANYTHING FOR ME TO EXTRACT THE ANSWER FROM YOU.
RAVEN... PLEASE... DON'T.

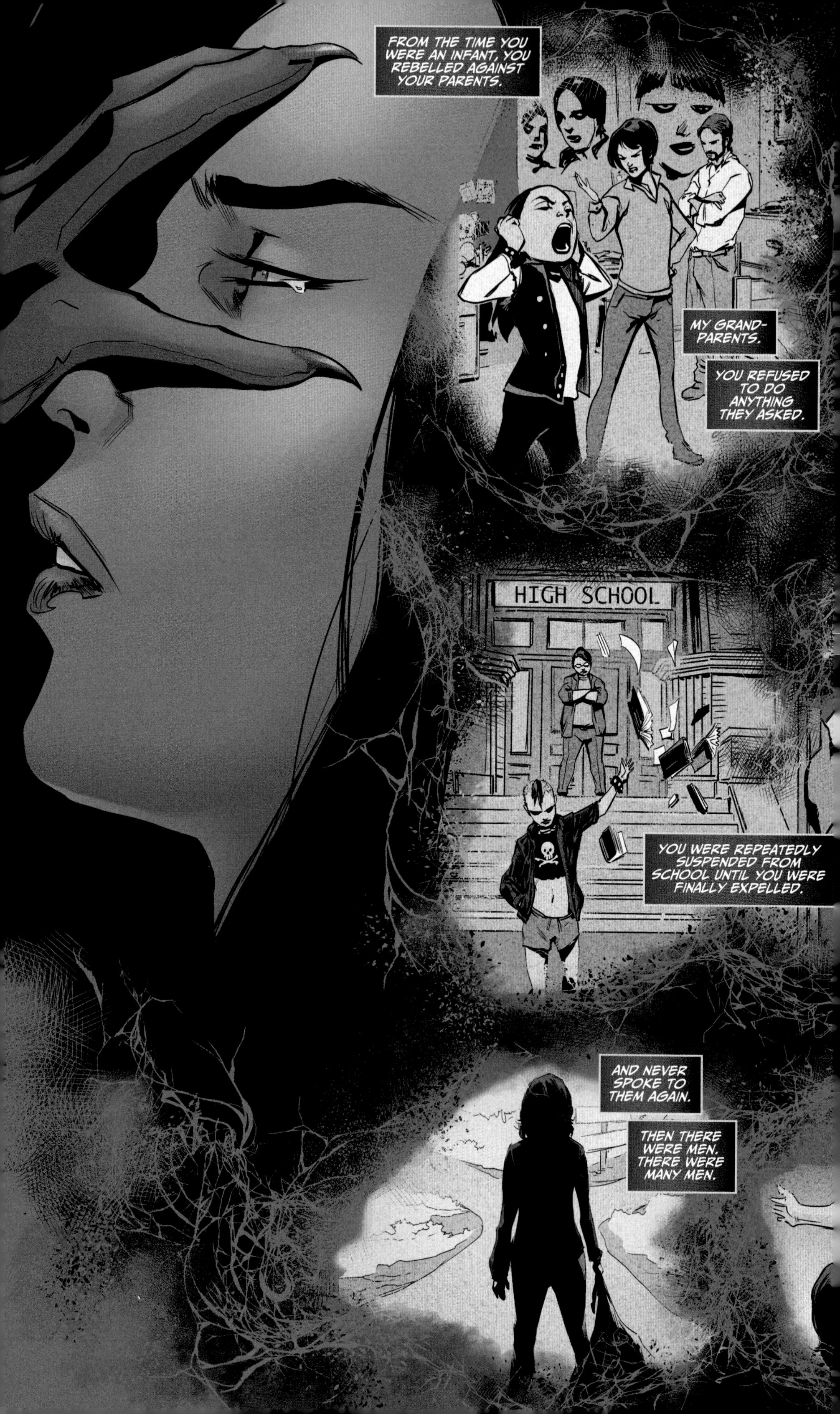
FROM THE TIME YOU WERE AN INFANT, YOU REBELLED AGAINST YOUR PARENTS.
MY GRAND-PARENTS.
YOU REFUSED TO DO ANYTHING THEY ASKED.
HIGH SCHOOL
YOU WERE REPEATEDLY SUSPENDED FROM SCHOOL UNTIL YOU WERE FINALLY EXPELLED.
AND NEVER SPOKE TO THEM AGAIN.
THEN THERE WERE MEN. THERE WERE MANY MEN.

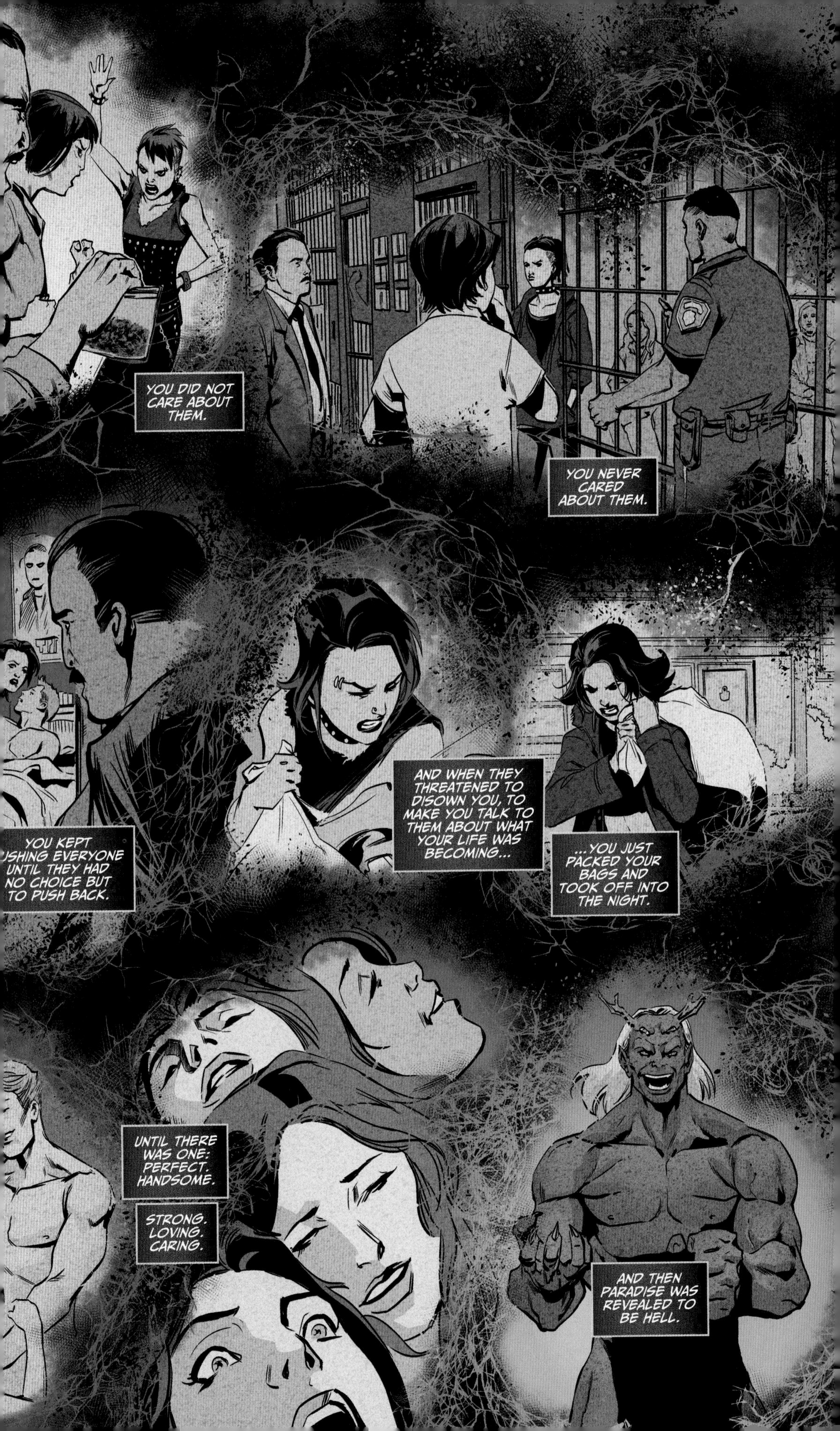
YOU DID NOT CARE ABOUT THEM.
YOU NEVER CARED ABOUT THEM.
YOU KEPT USHING EVERYONE UNTIL THEY HAD NO CHOICE BUT TO PUSH BACK.
AND WHEN THEY THREATENED TO DISOWN YOU, TO MAKE YOU TALK TO THEM ABOUT WHAT YOUR LIFE WAS BECOMING...
...YOU JUST PACKED YOUR BAGS AND TOOK OFF INTO THE NIGHT.
UNTIL THERE WAS ONE: PERFECT. HANDSOME.
STRONG. LOVING. CARING.
AND THEN PARADISE WAS REVEALED TO BE HELL.

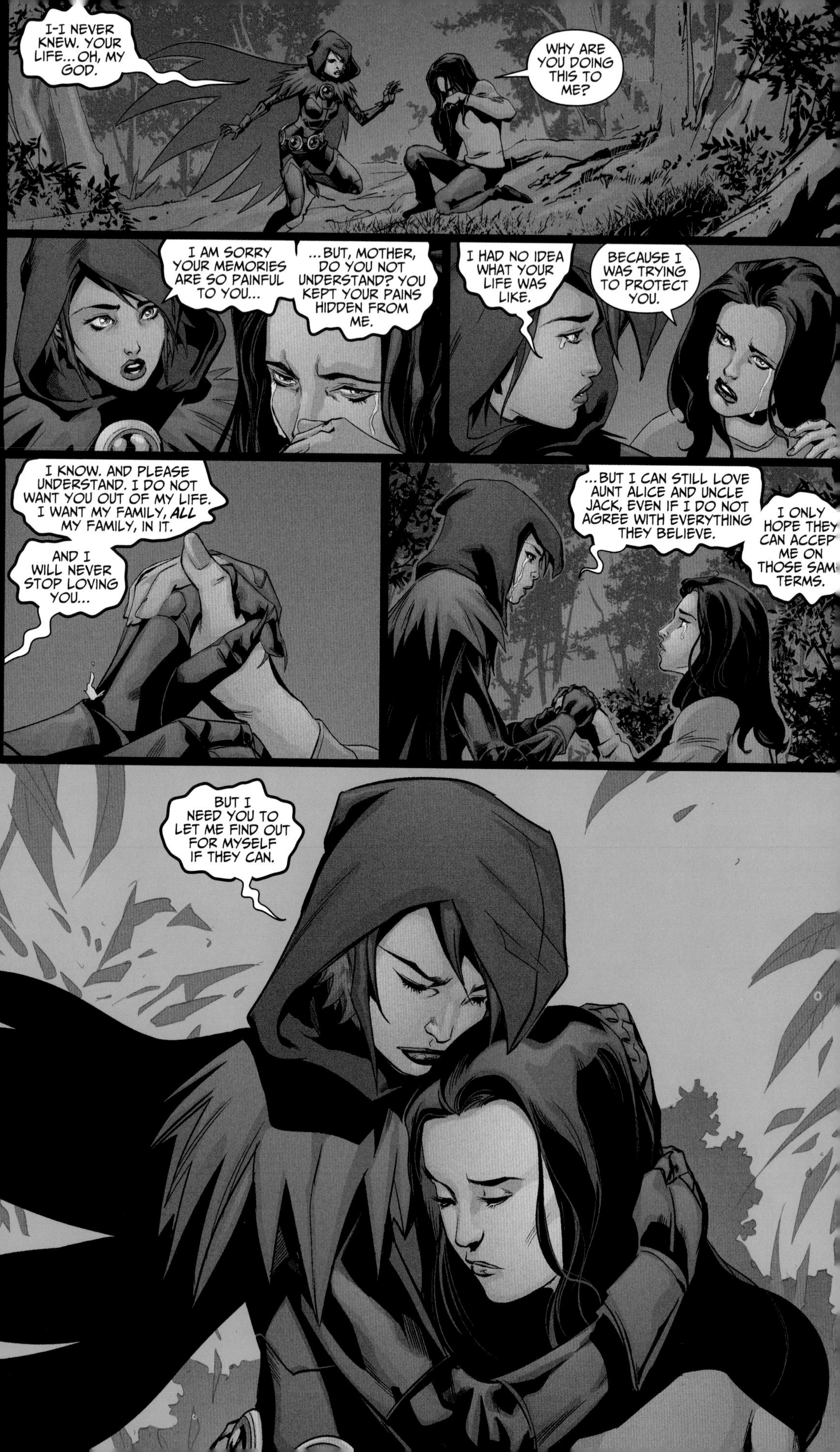
I-I NEVER KNEW. YOUR LIFE...OH, MY GOD.
WHY ARE YOU DOING THIS TO ME?
I AM SORRY YOUR MEMORIES ARE SO PAINFUL TO YOU...
...BUT, MOTHER, DO YOU NOT UNDERSTAND? YOU KEPT YOUR PAINS HIDDEN FROM ME.
I HAD NO IDEA WHAT YOUR LIFE WAS LIKE.
BECAUSE I WAS TRYING TO PROTECT YOU.
I KNOW. AND PLEASE UNDERSTAND. I DO NOT WANT YOU OUT OF MY LIFE. I WANT MY FAMILY, ALL MY FAMILY, IN IT.
AND I WILL NEVER STOP LOVING YOU...
...BUT I CAN STILL LOVE AUNT ALICE AND UNCLE JACK, EVEN IF I DO NOT AGREE WITH EVERYTHING THEY BELIEVE.
I ONLY HOPE THEY CAN ACCEP ME ON THOSE SAM TERMS.
BUT I NEED YOU TO LET ME FIND OUT FOR MYSELF IF THEY CAN.

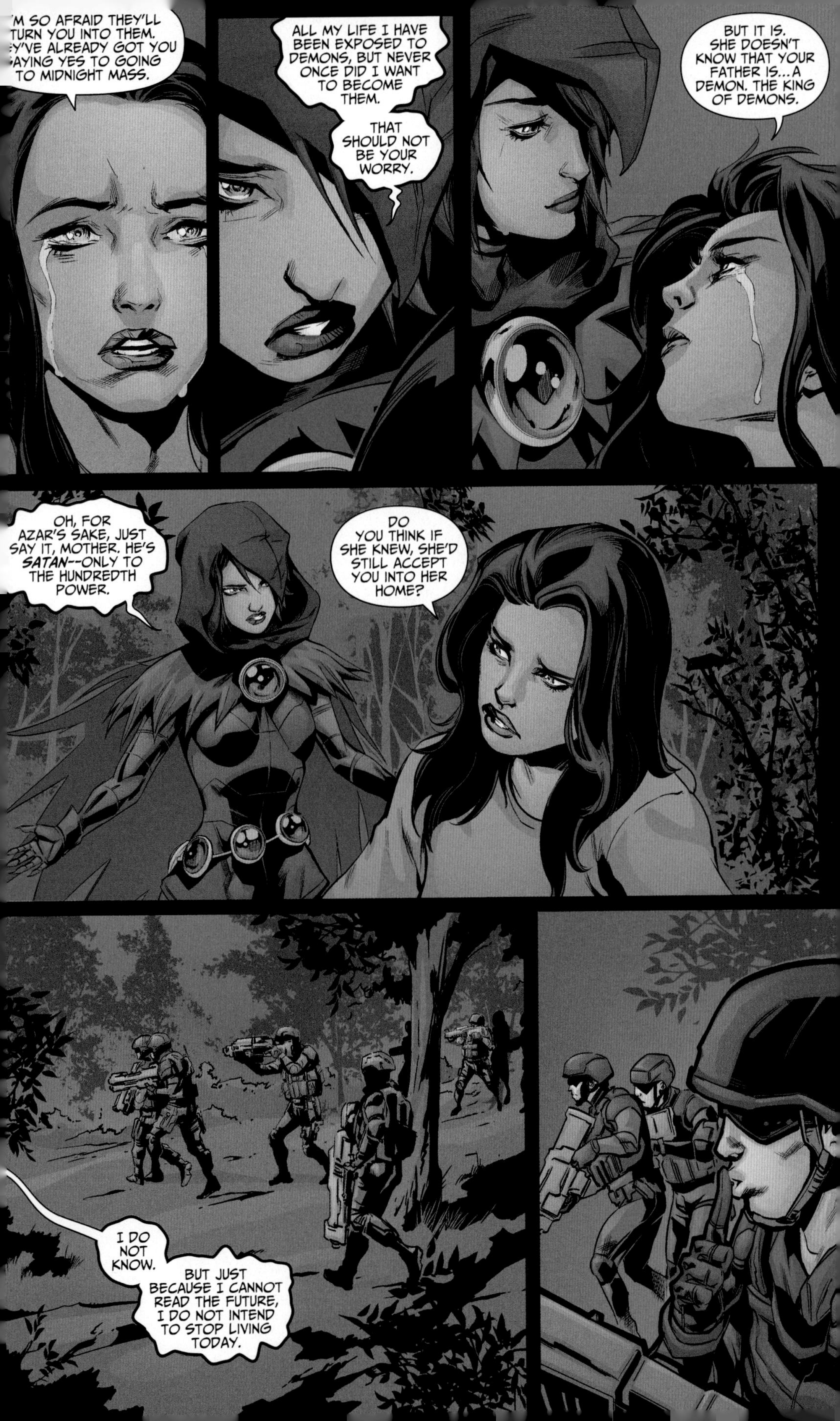
I'M SO AFRAID THEY'LL TURN YOU INTO THEM. THEY'VE ALREADY GOT YOU SAYING YES TO GOING TO MIDNIGHT MASS.
ALL MY LIFE I HAVE BEEN EXPOSED TO DEMONS, BUT NEVER ONCE DID I WANT TO BECOME THEM.
THAT SHOULD NOT BE YOUR WORRY.
BUT IT IS. SHE DOESN'T KNOW THAT YOUR FATHER IS...A DEMON. THE KING OF DEMONS.
OH, FOR AZAR'S SAKE, JUST SAY IT, MOTHER. HE'S *SATAN*--ONLY TO THE HUNDREDTH POWER.
DO YOU THINK IF SHE KNEW, SHE'D STILL ACCEPT YOU INTO HER HOME?
I DO NOT KNOW.
BUT JUST BECAUSE I CANNOT READ THE FUTURE, I DO NOT INTEND TO STOP LIVING TODAY.

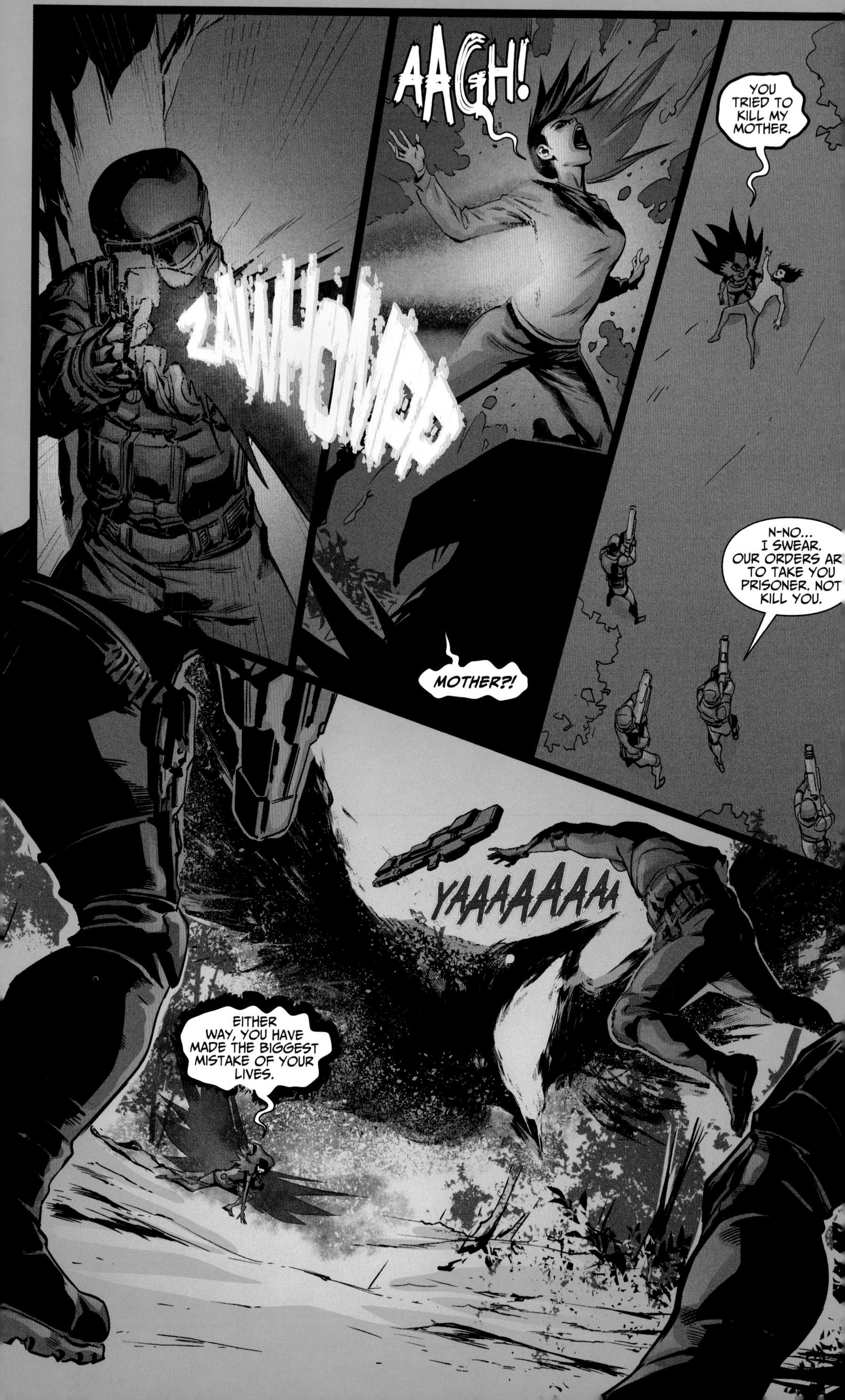
ZAWHOMPP
AAGH!
MOTHER?!
YOU TRIED TO KILL MY MOTHER.
N-NO... I SWEAR. OUR ORDERS AR TO TAKE YOU PRISONER. NOT KILL YOU.
YAAAAAAA
EITHER WAY, YOU HAVE MADE THE BIGGEST MISTAKE OF YOUR LIVES.

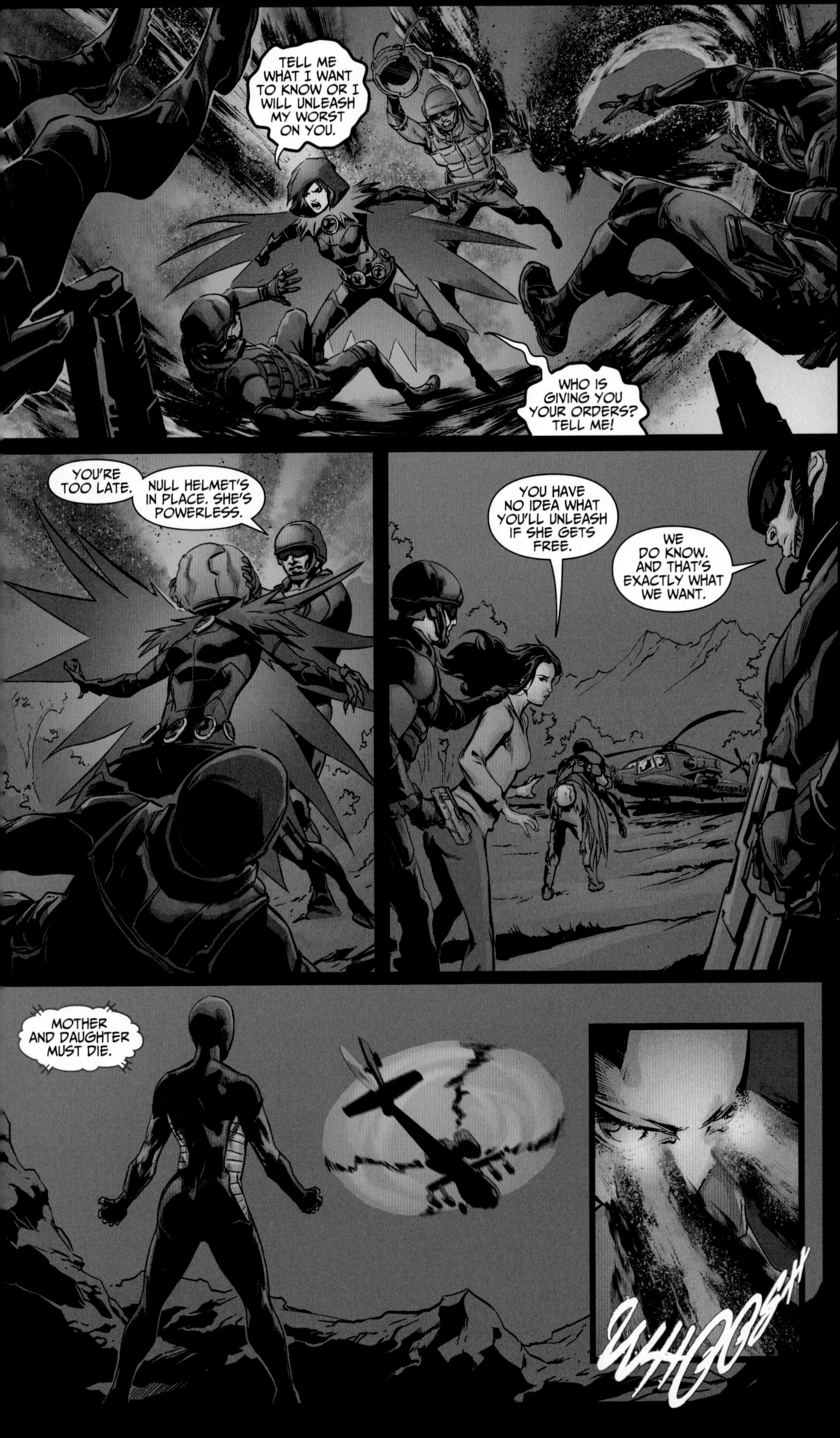
TELL ME WHAT I WANT TO KNOW OR I WILL UNLEASH MY WORST ON YOU.
WHO IS GIVING YOU YOUR ORDERS? TELL ME!
YOU'RE TOO LATE.
NULL HELMET'S IN PLACE. SHE'S POWERLESS.
YOU HAVE NO IDEA WHAT YOU'LL UNLEASH IF SHE GETS FREE.
WE DO KNOW. AND THAT'S EXACTLY WHAT WE WANT.
MOTHER AND DAUGHTER MUST DIE.
WHOOSH

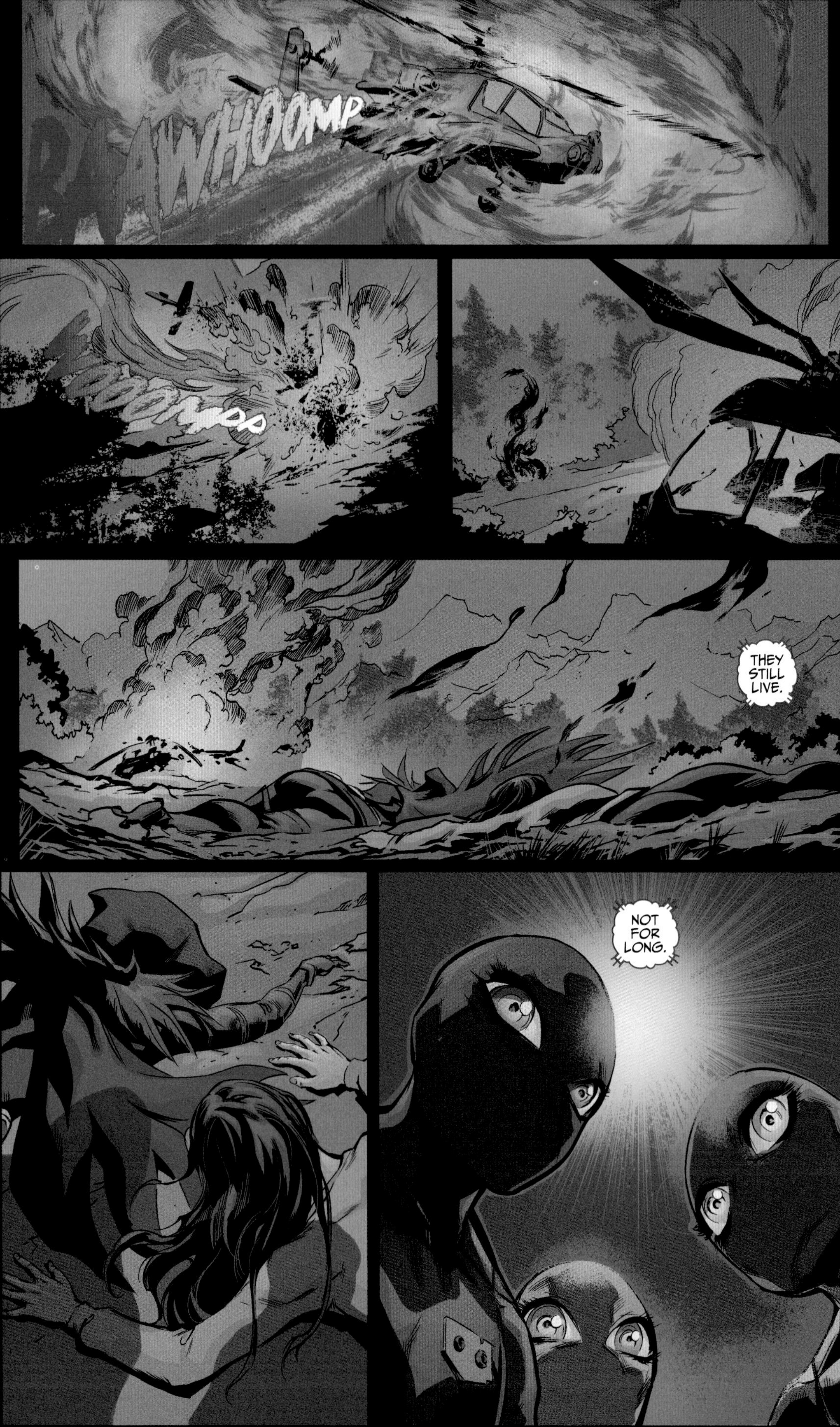
BRAWHOOMP
WHOOOOMPP
THEY STILL LIVE.
NOT FOR LONG.

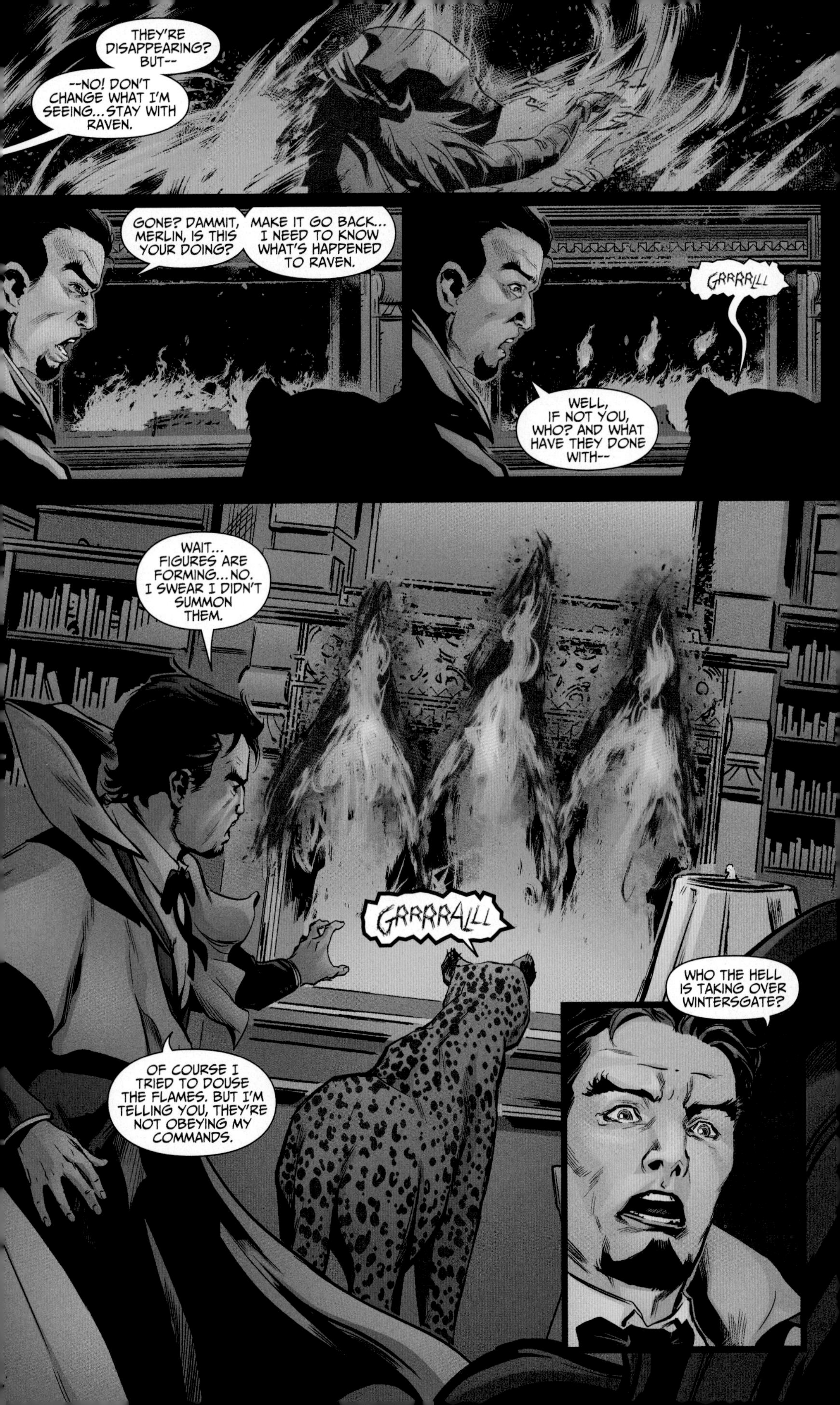

THEY'RE DISAPPEARING? BUT--
--NO! DON'T CHANGE WHAT I'M SEEING...STAY WITH RAVEN.
GONE? DAMMIT, MERLIN, IS THIS YOUR DOING?
MAKE IT GO BACK... I NEED TO KNOW WHAT'S HAPPENED TO RAVEN.
GRRRRLLL
WELL, IF NOT YOU, WHO? AND WHAT HAVE THEY DONE WITH--
WAIT... FIGURES ARE FORMING...NO. I SWEAR I DIDN'T SUMMON THEM.
GRRRRALLL
OF COURSE I TRIED TO DOUSE THE FLAMES. BUT I'M TELLING YOU, THEY'RE NOT OBEYING MY COMMANDS.
WHO THE HELL IS TAKING OVER WINTERSGATE?

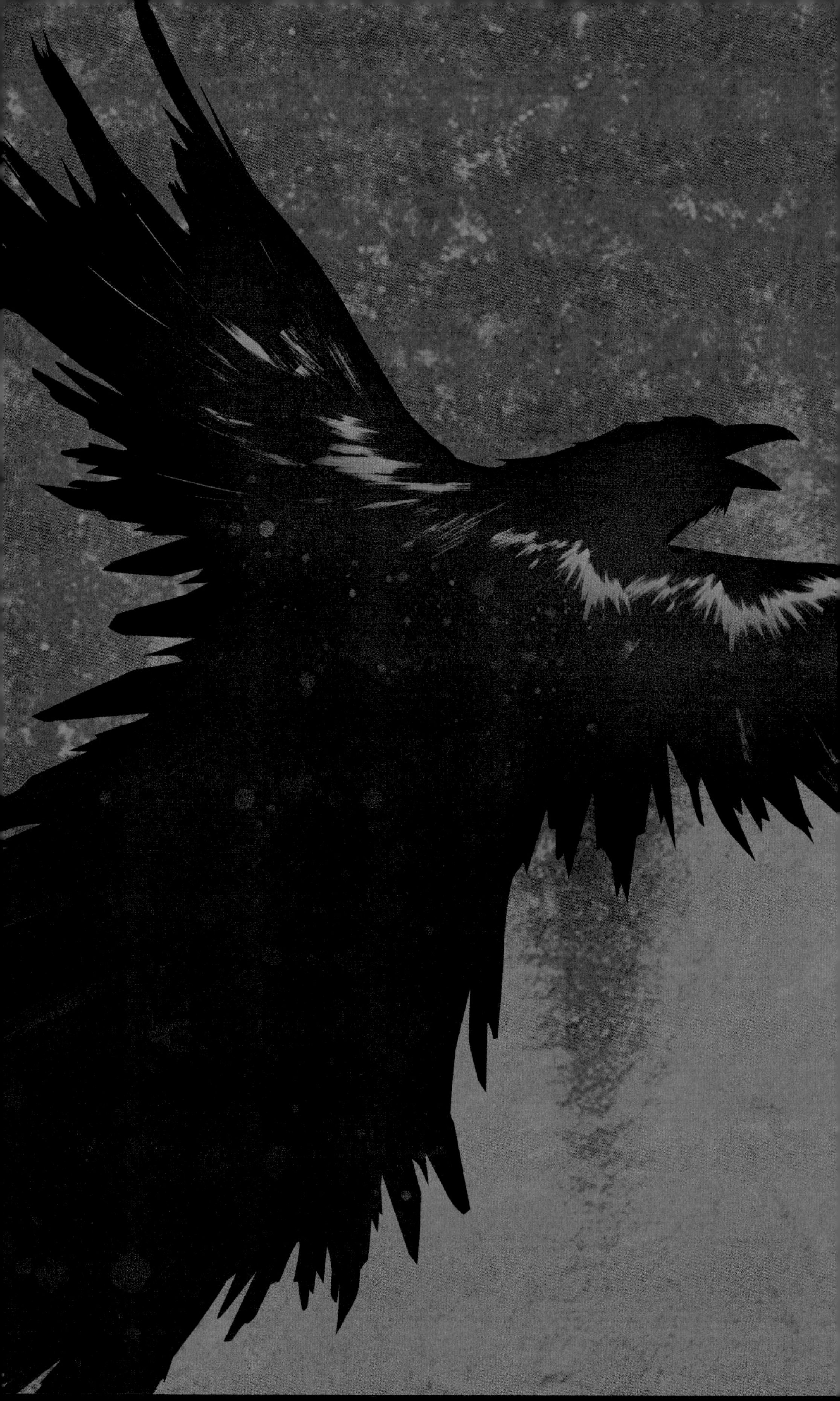

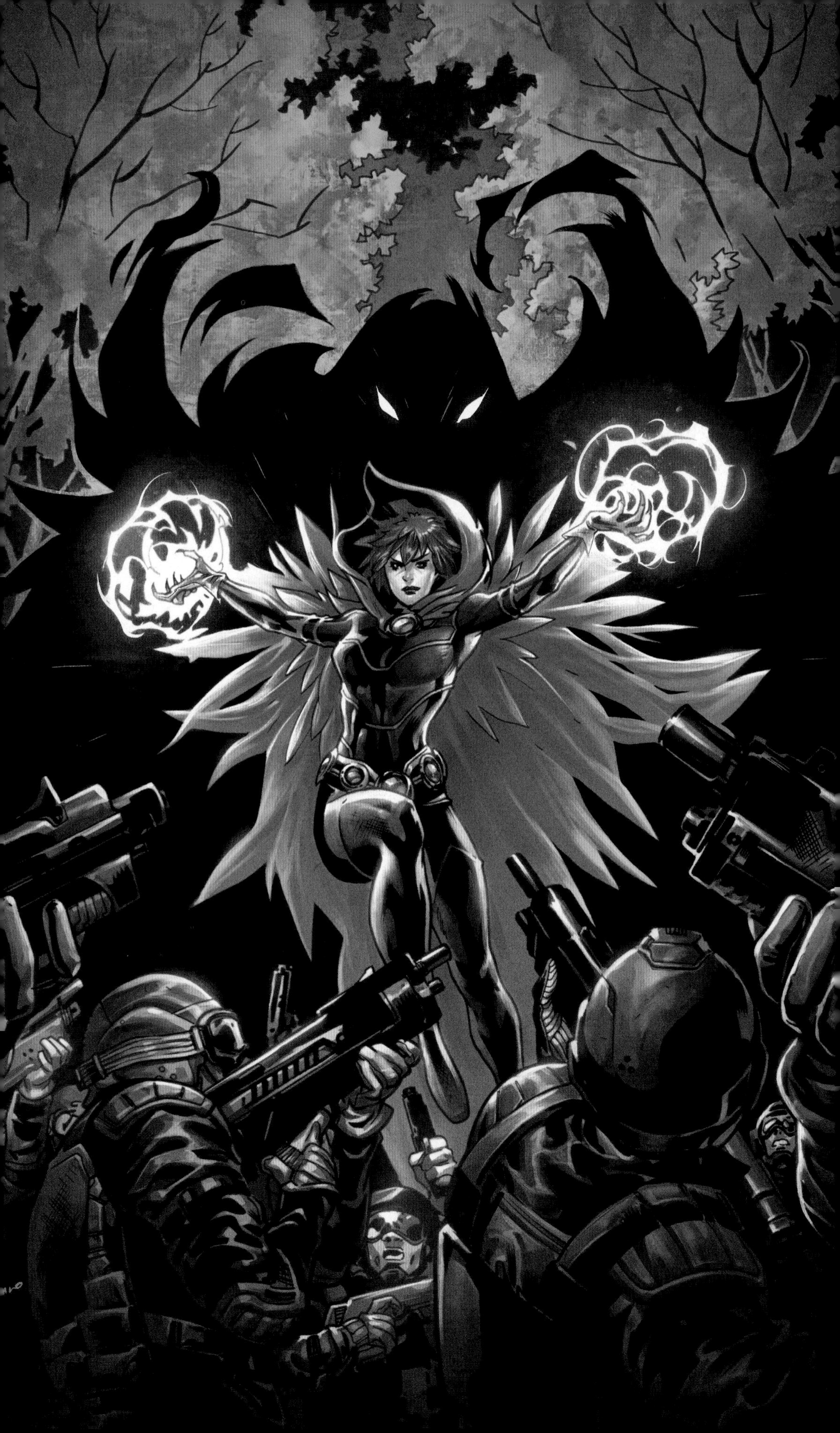

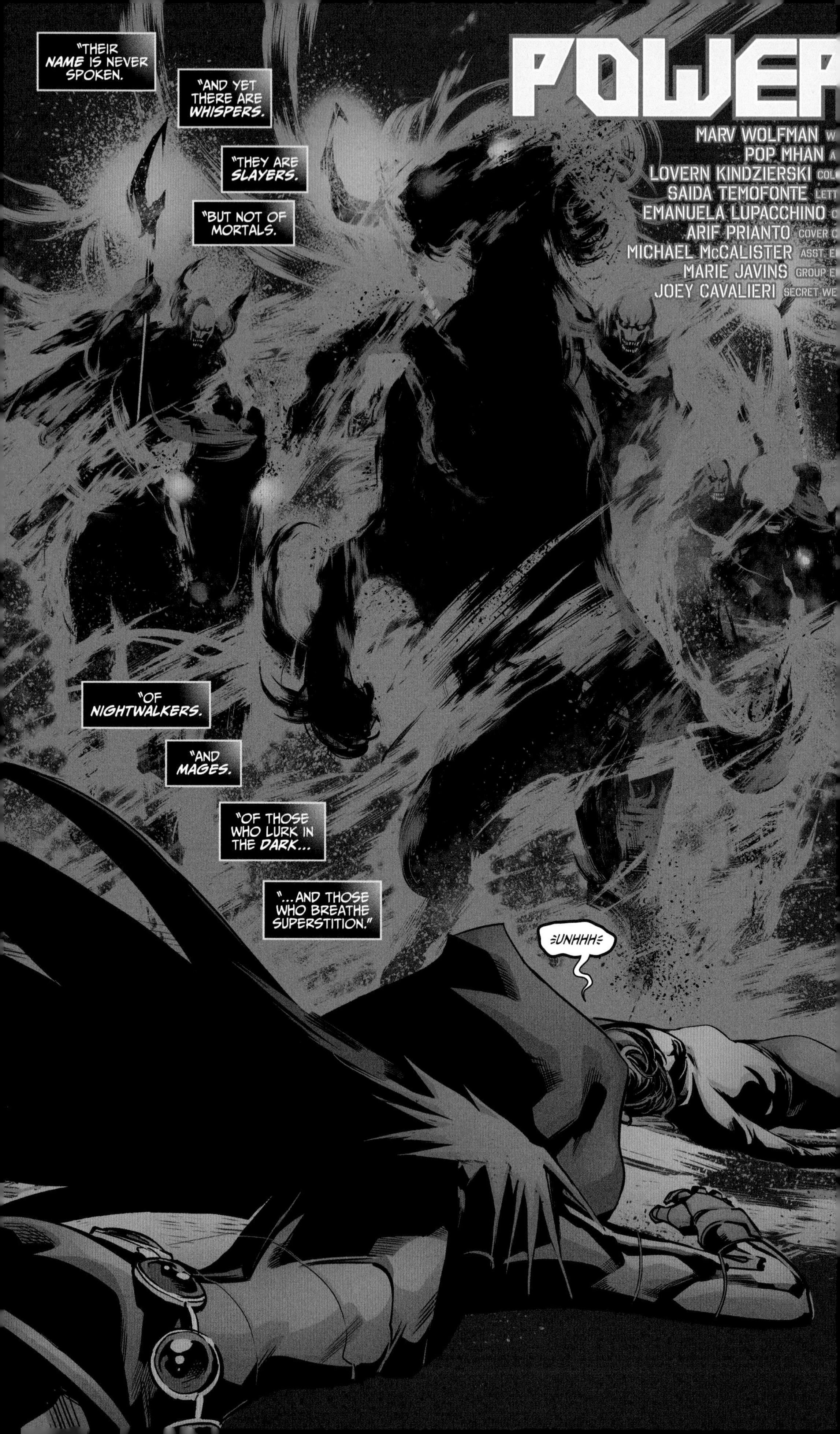

"THEIR NAME IS NEVER SPOKEN.
"AND YET THERE ARE WHISPERS.
"THEY ARE SLAYERS.
"BUT NOT OF MORTALS.
POWE
MARV WOLFMAN
POP MHAN
LOVERN KINDZIERSKI
SAIDA TEMOFONTE
EMANUELA LUPACCHINO
ARIF PRIANTO COVER
MICHAEL McCALISTER
MARIE JAVINS
JOEY CAVALIERI
"OF NIGHTWALKERS.
"AND MAGES.
"OF THOSE WHO LURK IN THE DARK...
"...AND THOSE WHO BREATHE SUPERSTITION."
UNHHH

"THEY CANNOT BE SEEN...

"...UNTIL IT IS TOO LATE.

"THEY ARE...

THE SHADOW-RIDERS!

"PRAY THEY DO NOT COME FOR YOU."

...M-MOTHER...? M-M-MOTHER...?

ARE YOU...ARE YOU THERE?

M-M-MOTHER...?!

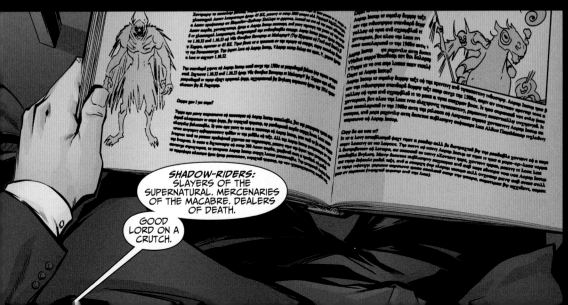

SHADOW-RIDERS: SLAYERS OF THE SUPERNATURAL. MERCENARIES OF THE MACABRE. DEALERS OF DEATH.

GOOD LORD ON A CRUTCH.

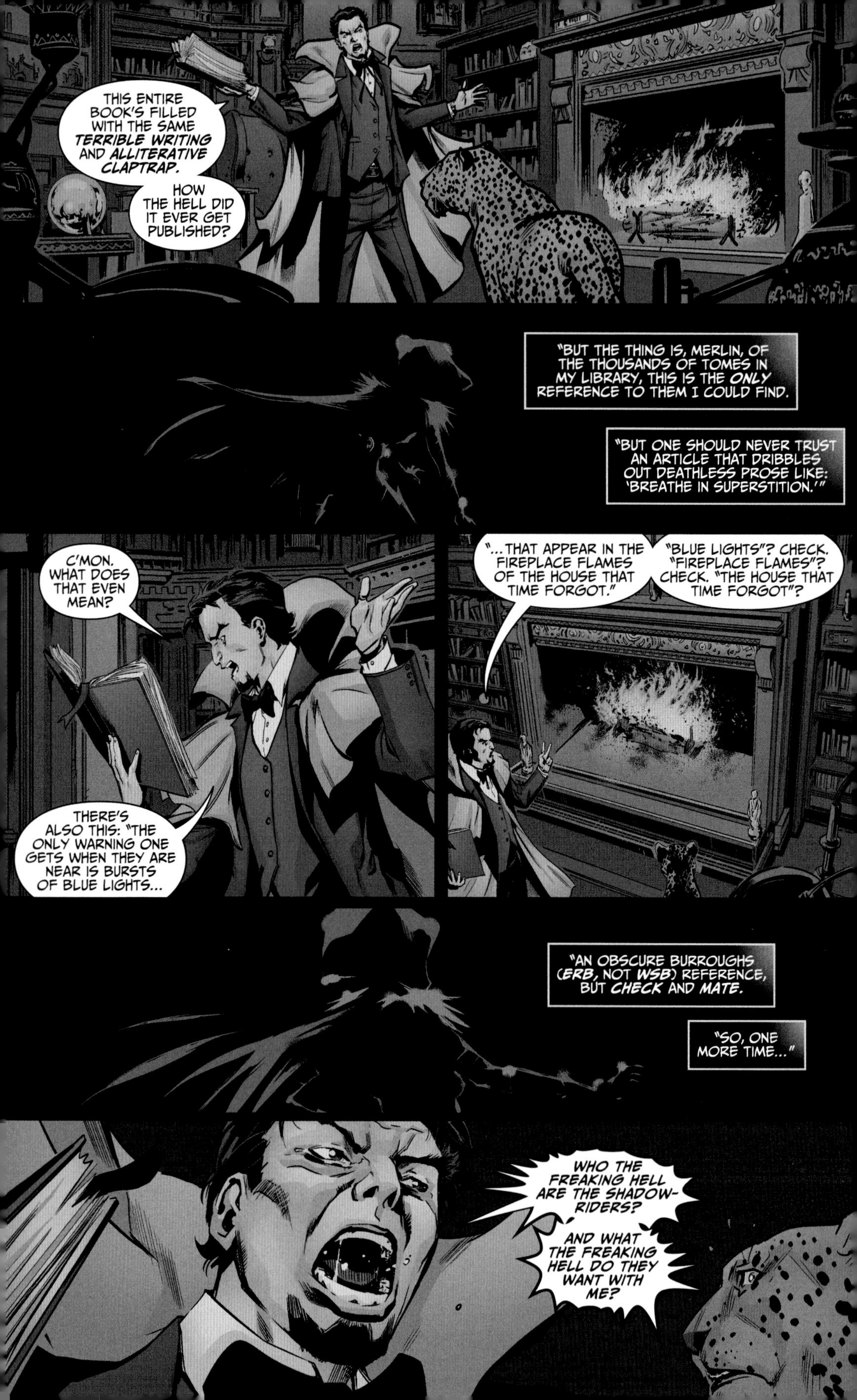
THIS ENTIRE BOOK'S FILLED WITH THE SAME TERRIBLE WRITING AND ALLITERATIVE CLAPTRAP.
HOW THE HELL DID IT EVER GET PUBLISHED?
"BUT THE THING IS, MERLIN, OF THE THOUSANDS OF TOMES IN MY LIBRARY, THIS IS THE ONLY REFERENCE TO THEM I COULD FIND.
"BUT ONE SHOULD NEVER TRUST AN ARTICLE THAT DRIBBLES OUT DEATHLESS PROSE LIKE: 'BREATHE IN SUPERSTITION.'"
C'MON. WHAT DOES THAT EVEN MEAN?
THERE'S ALSO THIS: "THE ONLY WARNING ONE GETS WHEN THEY ARE NEAR IS BURSTS OF BLUE LIGHTS...
"...THAT APPEAR IN THE FIREPLACE FLAMES OF THE HOUSE THAT TIME FORGOT."
"BLUE LIGHTS"? CHECK. "FIREPLACE FLAMES"? CHECK. "THE HOUSE THAT TIME FORGOT"?
"AN OBSCURE BURROUGHS (ERB, NOT WSB) REFERENCE, BUT CHECK AND MATE.
"SO, ONE MORE TIME..."
WHO THE FREAKING HELL ARE THE SHADOW-RIDERS?
AND WHAT THE FREAKING HELL DO THEY WANT WITH ME?

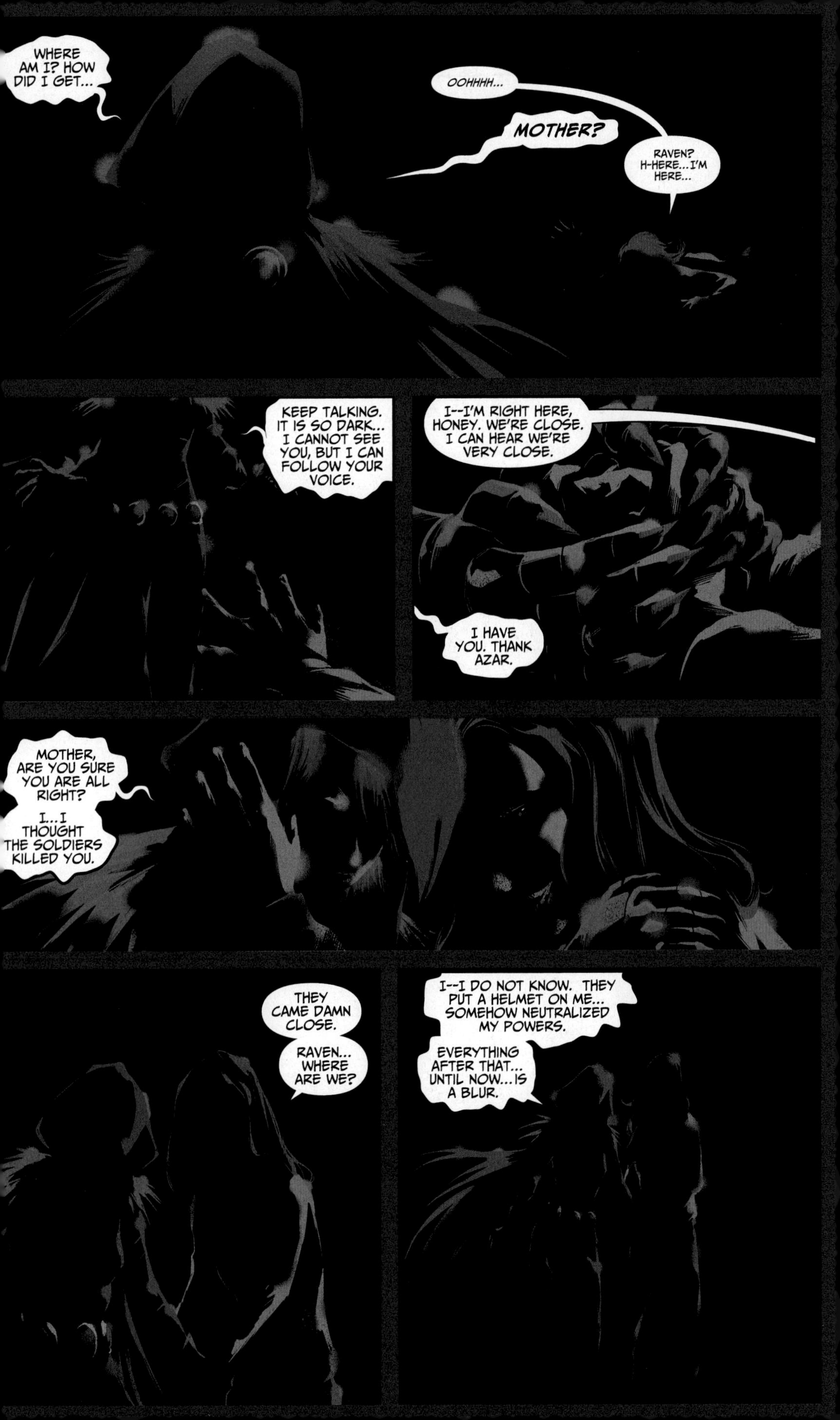
WHERE AM I? HOW DID I GET...
OOHHHH...
MOTHER?
RAVEN? H-HERE...I'M HERE...
KEEP TALKING. IT IS SO DARK... I CANNOT SEE YOU, BUT I CAN FOLLOW YOUR VOICE.
I--I'M RIGHT HERE, HONEY. WE'RE CLOSE. I CAN HEAR WE'RE VERY CLOSE.
I HAVE YOU. THANK AZAR.
MOTHER, ARE YOU SURE YOU ARE ALL RIGHT?
I...I THOUGHT THE SOLDIERS KILLED YOU.
THEY CAME DAMN CLOSE.
RAVEN... WHERE ARE WE?
I--I DO NOT KNOW. THEY PUT A HELMET ON ME... SOMEHOW NEUTRALIZED MY POWERS.
EVERYTHING AFTER THAT... UNTIL NOW...IS A BLUR.

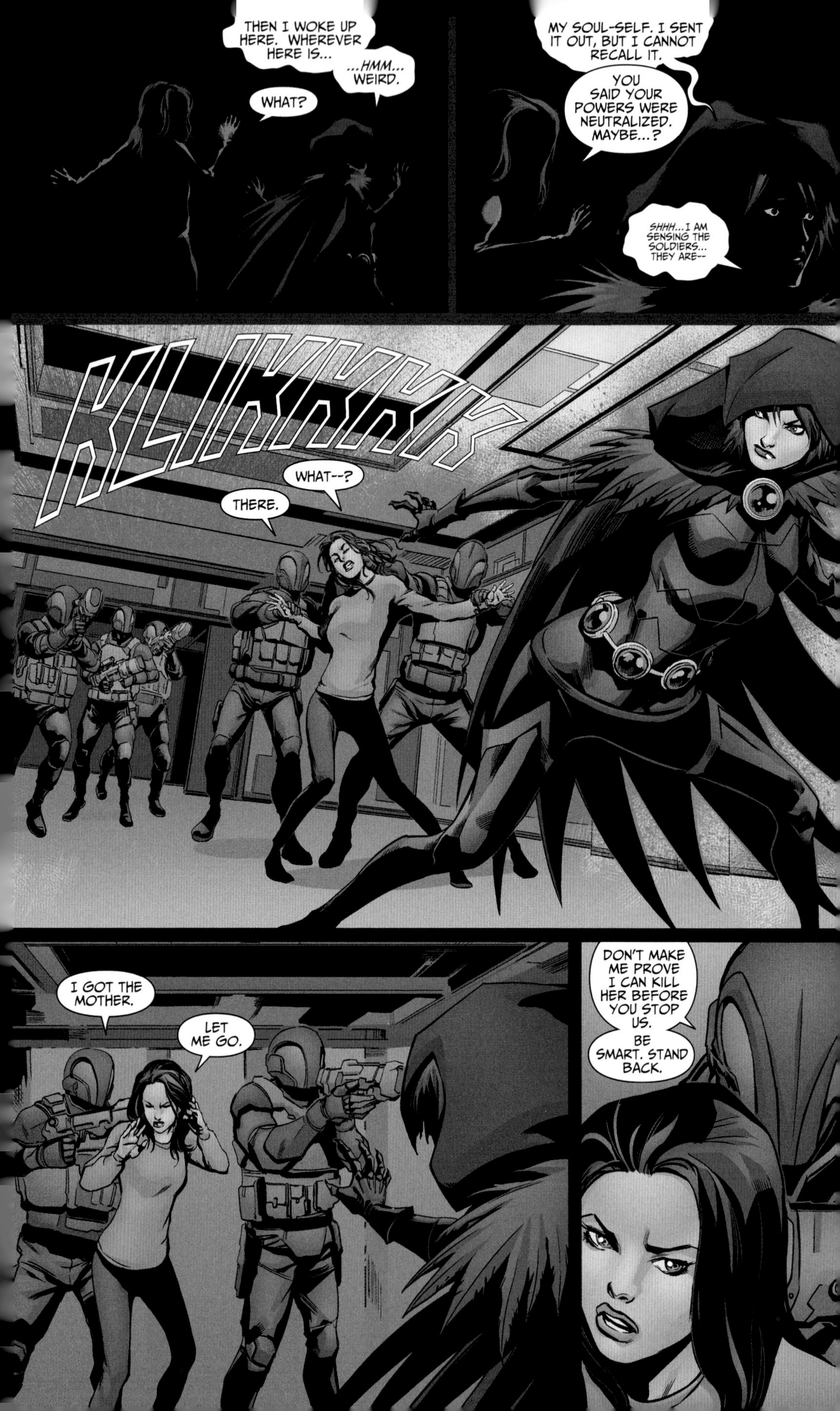
THEN I WOKE UP HERE. WHEREVER HERE IS...
...HMM... WEIRD.
WHAT?
MY SOUL-SELF. I SENT IT OUT, BUT I CANNOT RECALL IT.
YOU SAID YOUR POWERS WERE NEUTRALIZED. MAYBE...?
SHHH... I AM SENSING THE SOLDIERS... THEY ARE--
KLIKKKK
THERE.
WHAT--?
I GOT THE MOTHER.
LET ME GO.
DON'T MAKE ME PROVE I CAN KILL HER BEFORE YOU STOP US.
BE SMART. STAND BACK.

EVEN WITHOUT MY SOUL-SELF, I CAN EASILY DEFEAT THEM. BUT I NEED TO KNOW WHY THEY ARE PURSUING ME.

DOWN THE CORRIDOR. C'MON. LET'S GO.

WHERE ARE WE?

OKAY. DO NOT HURT HER. SHE IS THE ONLY MOTHER I HAVE.

rrowTek
Bay, California

THE NEXUS OF EVERYTHING BIZARRO.

ABOUT TIME. WE'VE BEEN WAITING FOREVER TO GET YOU BOTH HERE.

I WOULD HAVE COME SOONER IF YOU HAD CALLED. YOU KNOW HOW MUCH I LIKE TO PARTY.

NOT.

I AM SO LEARNING HOW TO LIE AND ACT TOUGH. THANK YOU, GARFIELD LOGAN, MENTOR OF MISCHIEF.

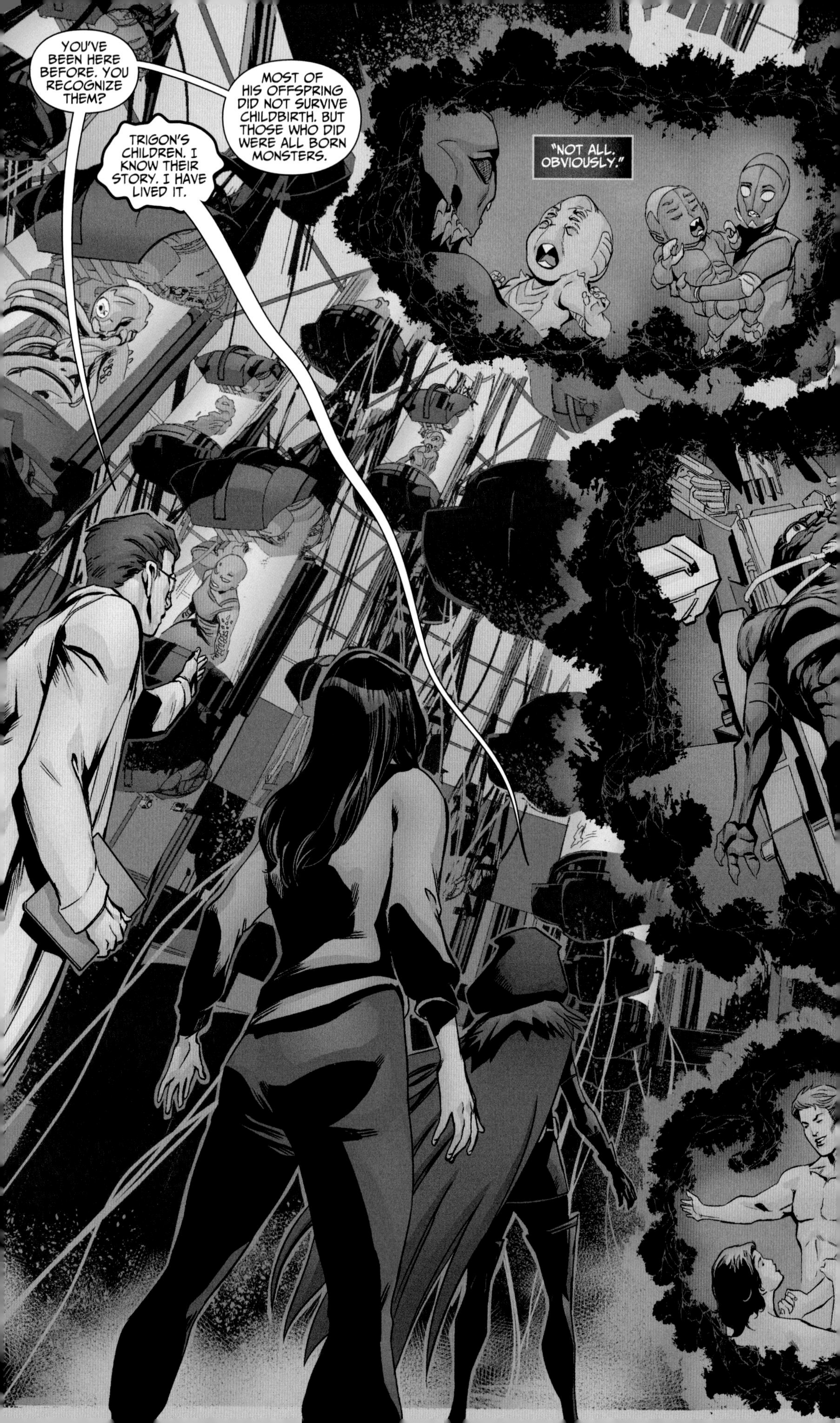
YOU'VE BEEN HERE BEFORE. YOU RECOGNIZE THEM?
TRIGON'S CHILDREN. I KNOW THEIR STORY. I HAVE LIVED IT.
MOST OF HIS OFFSPRING DID NOT SURVIVE CHILDBIRTH. BUT THOSE WHO DID WERE ALL BORN MONSTERS.
"NOT ALL. OBVIOUSLY."

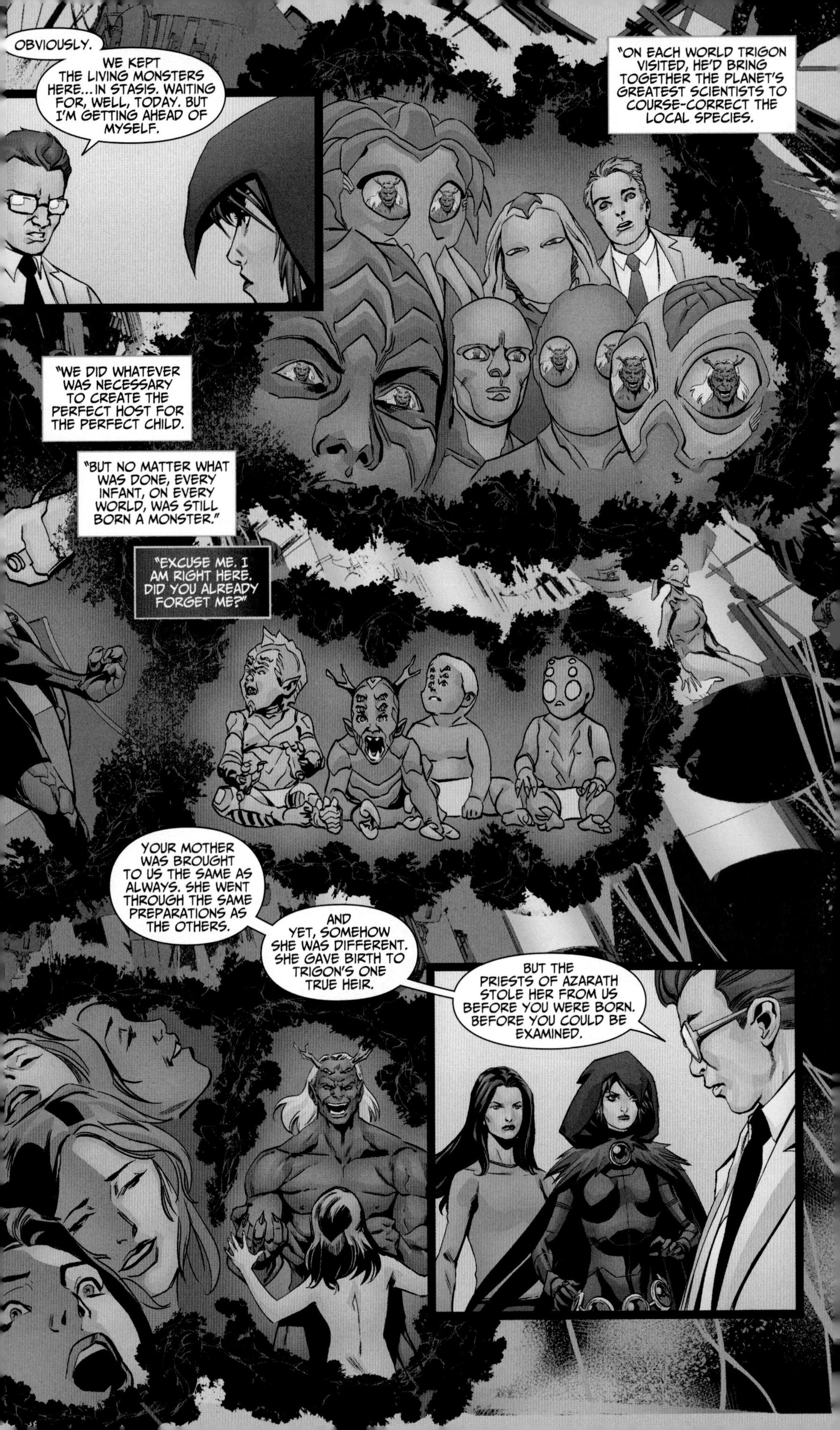
OBVIOUSLY.
WE KEPT THE LIVING MONSTERS HERE...IN STASIS. WAITING FOR, WELL, TODAY. BUT I'M GETTING AHEAD OF MYSELF.
"ON EACH WORLD TRIGON VISITED, HE'D BRING TOGETHER THE PLANET'S GREATEST SCIENTISTS TO COURSE-CORRECT THE LOCAL SPECIES.
"WE DID WHATEVER WAS NECESSARY TO CREATE THE PERFECT HOST FOR THE PERFECT CHILD.
"BUT NO MATTER WHAT WAS DONE, EVERY INFANT, ON EVERY WORLD, WAS STILL BORN A MONSTER."
"EXCUSE ME. I AM RIGHT HERE. DID YOU ALREADY FORGET ME?"
YOUR MOTHER WAS BROUGHT TO US THE SAME AS ALWAYS. SHE WENT THROUGH THE SAME PREPARATIONS AS THE OTHERS.
AND YET, SOMEHOW SHE WAS DIFFERENT. SHE GAVE BIRTH TO TRIGON'S ONE TRUE HEIR.
BUT THE PRIESTS OF AZARATH STOLE HER FROM US BEFORE YOU WERE BORN. BEFORE YOU COULD BE EXAMINED.

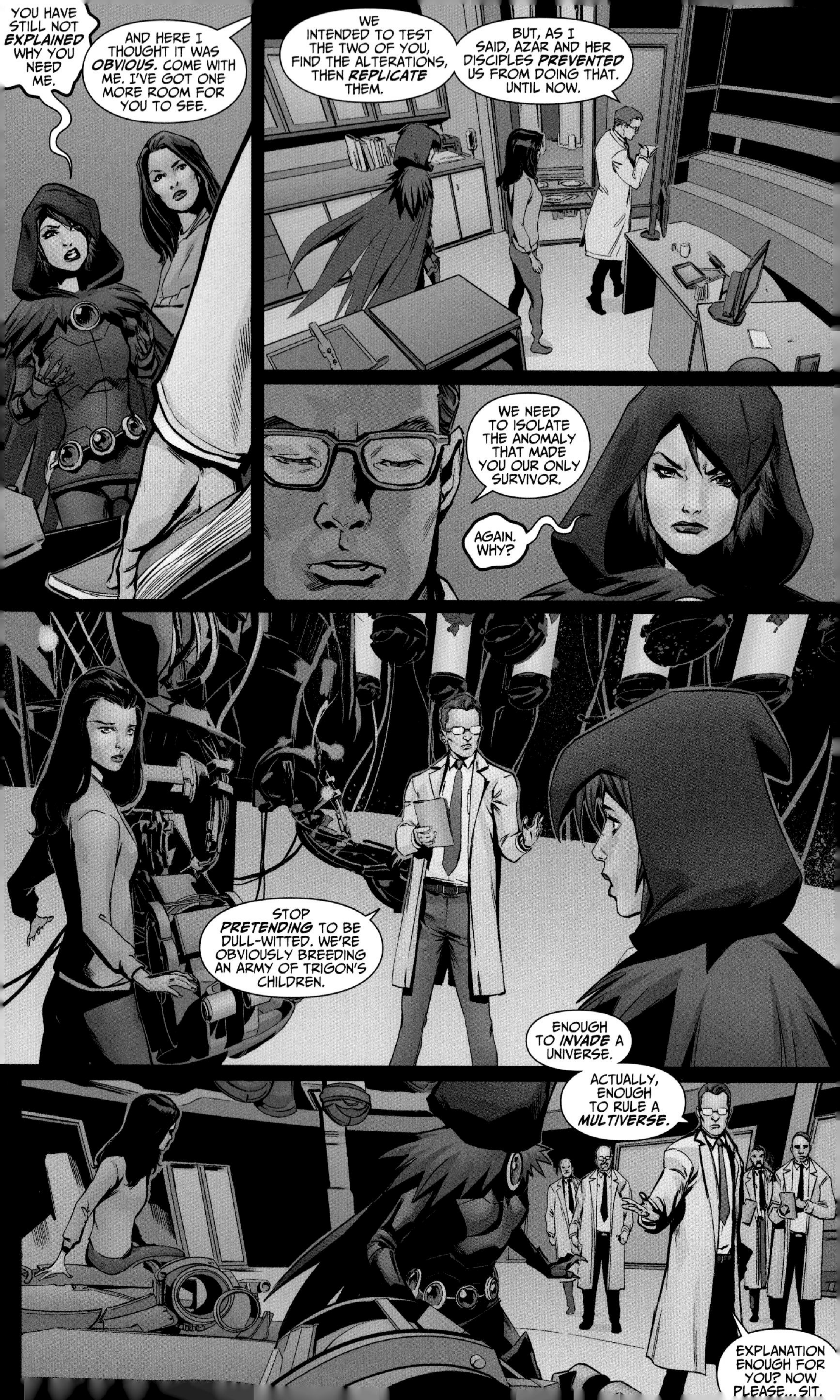
YOU HAVE STILL NOT EXPLAINED WHY YOU NEED ME.
AND HERE I THOUGHT IT WAS OBVIOUS. COME WITH ME. I'VE GOT ONE MORE ROOM FOR YOU TO SEE.
WE INTENDED TO TEST THE TWO OF YOU, FIND THE ALTERATIONS, THEN REPLICATE THEM.
BUT, AS I SAID, AZAR AND HER DISCIPLES PREVENTED US FROM DOING THAT. UNTIL NOW.
WE NEED TO ISOLATE THE ANOMALY THAT MADE YOU OUR ONLY SURVIVOR.
AGAIN. WHY?
STOP PRETENDING TO BE DULL-WITTED. WE'RE OBVIOUSLY BREEDING AN ARMY OF TRIGON'S CHILDREN.
ENOUGH TO INVADE A UNIVERSE.
ACTUALLY, ENOUGH TO RULE A MULTIVERSE.
EXPLANATION ENOUGH FOR YOU? NOW PLEASE... SIT.

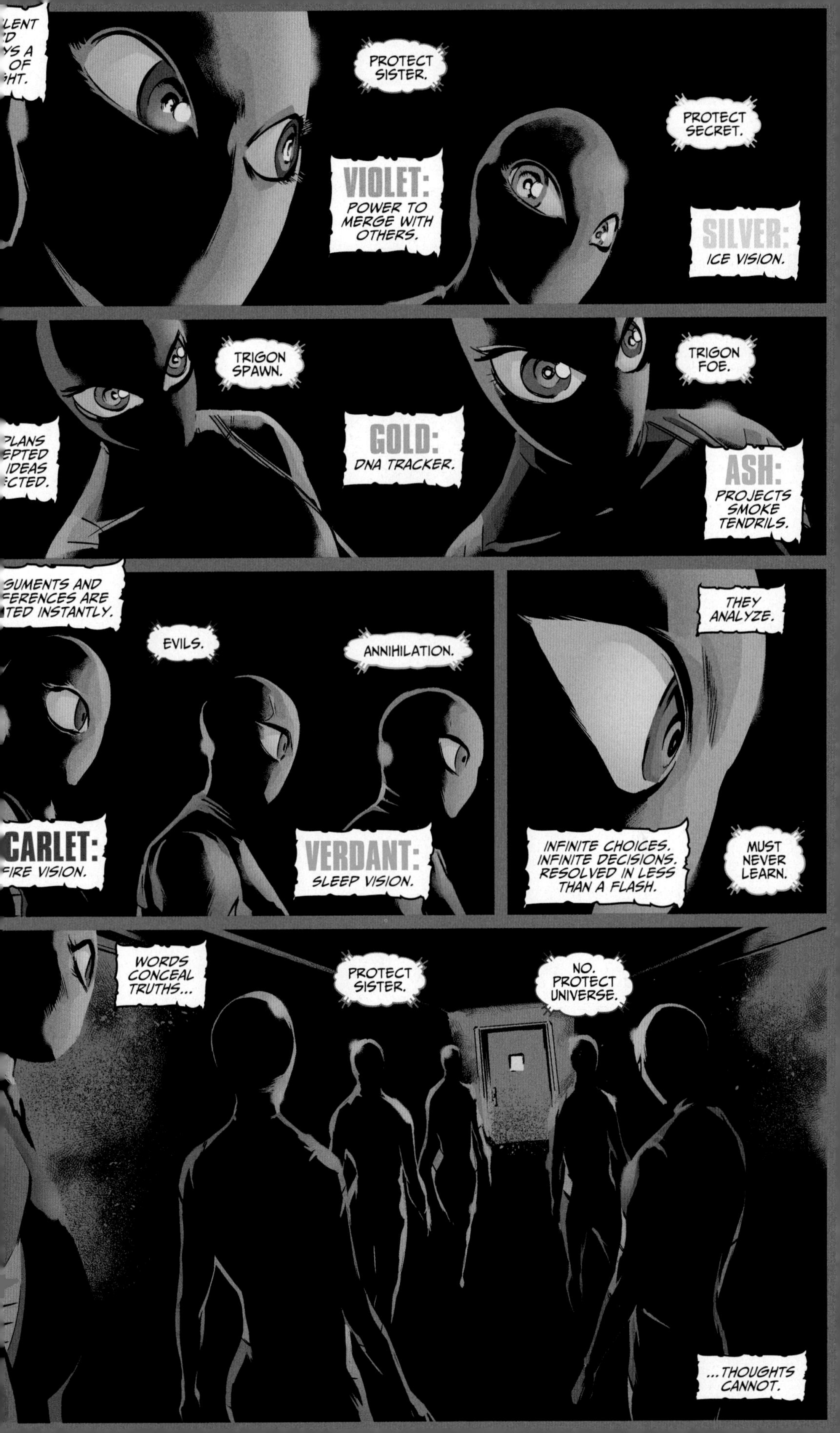
PROTECT SISTER.
VIOLET: POWER TO MERGE WITH OTHERS.
PROTECT SECRET.
SILVER: ICE VISION.
TRIGON SPAWN.
GOLD: DNA TRACKER.
TRIGON FOE.
ASH: PROJECTS SMOKE TENDRILS.
EVILS.
ANNIHILATION.
VERDANT: SLEEP VISION.
THEY ANALYZE.
INFINITE CHOICES. INFINITE DECISIONS. RESOLVED IN LESS THAN A FLASH.
MUST NEVER LEARN.
WORDS CONCEAL TRUTHS...
PROTECT SISTER.
NO. PROTECT UNIVERSE.
...THOUGHTS CANNOT.

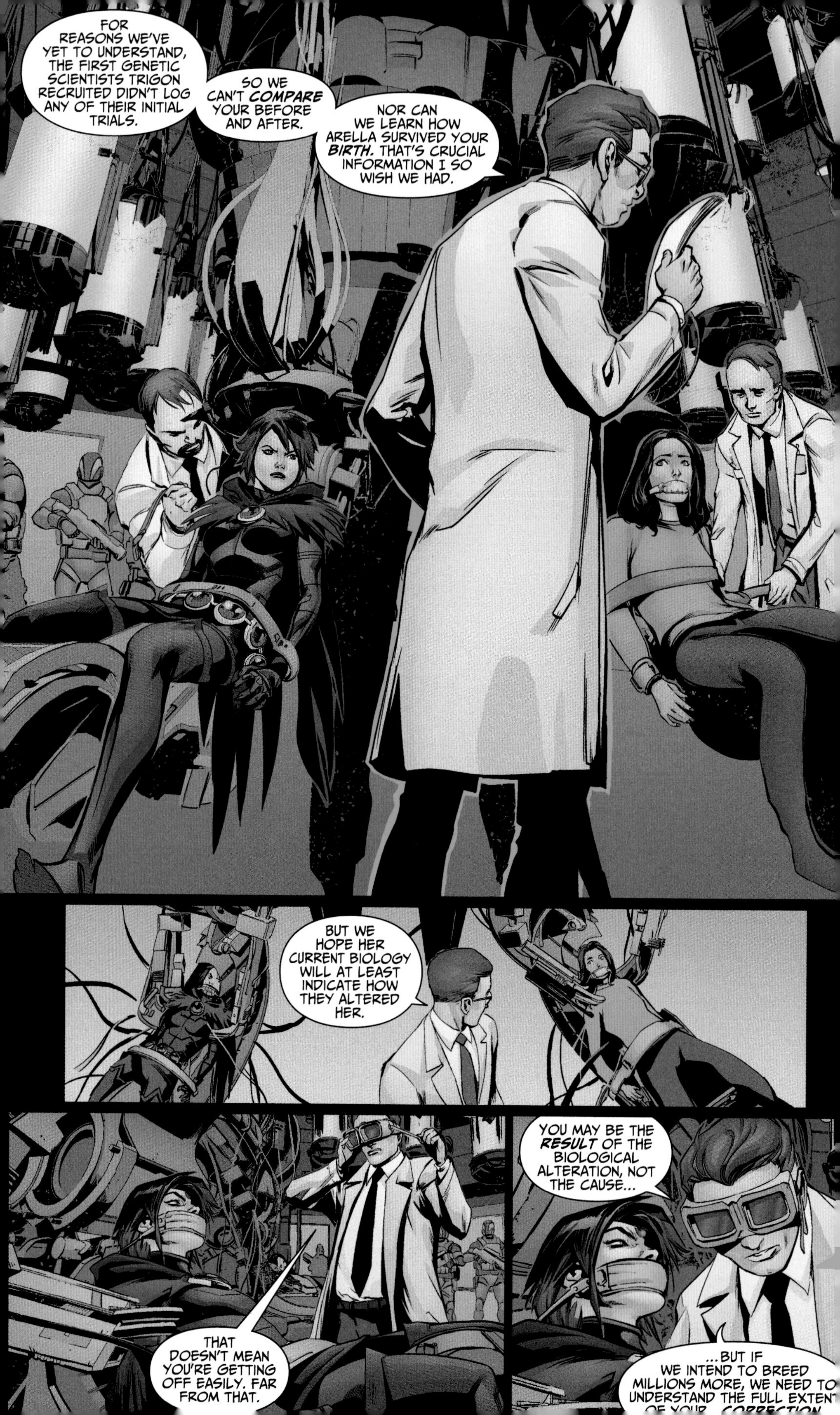
FOR REASONS WE'VE YET TO UNDERSTAND, THE FIRST GENETIC SCIENTISTS TRIGON RECRUITED DIDN'T LOG ANY OF THEIR INITIAL TRIALS.
SO WE CAN'T COMPARE YOUR BEFORE AND AFTER.
NOR CAN WE LEARN HOW ARELLA SURVIVED YOUR BIRTH. THAT'S CRUCIAL INFORMATION I SO WISH WE HAD.
BUT WE HOPE HER CURRENT BIOLOGY WILL AT LEAST INDICATE HOW THEY ALTERED HER.
THAT DOESN'T MEAN YOU'RE GETTING OFF EASILY. FAR FROM THAT.
YOU MAY BE THE RESULT OF THE BIOLOGICAL ALTERATION, NOT THE CAUSE...
...BUT IF WE INTEND TO BREED MILLIONS MORE, WE NEED TO UNDERSTAND THE FULL EXTENT

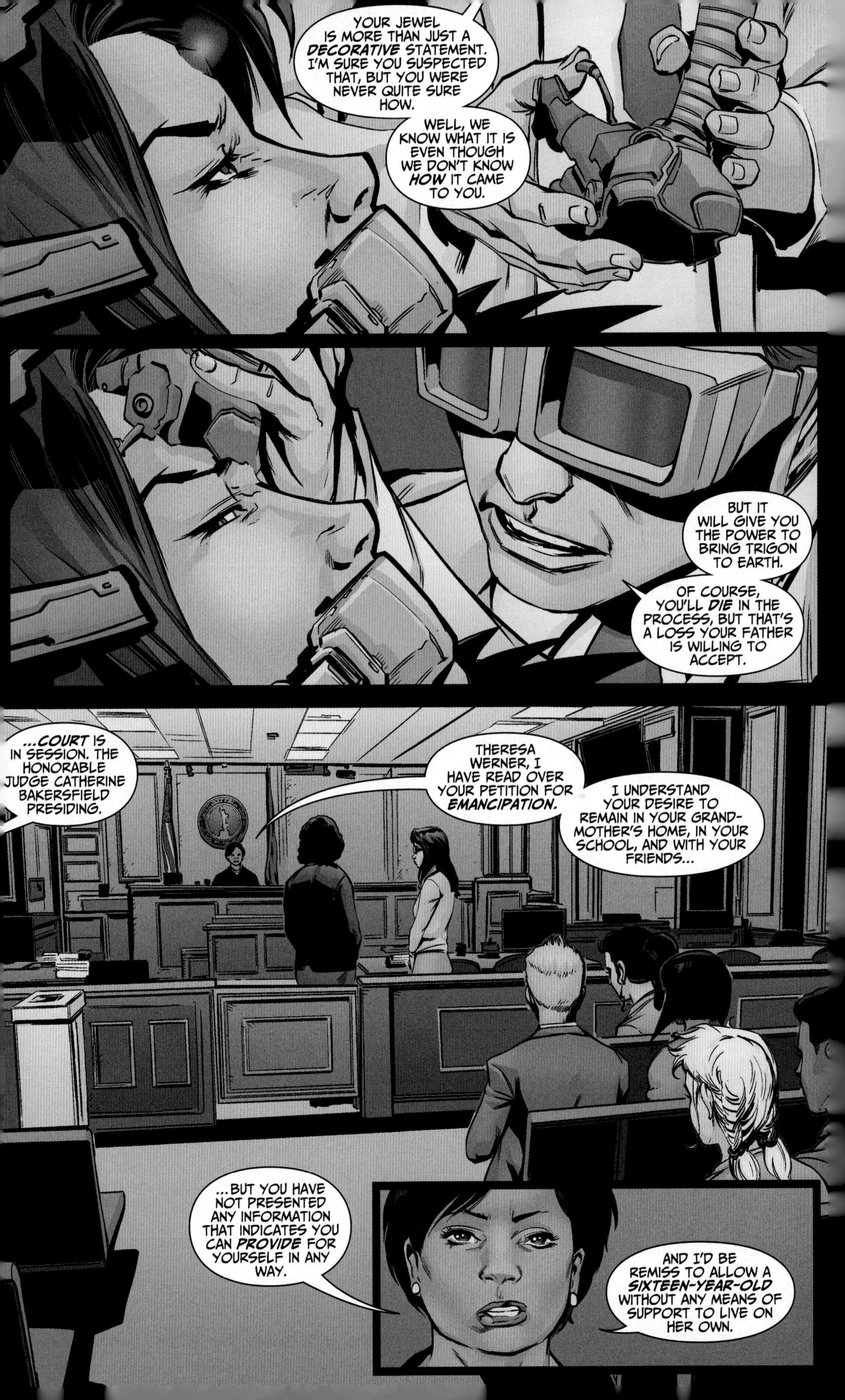

YOUR JEWEL IS MORE THAN JUST A DECORATIVE STATEMENT. I'M SURE YOU SUSPECTED THAT, BUT YOU WERE NEVER QUITE SURE HOW.
WELL, WE KNOW WHAT IT IS EVEN THOUGH WE DON'T KNOW HOW IT CAME TO YOU.
BUT IT WILL GIVE YOU THE POWER TO BRING TRIGON TO EARTH.
OF COURSE, YOU'LL DIE IN THE PROCESS, BUT THAT'S A LOSS YOUR FATHER IS WILLING TO ACCEPT.
...COURT IS IN SESSION. THE HONORABLE JUDGE CATHERINE BAKERSFIELD PRESIDING.
THERESA WERNER, I HAVE READ OVER YOUR PETITION FOR EMANCIPATION.
I UNDERSTAND YOUR DESIRE TO REMAIN IN YOUR GRAND-MOTHER'S HOME, IN YOUR SCHOOL, AND WITH YOUR FRIENDS...
...BUT YOU HAVE NOT PRESENTED ANY INFORMATION THAT INDICATES YOU CAN PROVIDE FOR YOURSELF IN ANY WAY.
AND I'D BE REMISS TO ALLOW A SIXTEEN-YEAR-OLD WITHOUT ANY MEANS OF SUPPORT TO LIVE ON HER OWN.

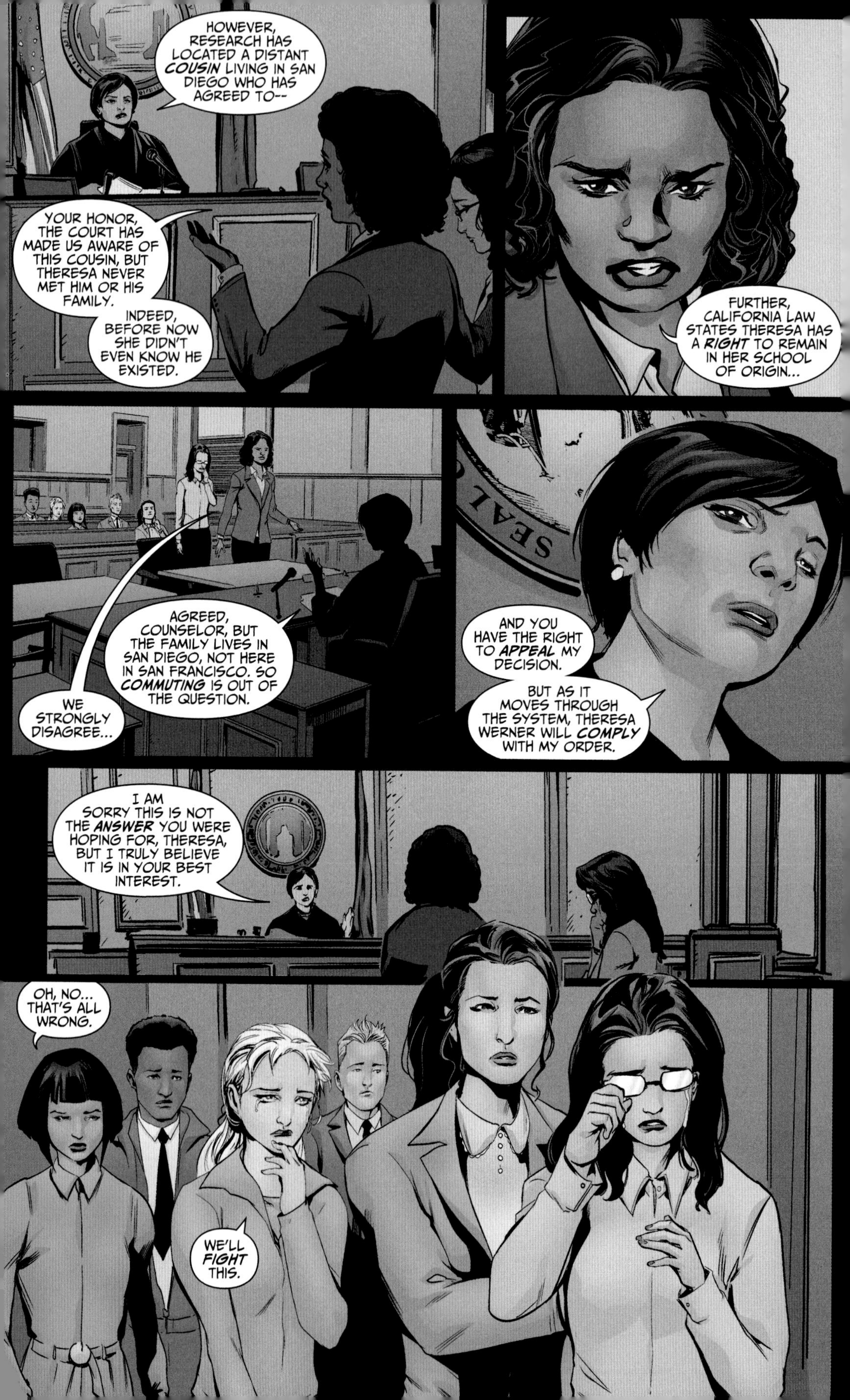
HOWEVER, RESEARCH HAS LOCATED A DISTANT COUSIN LIVING IN SAN DIEGO WHO HAS AGREED TO--
YOUR HONOR, THE COURT HAS MADE US AWARE OF THIS COUSIN, BUT THERESA NEVER MET HIM OR HIS FAMILY.
INDEED, BEFORE NOW SHE DIDN'T EVEN KNOW HE EXISTED.
FURTHER, CALIFORNIA LAW STATES THERESA HAS A RIGHT TO REMAIN IN HER SCHOOL OF ORIGIN...
WE STRONGLY DISAGREE...
AGREED, COUNSELOR, BUT THE FAMILY LIVES IN SAN DIEGO, NOT HERE IN SAN FRANCISCO. SO COMMUTING IS OUT OF THE QUESTION.
AND YOU HAVE THE RIGHT TO APPEAL MY DECISION.
BUT AS IT MOVES THROUGH THE SYSTEM, THERESA WERNER WILL COMPLY WITH MY ORDER.
I AM SORRY THIS IS NOT THE ANSWER YOU WERE HOPING FOR, THERESA, BUT I TRULY BELIEVE IT IS IN YOUR BEST INTEREST.
OH, NO... THAT'S ALL WRONG.
WE'LL FIGHT THIS.

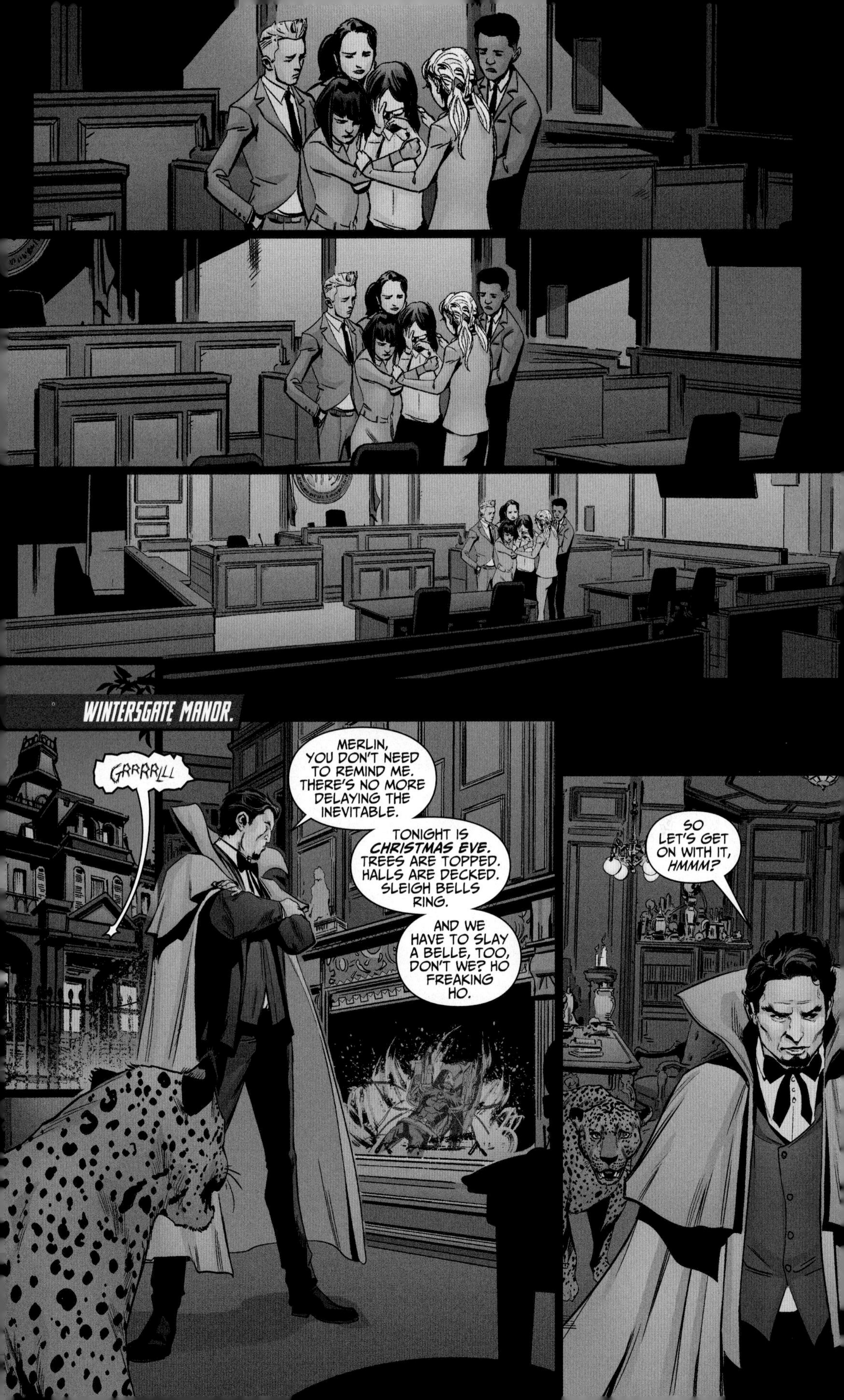

WINTERSGATE MANOR.
GRRRRLLL
MERLIN, YOU DON'T NEED TO REMIND ME. THERE'S NO MORE DELAYING THE INEVITABLE.
TONIGHT IS CHRISTMAS EVE. TREES ARE TOPPED. HALLS ARE DECKED. SLEIGH BELLS RING.
AND WE HAVE TO SLAY A BELLE, TOO, DON'T WE? HO FREAKING HO.
SO LET'S GET ON WITH IT, HMMM?

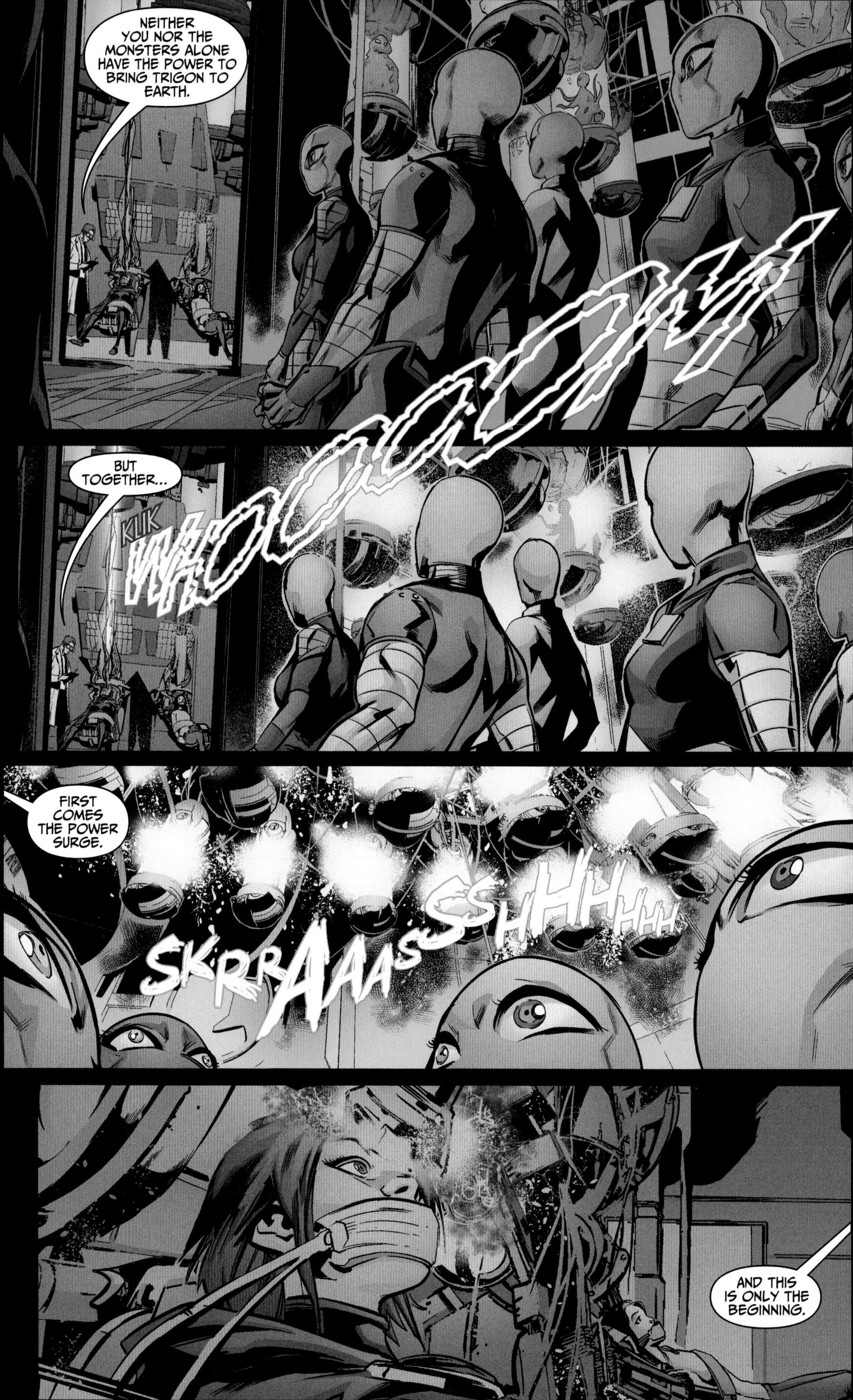
NEITHER YOU NOR THE MONSTERS ALONE HAVE THE POWER TO BRING TRIGON TO EARTH.
BUT TOGETHER...
KLIK
WHOOOOOOM
FIRST COMES THE POWER SURGE.
SKRRAAASSSHHHHHH
AND THIS IS ONLY THE BEGINNING.

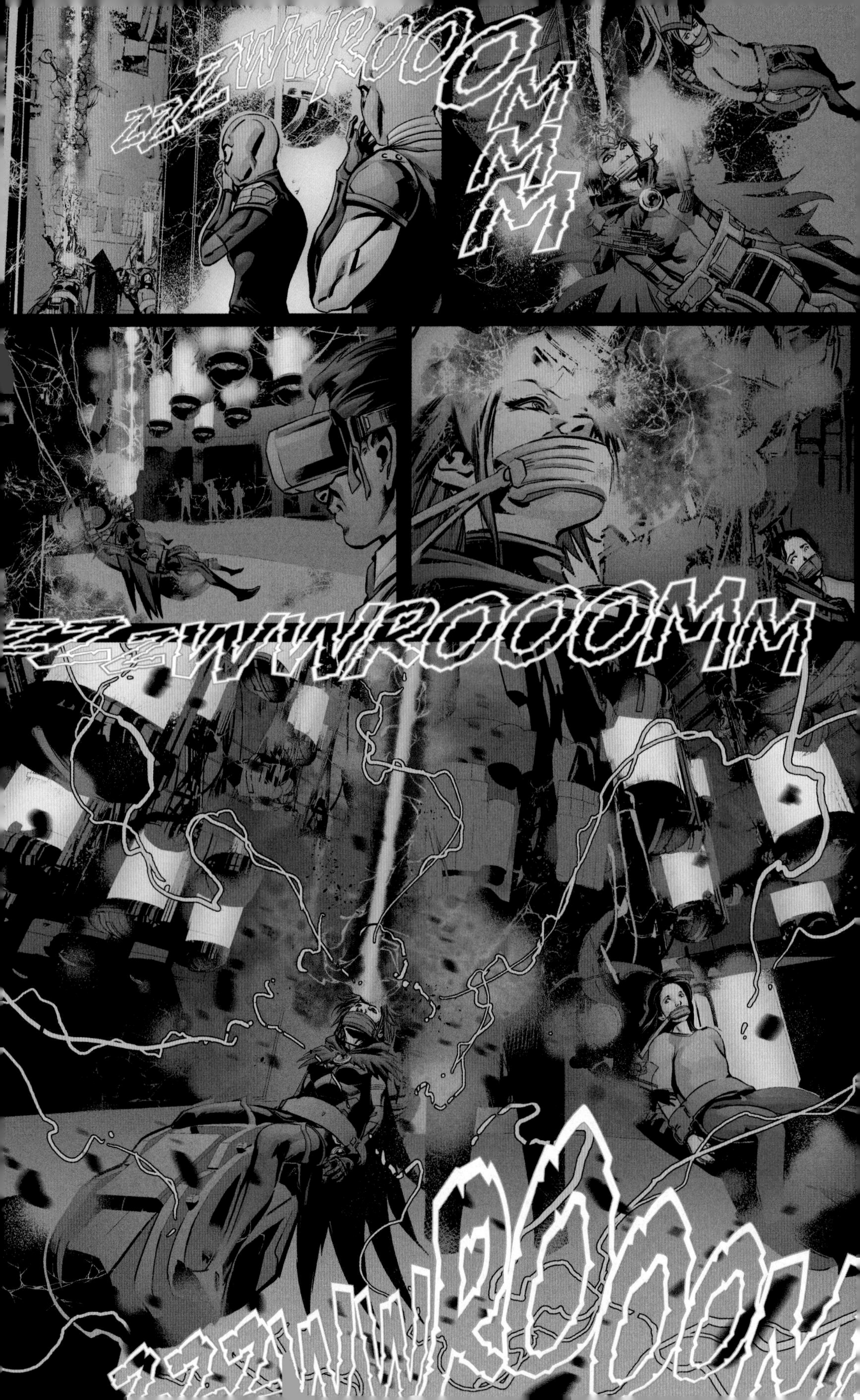
zzZWWROOOMMM
ZZZWWROOOMM

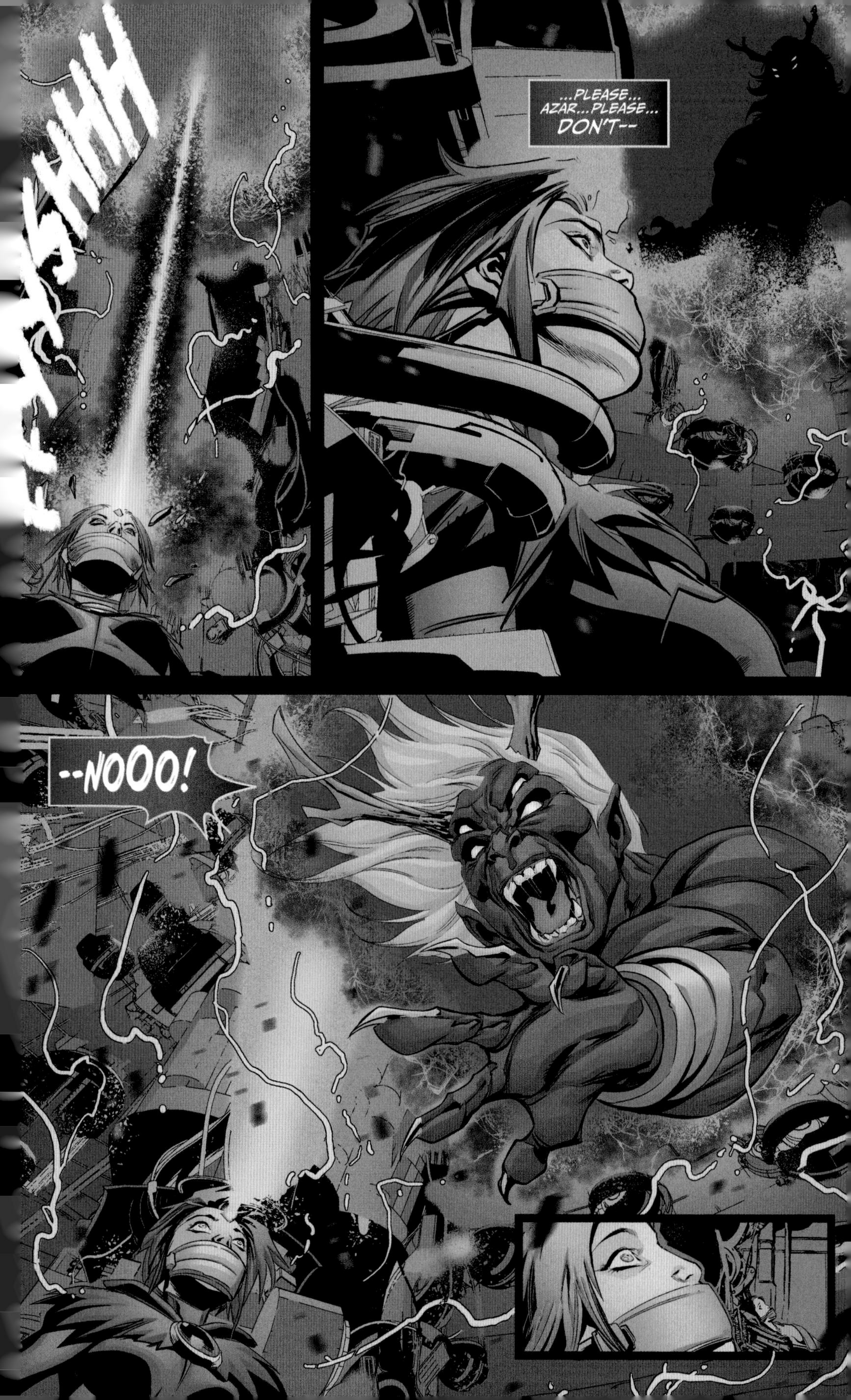
FFSSHHH
...PLEASE... AZAR...PLEASE... DON'T--
--NOOO!

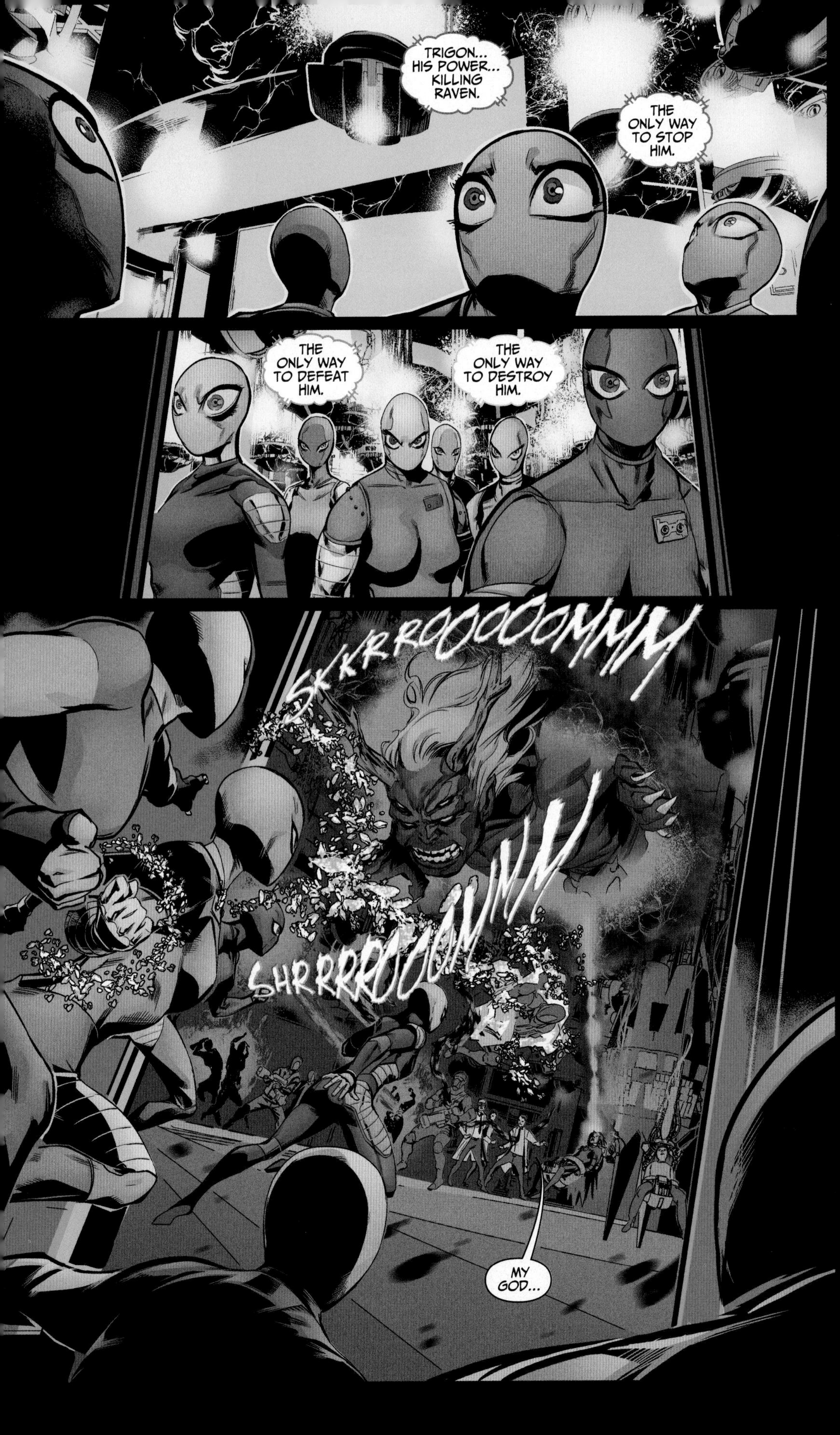
TRIGON... HIS POWER... KILLING RAVEN.
THE ONLY WAY TO STOP HIM.
THE ONLY WAY TO DEFEAT HIM.
THE ONLY WAY TO DESTROY HIM.
SKKRROOOOOMMM
SHRRRROOOMMM
MY GOD...

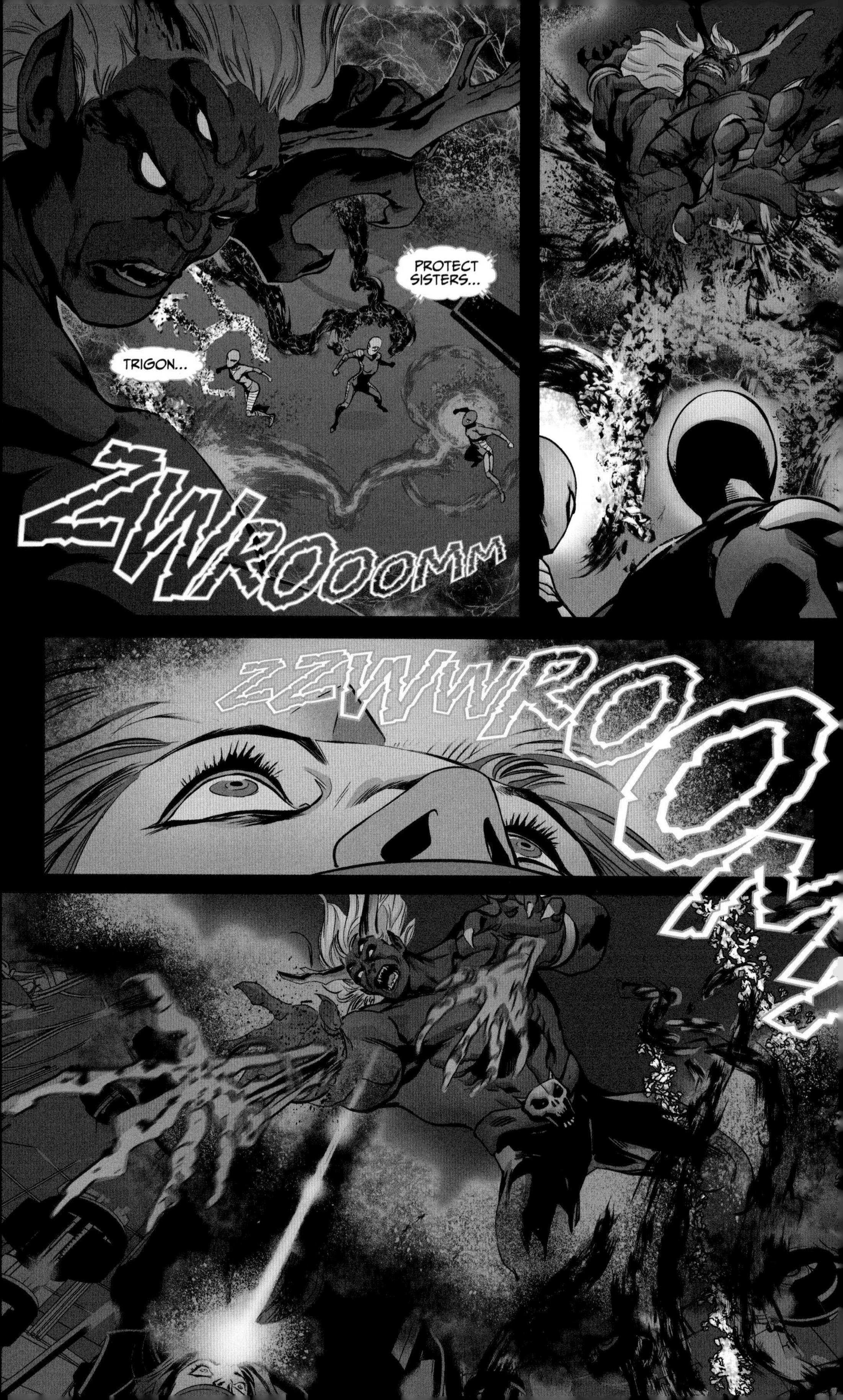
PROTECT SISTERS...
TRIGON...
ZWROOOMM
ZZWWROOOM

SKKRROOOOOOO
GOLD!
CLOSE PORTAL...
...THROUGH RAVEN...
MERGE...
...BECOME...
...I AM...
...RAVEN.

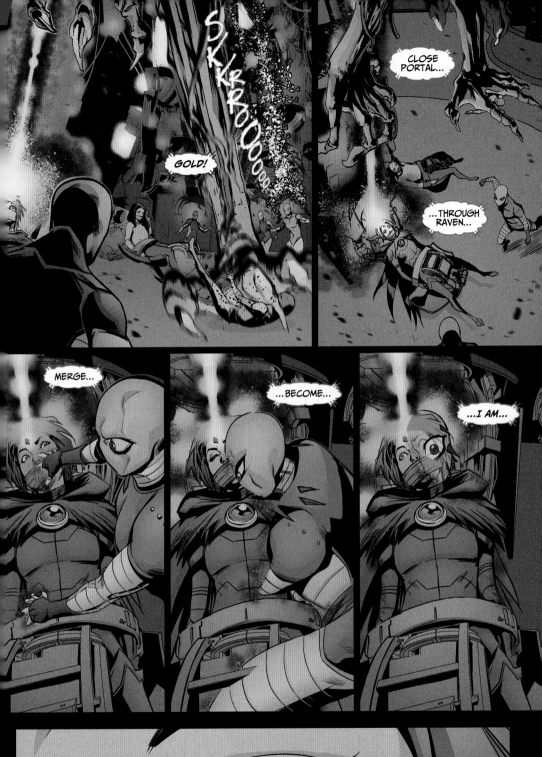

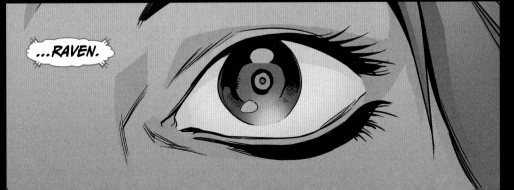

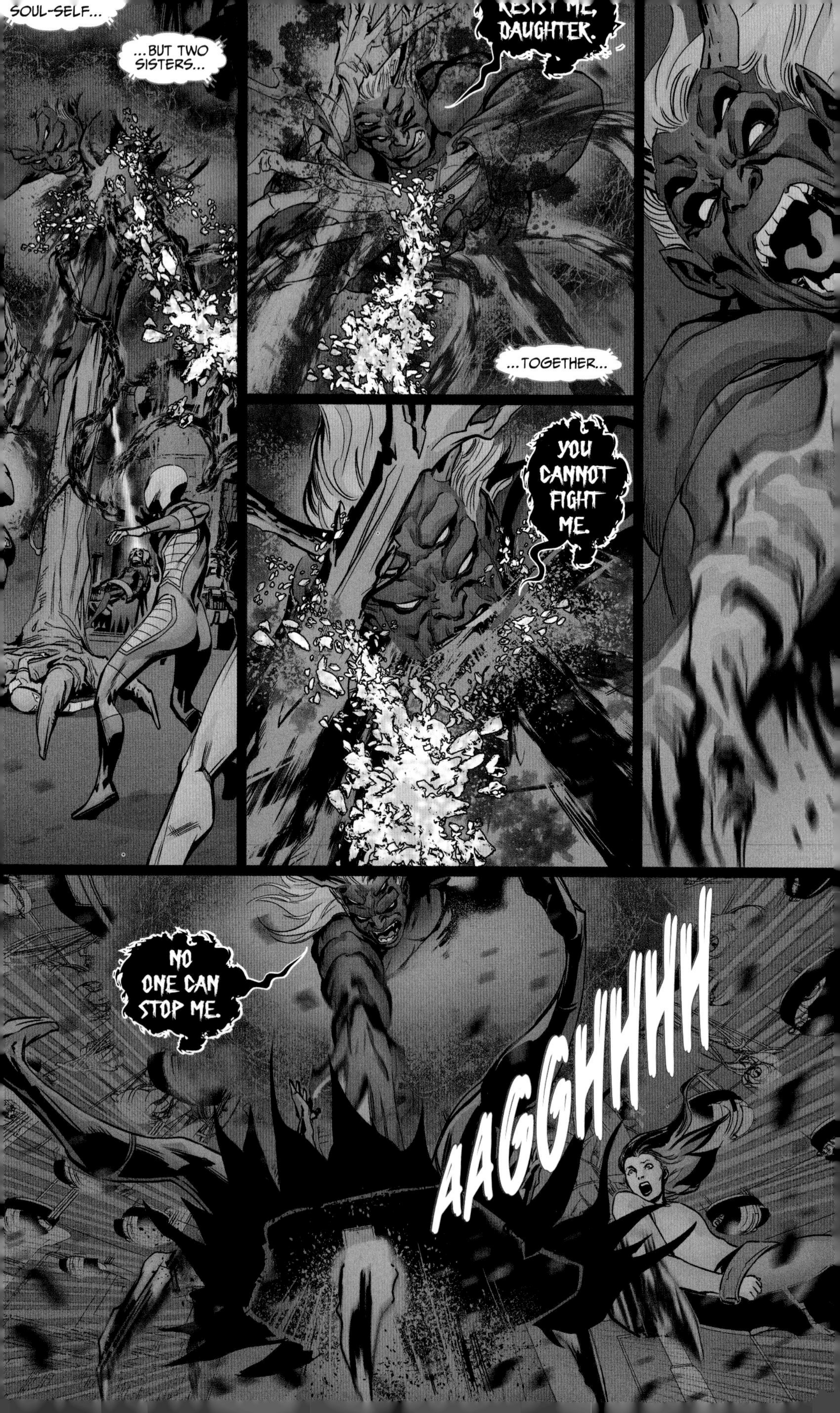
SOUL-SELF...
...BUT TWO SISTERS...
RESIST ME, DAUGHTER.
...TOGETHER...
YOU CANNOT FIGHT ME.
NO ONE CAN STOP ME.
AAGGHHHH

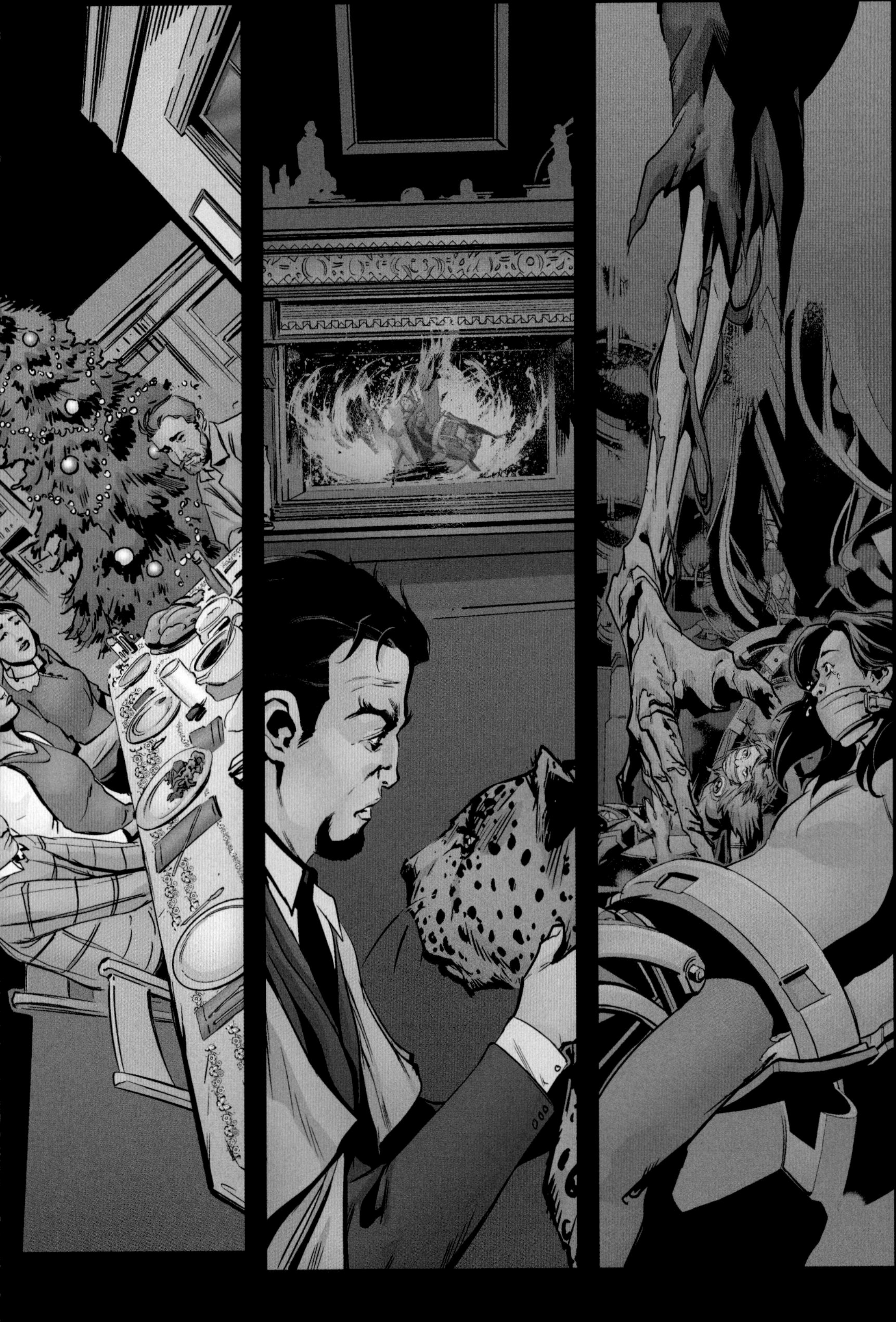

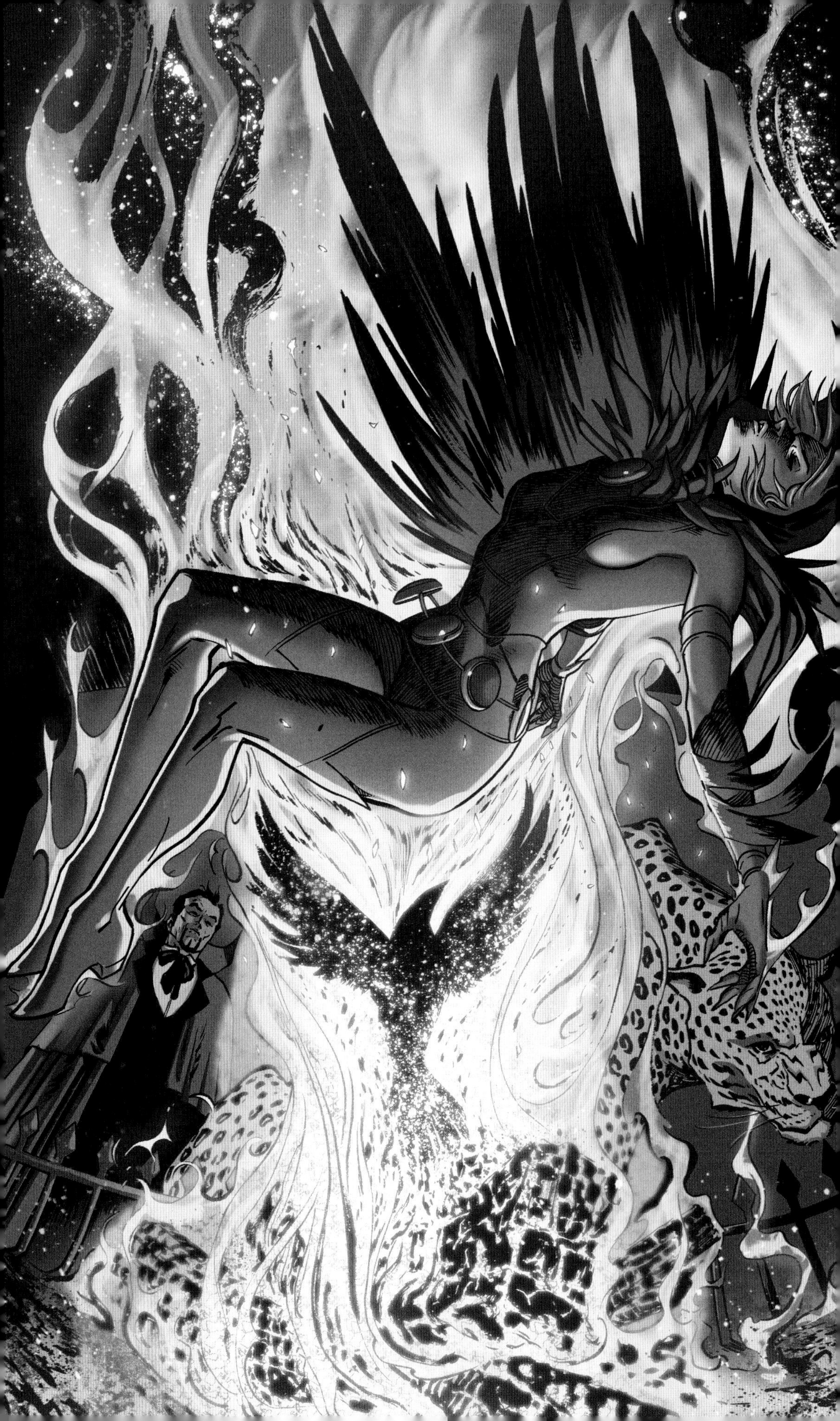

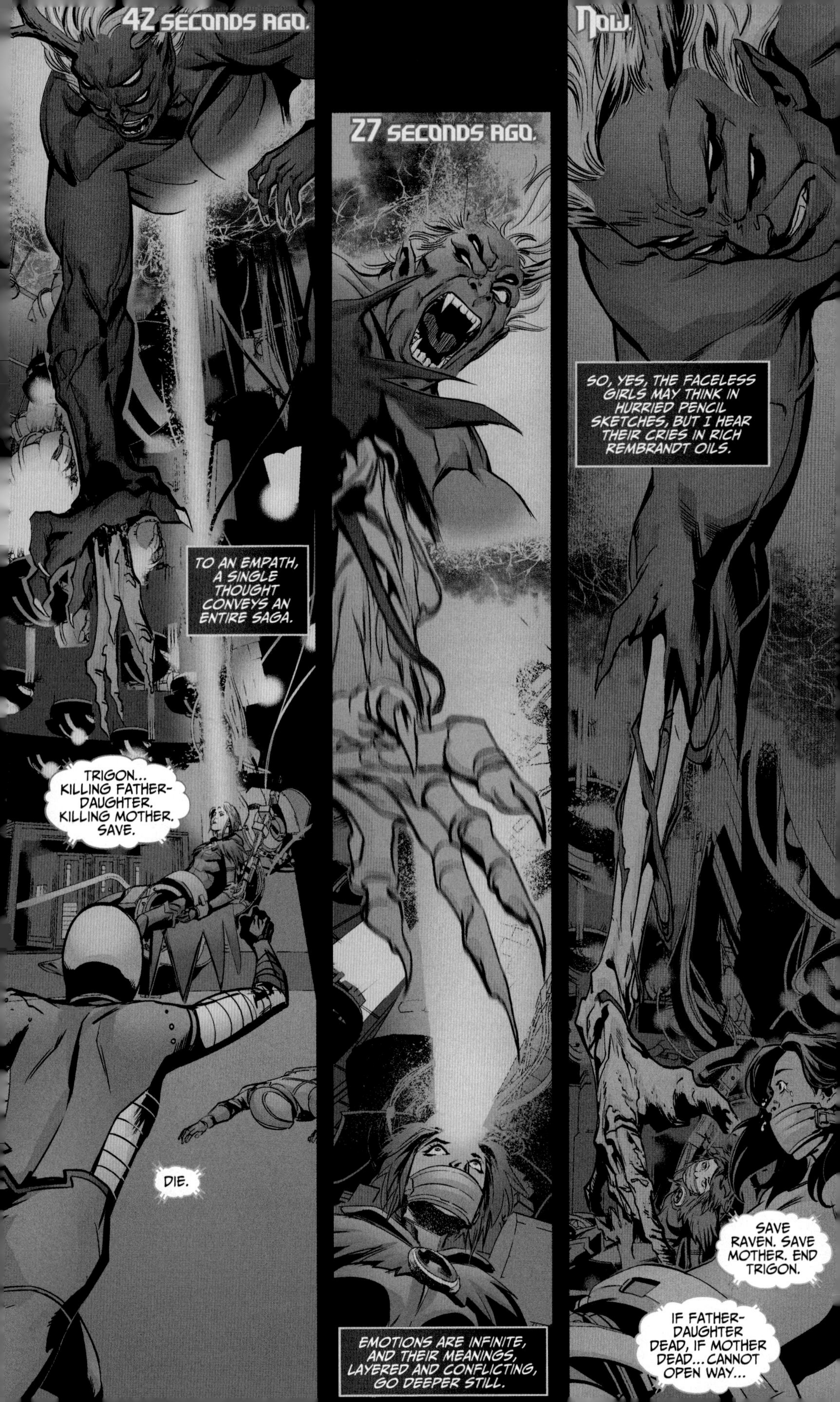
42 SECONDS AGO.
TO AN EMPATH, A SINGLE THOUGHT CONVEYS AN ENTIRE SAGA.
TRIGON... KILLING FATHER-DAUGHTER. KILLING MOTHER. SAVE.
DIE.
27 SECONDS AGO.
EMOTIONS ARE INFINITE, AND THEIR MEANINGS, LAYERED AND CONFLICTING, GO DEEPER STILL.
NOW.
SO, YES, THE FACELESS GIRLS MAY THINK IN HURRIED PENCIL SKETCHES, BUT I HEAR THEIR CRIES IN RICH REMBRANDT OILS.
SAVE RAVEN. SAVE MOTHER. END TRIGON.
IF FATHER-DAUGHTER DEAD, IF MOTHER DEAD... CANNOT OPEN WAY...

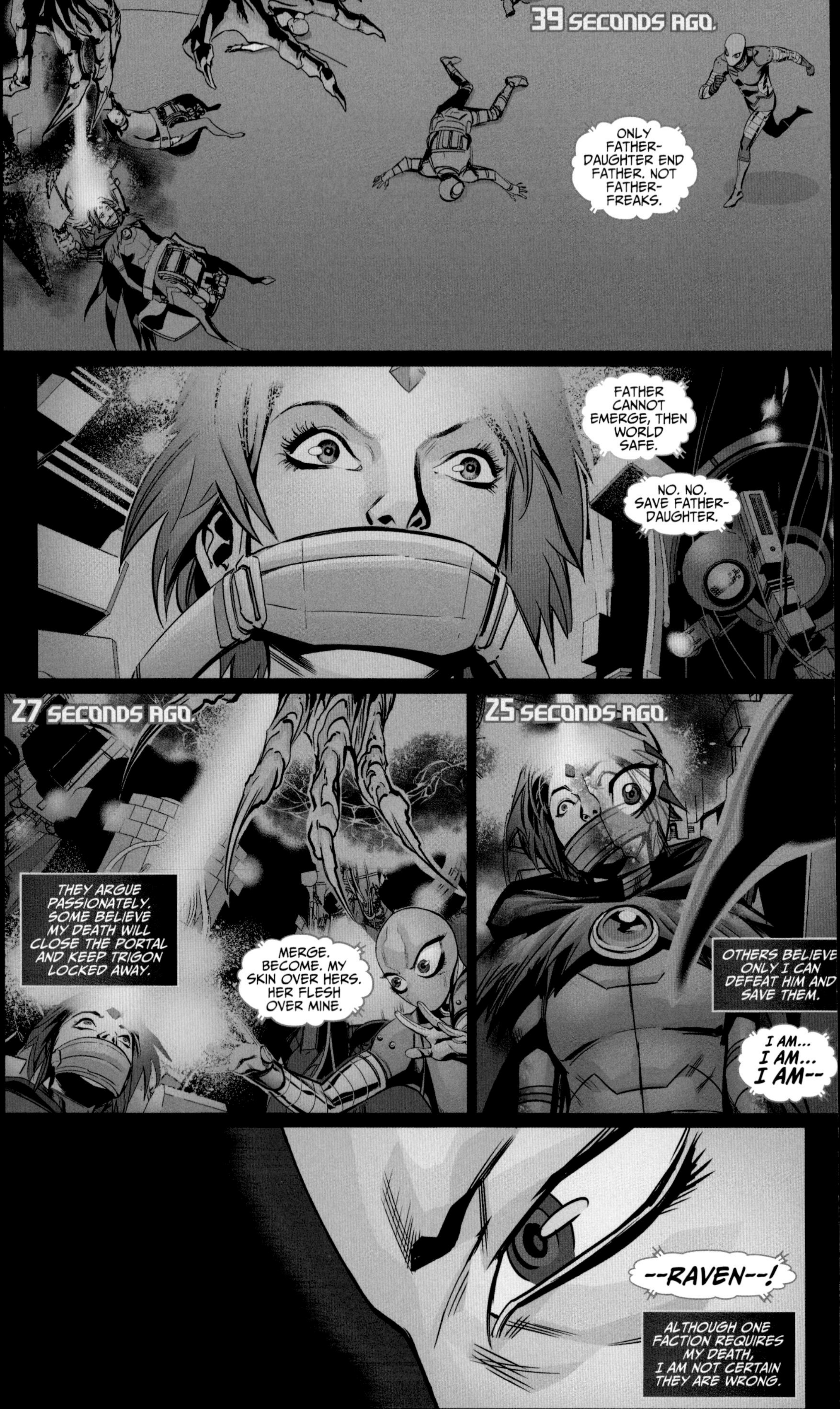
39 SECONDS AGO.
ONLY FATHER-DAUGHTER END FATHER. NOT FATHER-FREAKS.
FATHER CANNOT EMERGE, THEN WORLD SAFE.
NO. NO. SAVE FATHER-DAUGHTER.
27 SECONDS AGO.
THEY ARGUE PASSIONATELY. SOME BELIEVE MY DEATH WILL CLOSE THE PORTAL AND KEEP TRIGON LOCKED AWAY.
MERGE. BECOME. MY SKIN OVER HERS. HER FLESH OVER MINE.
25 SECONDS AGO.
OTHERS BELIEVE ONLY I CAN DEFEAT HIM AND SAVE THEM.
I AM... I AM... I AM--
--RAVEN--!
ALTHOUGH ONE FACTION REQUIRES MY DEATH, I AM NOT CERTAIN THEY ARE WRONG.

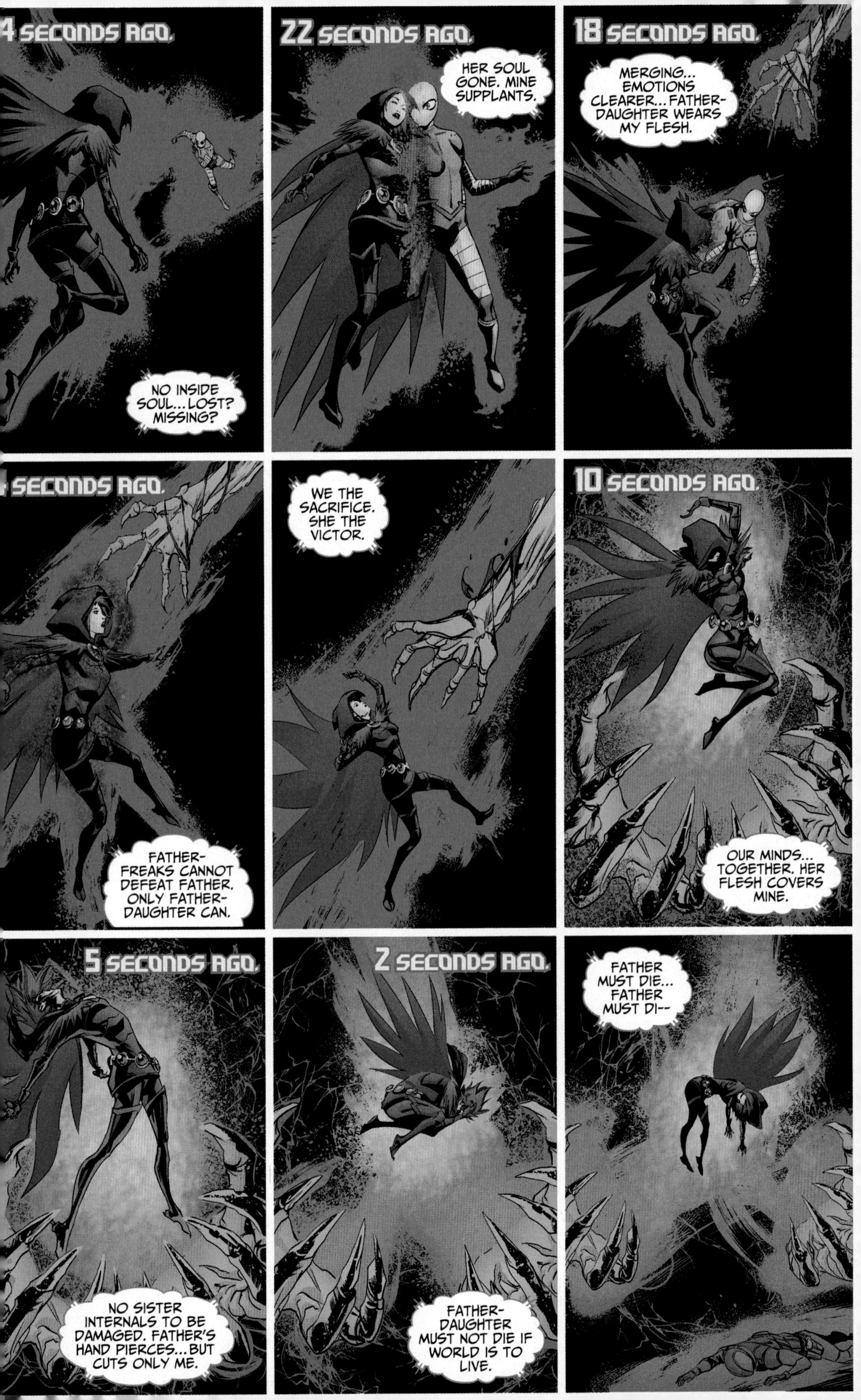
4 SECONDS AGO.
NO INSIDE SOUL... LOST? MISSING?
22 SECONDS AGO.
HER SOUL GONE. MINE SUPPLANTS.
18 SECONDS AGO.
MERGING... EMOTIONS CLEARER... FATHER-DAUGHTER WEARS MY FLESH.
4 SECONDS AGO.
FATHER-FREAKS CANNOT DEFEAT FATHER. ONLY FATHER-DAUGHTER CAN.
WE THE SACRIFICE. SHE THE VICTOR.
10 SECONDS AGO.
OUR MINDS... TOGETHER. HER FLESH COVERS MINE.
5 SECONDS AGO.
NO SISTER INTERNALS TO BE DAMAGED. FATHER'S HAND PIERCES... BUT CUTS ONLY ME.
2 SECONDS AGO.
FATHER-DAUGHTER MUST NOT DIE IF WORLD IS TO LIVE.
FATHER MUST DIE... FATHER MUST DI--

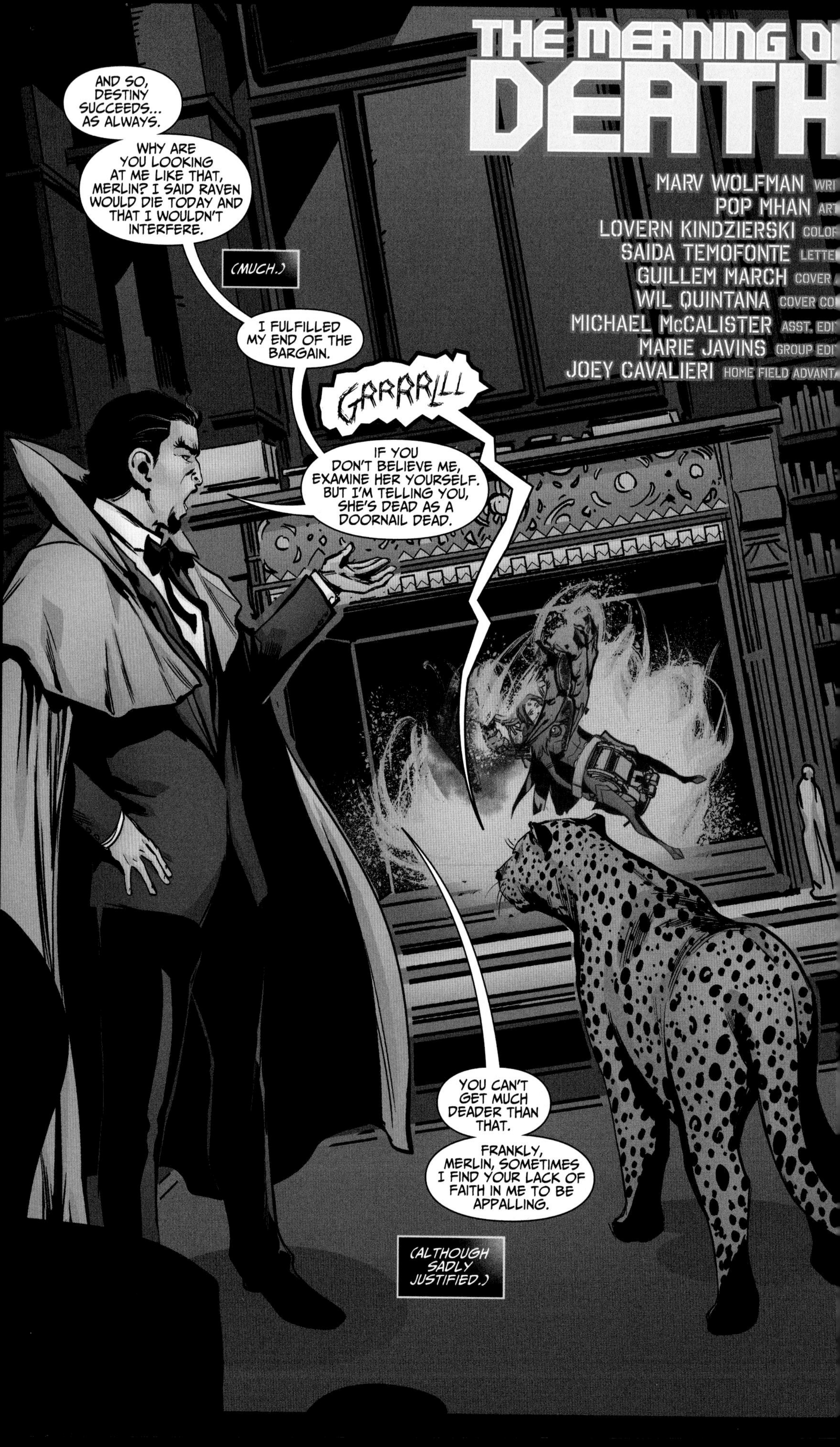
AND SO, DESTINY SUCCEEDS... AS ALWAYS.
WHY ARE YOU LOOKING AT ME LIKE THAT, MERLIN? I SAID RAVEN WOULD DIE TODAY AND THAT I WOULDN'T INTERFERE.
(MUCH.)
I FULFILLED MY END OF THE BARGAIN.
GRRRRLLL
IF YOU DON'T BELIEVE ME, EXAMINE HER YOURSELF. BUT I'M TELLING YOU, SHE'S DEAD AS A DOORNAIL DEAD.
YOU CAN'T GET MUCH DEADER THAN THAT.
FRANKLY, MERLIN, SOMETIMES I FIND YOUR LACK OF FAITH IN ME TO BE APPALLING.
(ALTHOUGH SADLY JUSTIFIED.)
THE MEANING OF
DEATH
MARV WOLFMAN
POP MHAN
LOVERN KINDZIERSKI
SAIDA TEMOFONTE
GUILLEM MARCH
WIL QUINTANA
MICHAEL McCALISTER
MARIE JAVINS
JOEY CAVALIERI

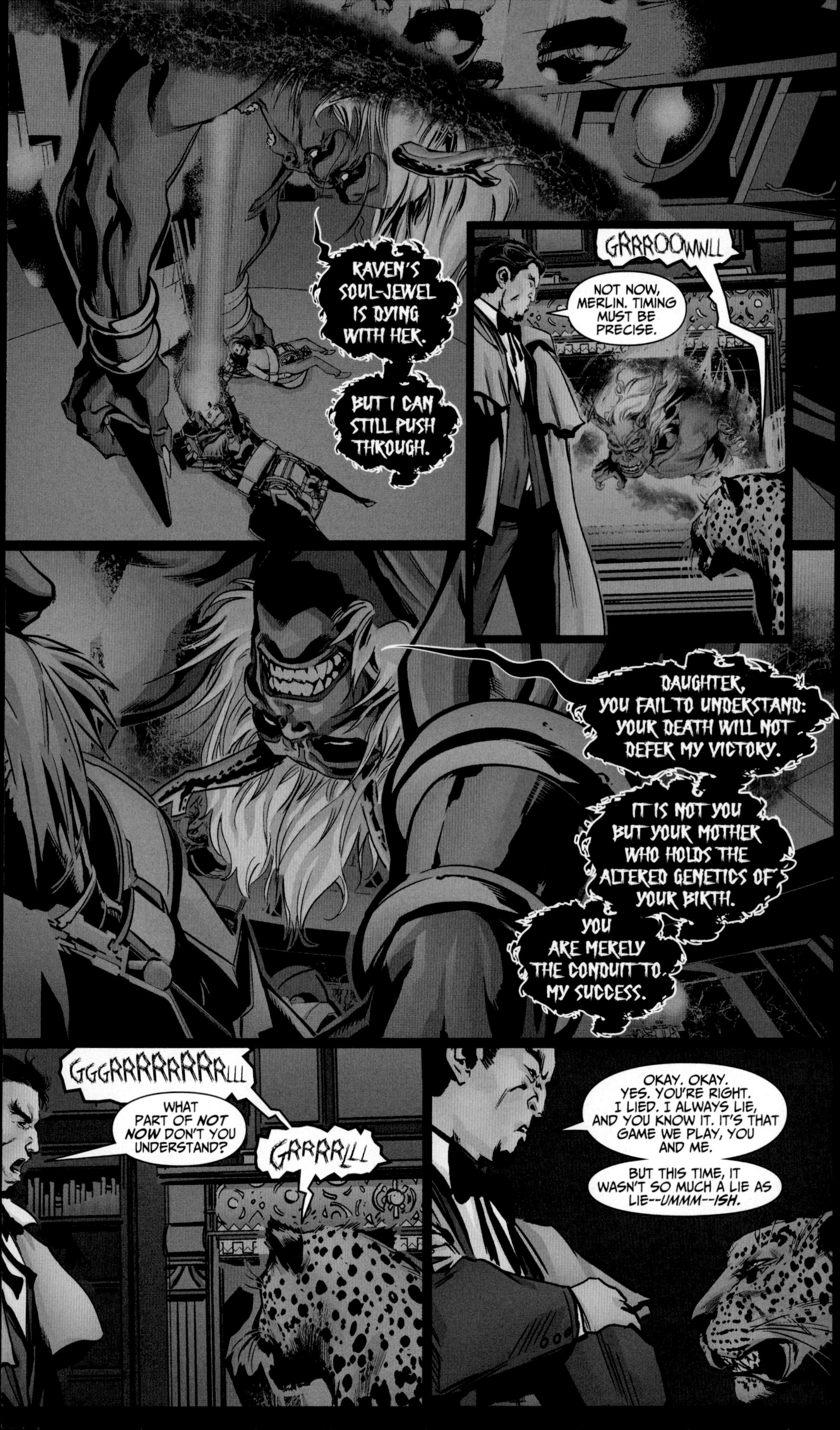
RAVEN'S SOUL-JEWEL IS DYING WITH HER.
BUT I CAN STILL PUSH THROUGH.
GRRROOWWLL
NOT NOW, MERLIN. TIMING MUST BE PRECISE.
DAUGHTER, YOU FAIL TO UNDERSTAND: YOUR DEATH WILL NOT DEFER MY VICTORY.
IT IS NOT YOU BUT YOUR MOTHER WHO HOLDS THE ALTERED GENETICS OF YOUR BIRTH.
YOU ARE MERELY THE CONDUIT TO MY SUCCESS.
GGGRRRRRRRRLLL
WHAT PART OF NOT NOW DON'T YOU UNDERSTAND?
GRRRRLLL
OKAY. OKAY. YES. YOU'RE RIGHT. I LIED. I ALWAYS LIE, AND YOU KNOW IT. IT'S THAT GAME WE PLAY, YOU AND ME.
BUT THIS TIME, IT WASN'T SO MUCH A LIE AS LIE--UMMM--ISH.

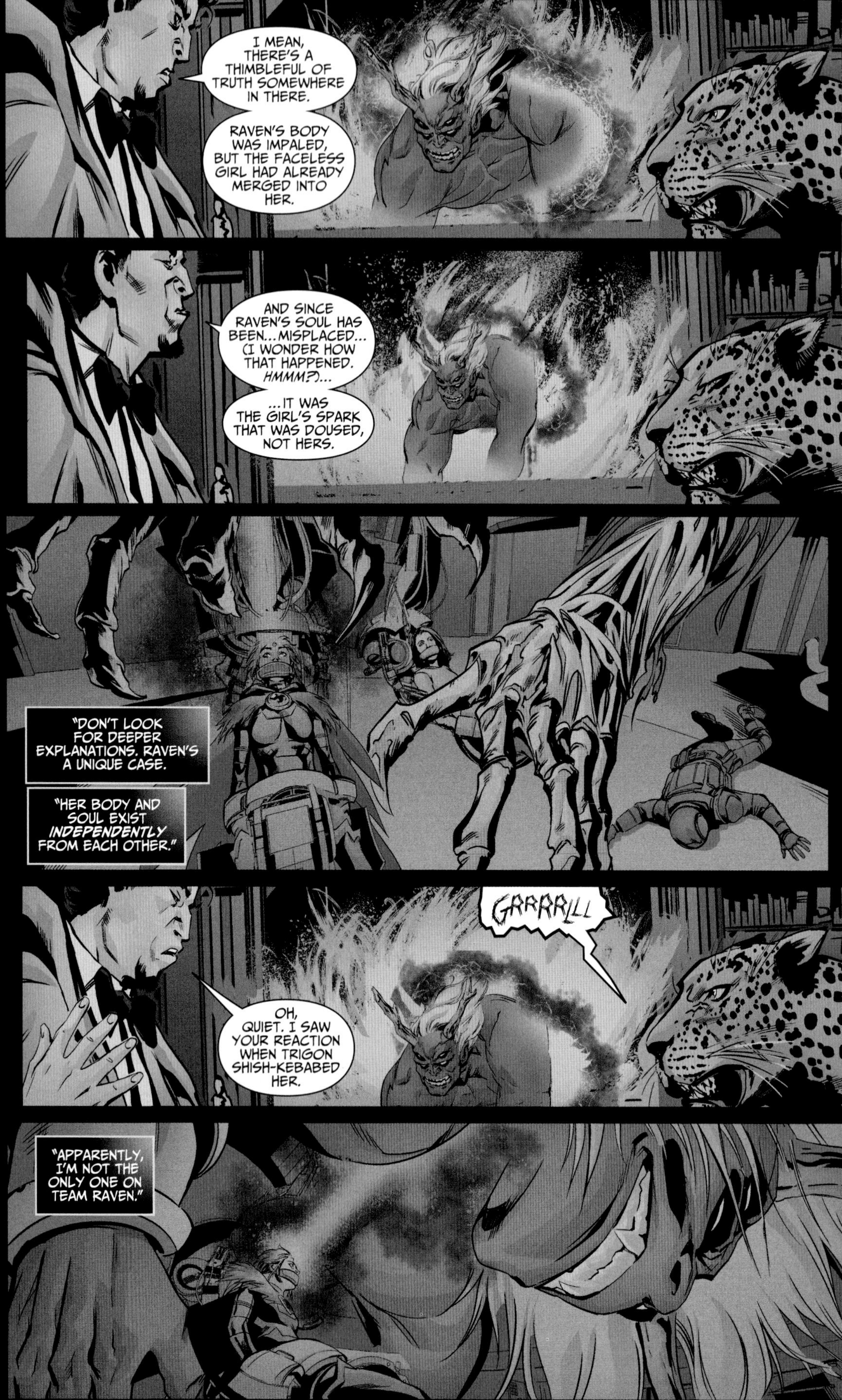
I MEAN, THERE'S A THIMBLEFUL OF TRUTH SOMEWHERE IN THERE.
RAVEN'S BODY WAS IMPALED, BUT THE FACELESS GIRL HAD ALREADY MERGED INTO HER.
AND SINCE RAVEN'S SOUL HAS BEEN...MISPLACED... (I WONDER HOW THAT HAPPENED. *HMMM?*)...
...IT WAS THE GIRL'S SPARK THAT WAS DOUSED, NOT HERS.
"DON'T LOOK FOR DEEPER EXPLANATIONS. RAVEN'S A UNIQUE CASE.
"HER BODY AND SOUL EXIST *INDEPENDENTLY* FROM EACH OTHER."
GRRRRLLL
OH, QUIET. I SAW YOUR REACTION WHEN TRIGON SHISH-KEBABED HER.
"APPARENTLY, I'M NOT THE ONLY ONE ON TEAM RAVEN."

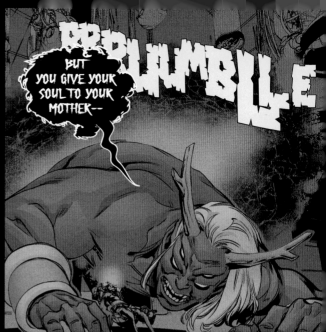

YOU ARE THE FLESH OF MY FLESH. YOU COULD HAVE RULED BESIDE ME.

BUT YOU GIVE YOUR SOUL TO YOUR MOTHER--

BRRUMBLE

WAIT!

SKROOM

I AM SENSING ANOTHER PLACE...

...OUTSIDE OF TIME... WITHOUT THE DAUGHTERS...

...WITHOUT RESISTANCE.

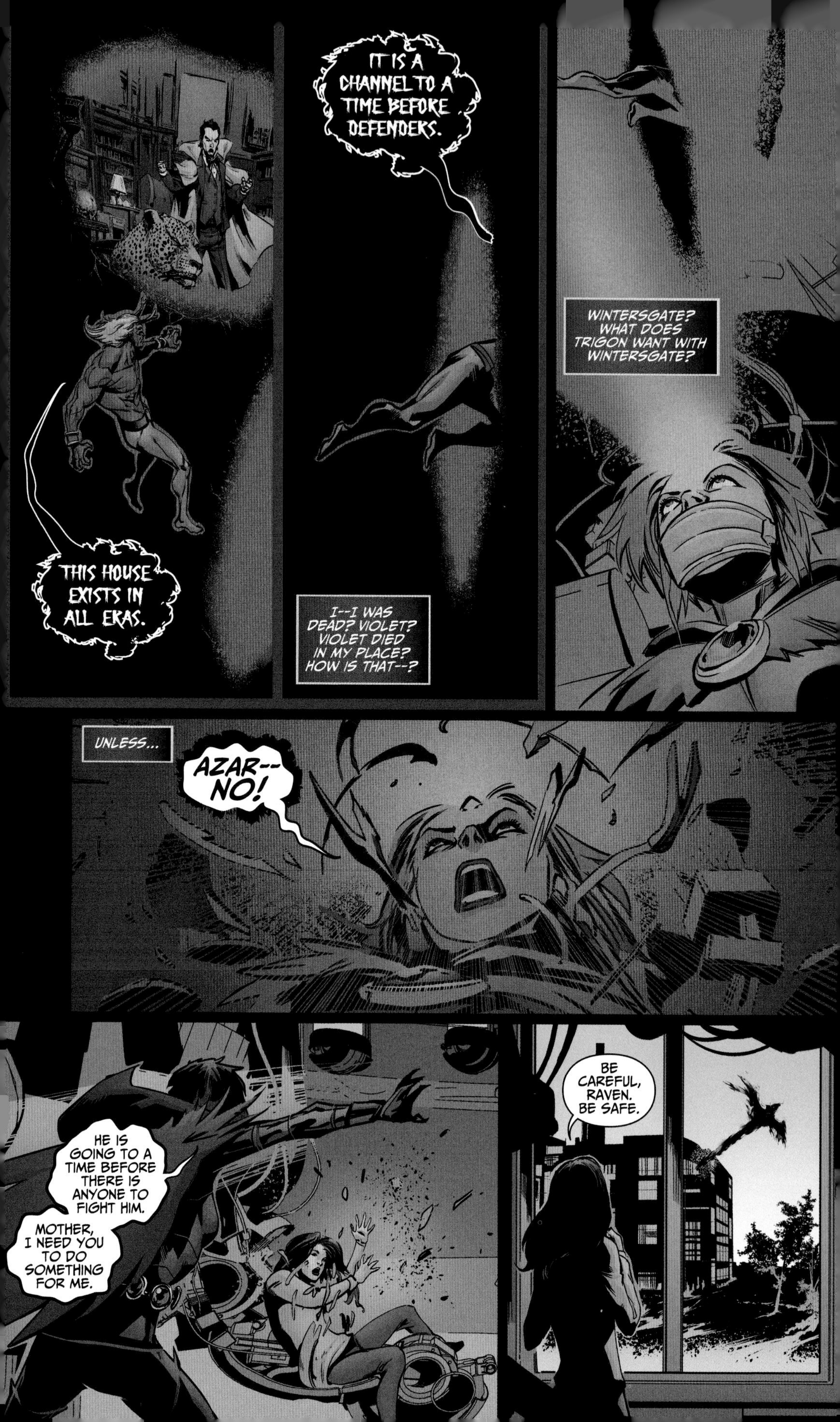
IT IS A CHANNEL TO A TIME BEFORE DEFENDERS.
THIS HOUSE EXISTS IN ALL ERAS.
I--I WAS DEAD? VIOLET? VIOLET DIED IN MY PLACE? HOW IS THAT--?
WINTERSGATE? WHAT DOES TRIGON WANT WITH WINTERSGATE?
UNLESS...
AZAR-- NO!
HE IS GOING TO A TIME BEFORE THERE IS ANYONE TO FIGHT HIM.
MOTHER, I NEED YOU TO DO SOMETHING FOR ME.
BE CAREFUL, RAVEN. BE SAFE.

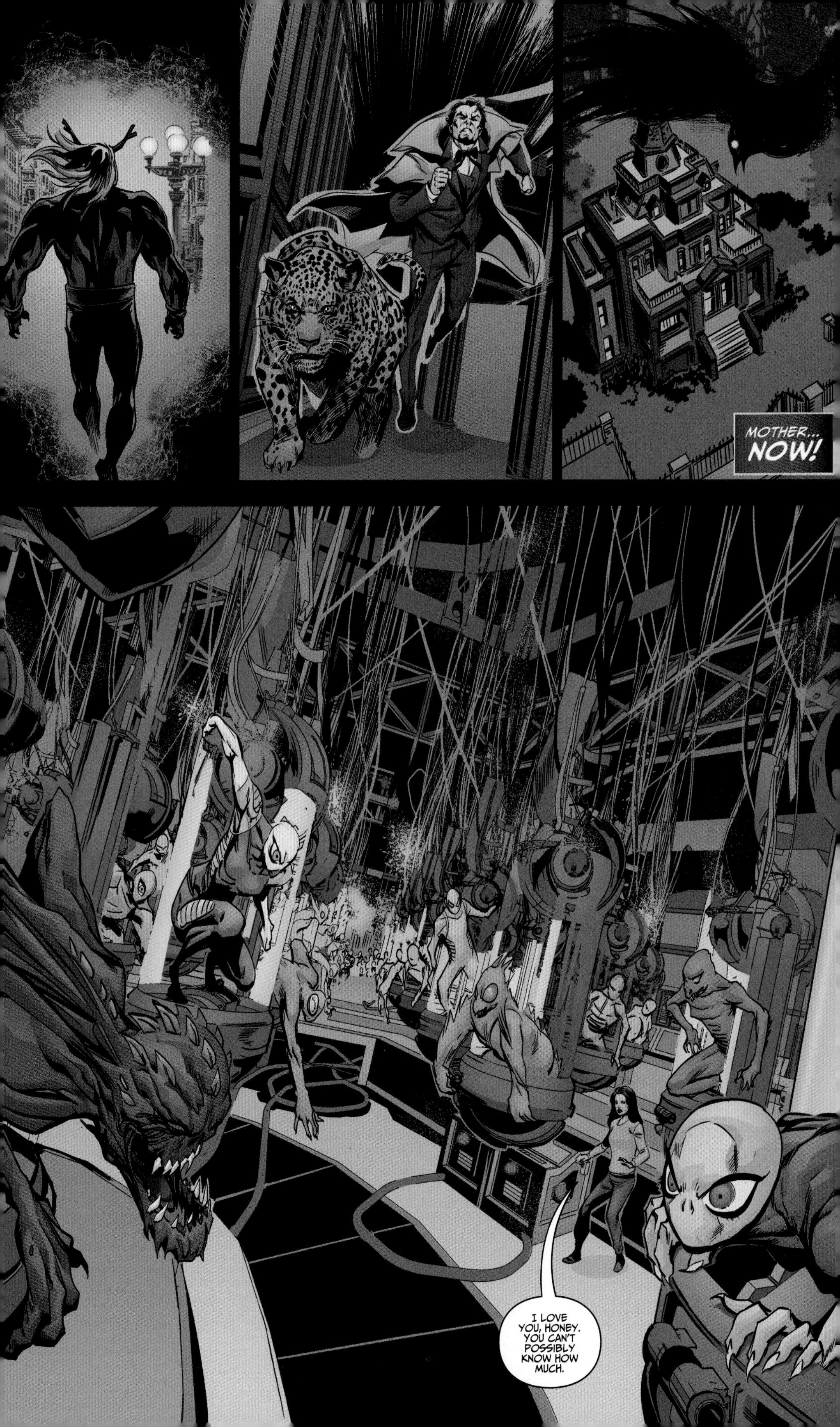
MOTHER... NOW!
I LOVE YOU, HONEY. YOU CAN'T POSSIBLY KNOW HOW MUCH.

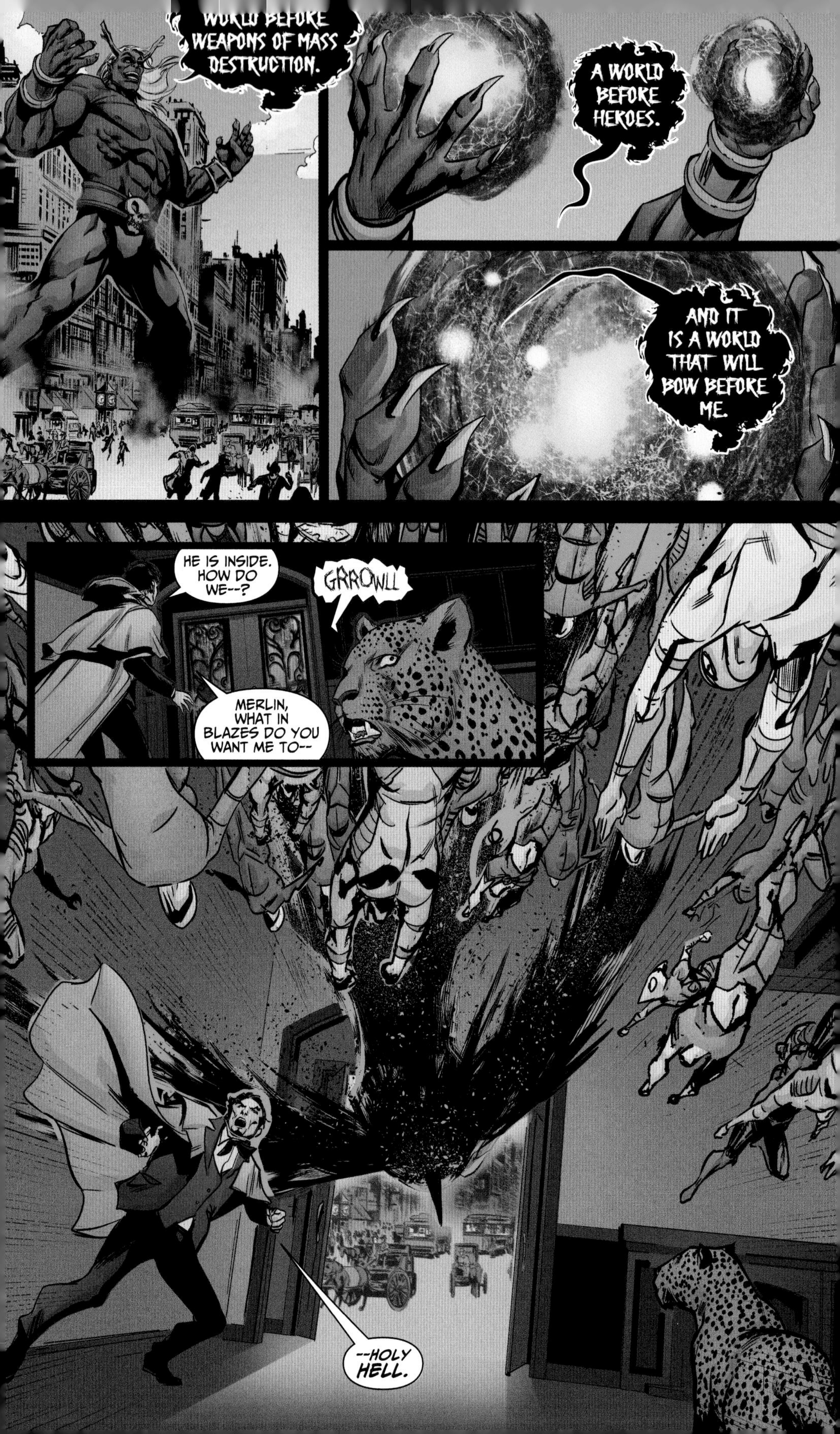
WORLD BEFORE WEAPONS OF MASS DESTRUCTION.
A WORLD BEFORE HEROES.
AND IT IS A WORLD THAT WILL BOW BEFORE ME.
HE IS INSIDE. HOW DO WE--?
GRROWLL
MERLIN, WHAT IN BLAZES DO YOU WANT ME TO--
--HOLY HELL.

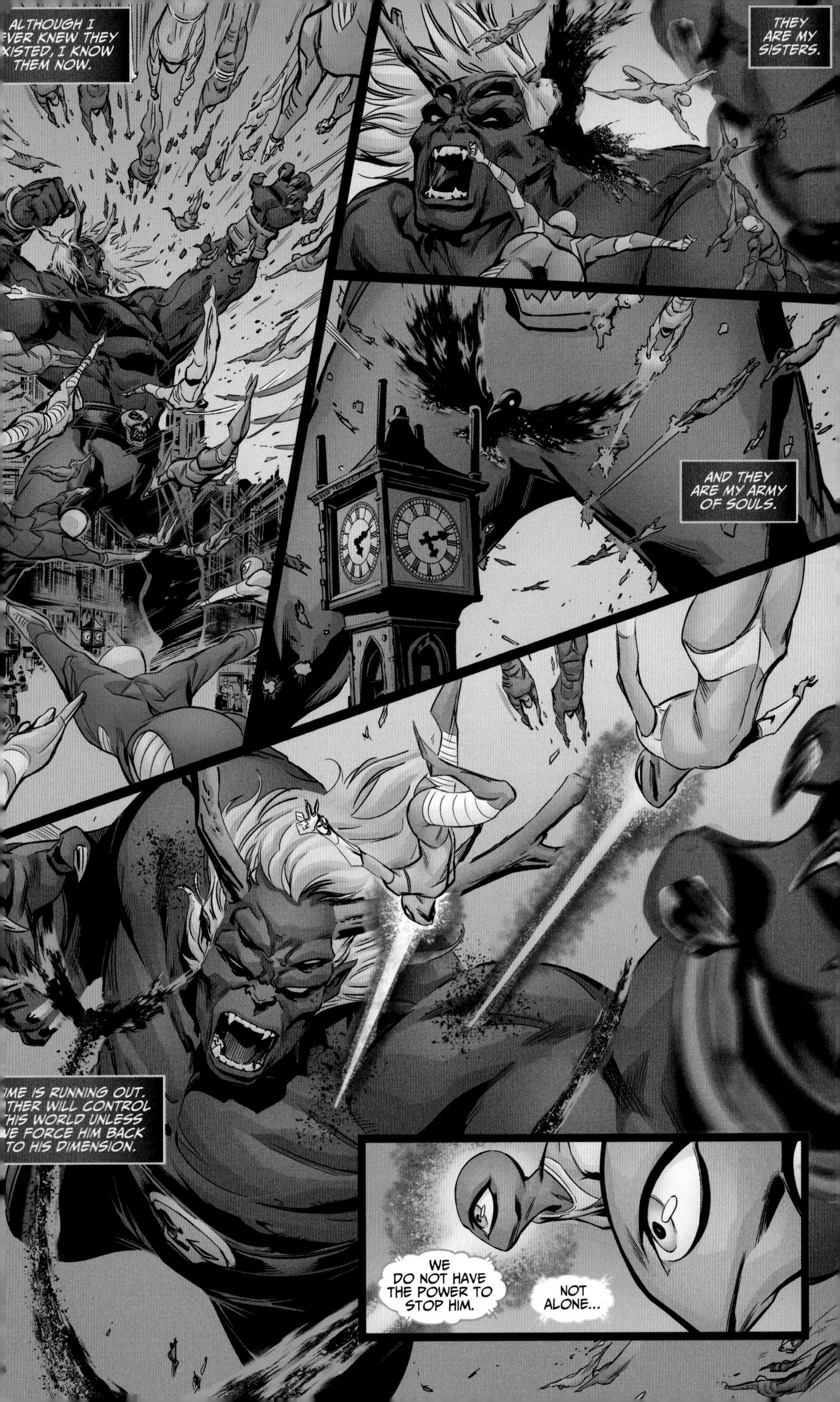
ALTHOUGH I
EVER KNEW THEY
XISTED, I KNOW
THEM NOW.
THEY
ARE MY
SISTERS.
AND THEY
ARE MY ARMY
OF SOULS.
IME IS RUNNING OUT.
THER WILL CONTROL
THIS WORLD UNLESS
VE FORCE HIM BACK
TO HIS DIMENSION.
WE
DO NOT HAVE
THE POWER TO
STOP HIM.
NOT
ALONE...

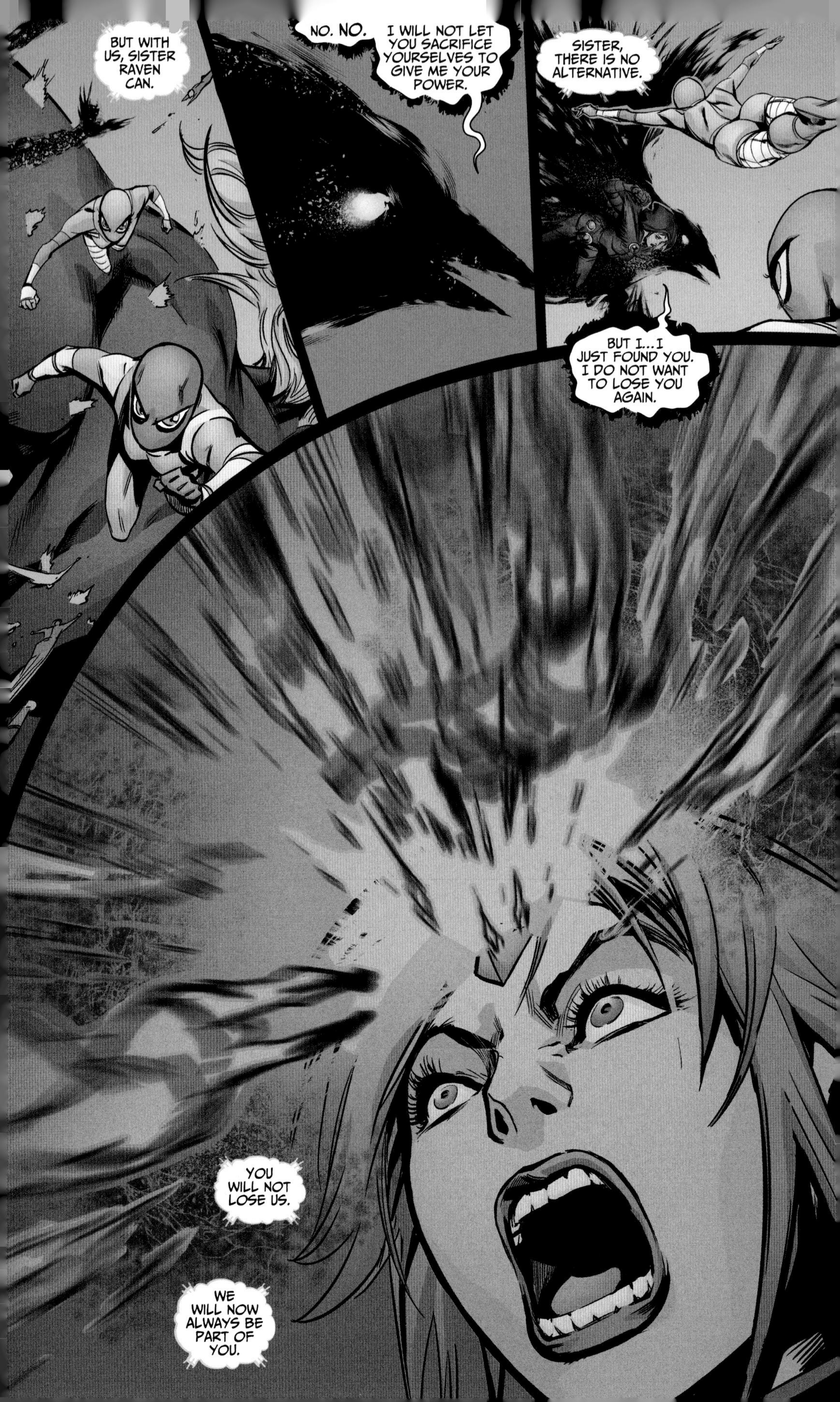
BUT WITH US, SISTER RAVEN CAN.
NO. NO.
I WILL NOT LET YOU SACRIFICE YOURSELVES TO GIVE ME YOUR POWER.
SISTER, THERE IS NO ALTERNATIVE.
BUT I...I JUST FOUND YOU. I DO NOT WANT TO LOSE YOU AGAIN.
YOU WILL NOT LOSE US.
WE WILL NOW ALWAYS BE PART OF YOU.

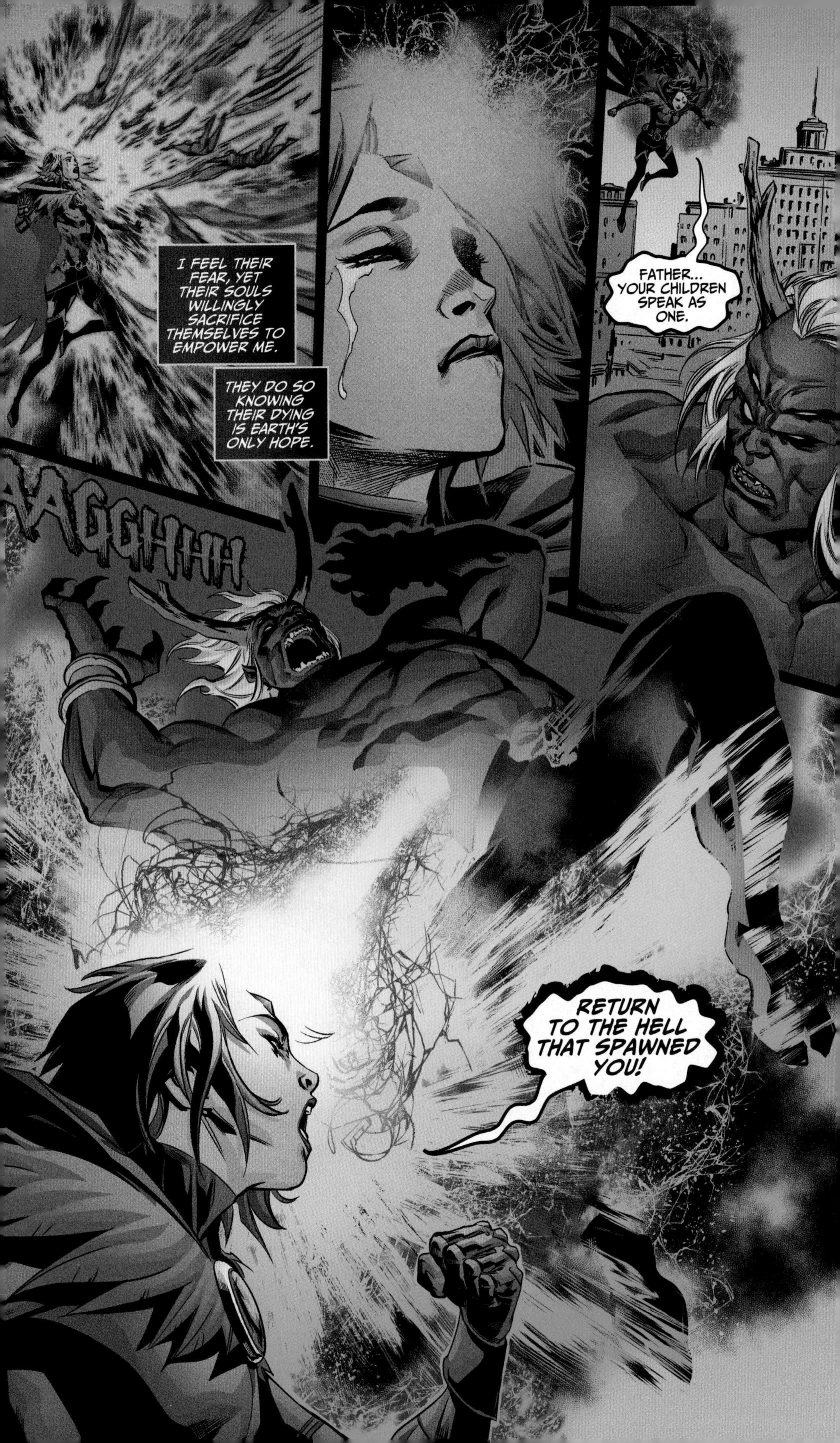
I FEEL THEIR FEAR, YET THEIR SOULS WILLINGLY SACRIFICE THEMSELVES TO EMPOWER ME.
THEY DO SO KNOWING THEIR DYING IS EARTH'S ONLY HOPE.
FATHER... YOUR CHILDREN SPEAK AS ONE.
AGGHHH
RETURN TO THE HELL THAT SPAWNED YOU!

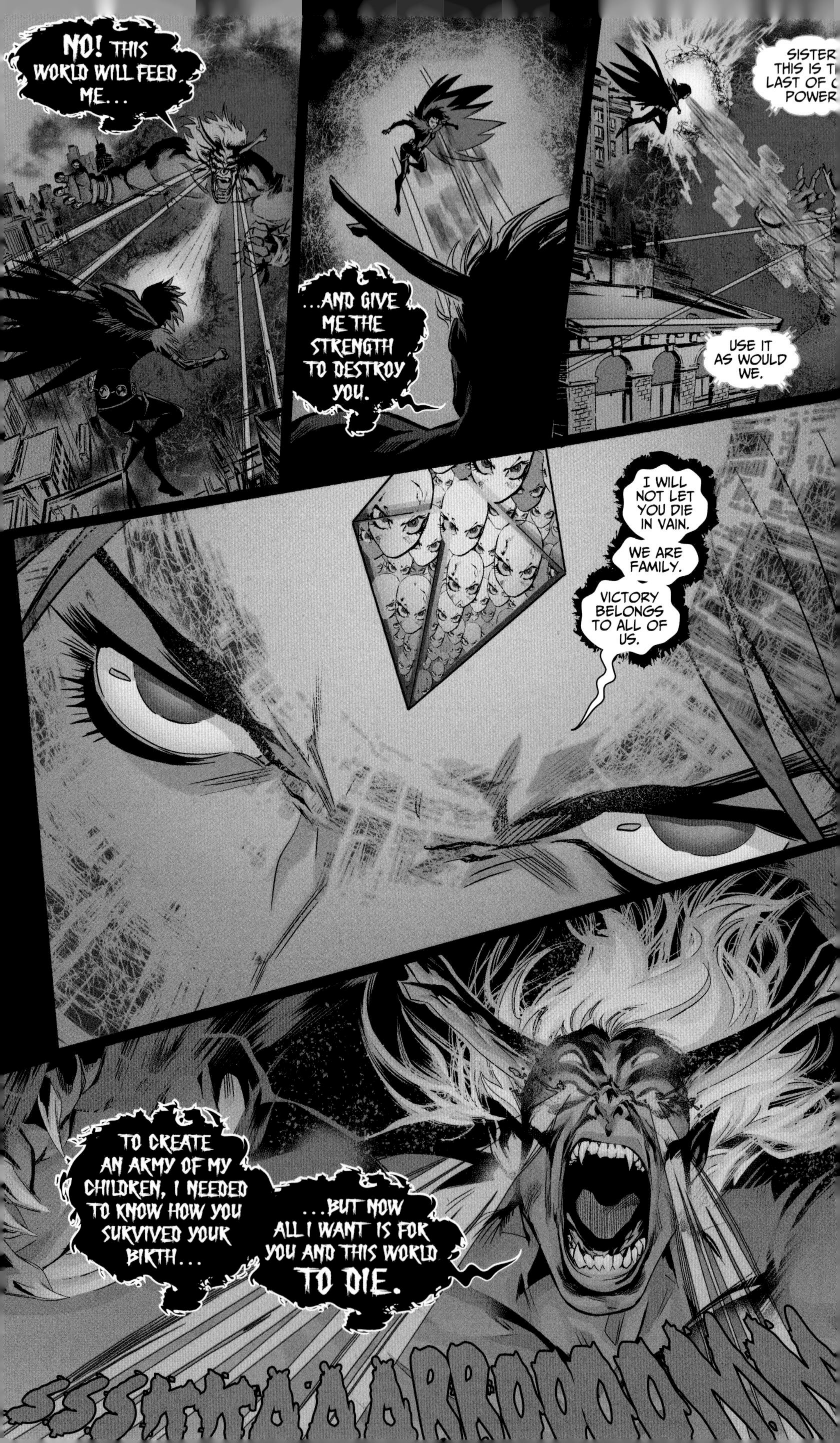
NO! THIS WORLD WILL FEED ME...
...AND GIVE ME THE STRENGTH TO DESTROY YOU.
SISTER THIS IS T LAST OF POWER
USE IT AS WOULD WE.
I WILL NOT LET YOU DIE IN VAIN.
WE ARE FAMILY.
VICTORY BELONGS TO ALL OF US.
TO CREATE AN ARMY OF MY CHILDREN, I NEEDED TO KNOW HOW YOU SURVIVED YOUR BIRTH...
...BUT NOW ALL I WANT IS FOR YOU AND THIS WORLD TO DIE.
SSSHHA-A-AARROOOOOM

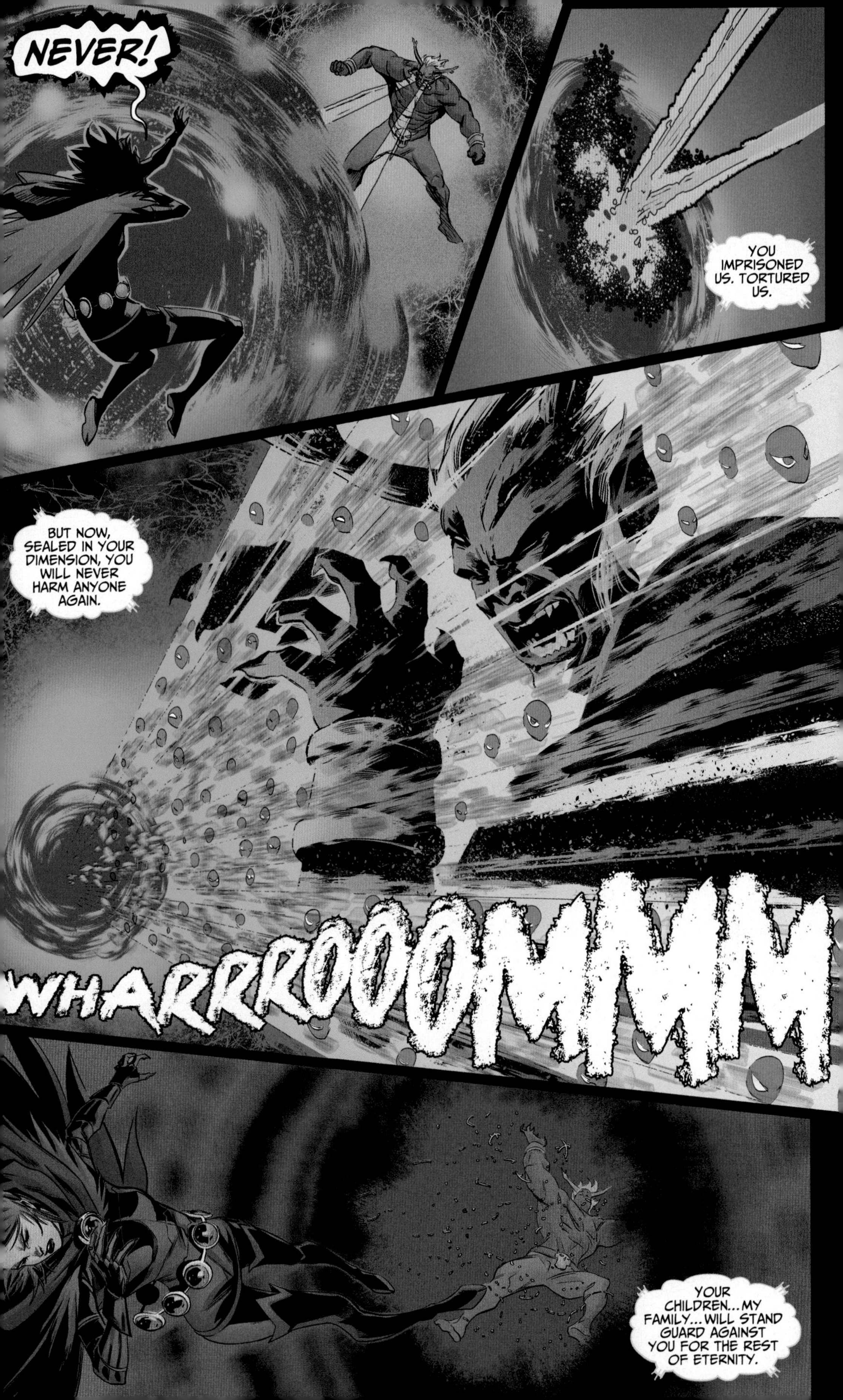
NEVER!
YOU IMPRISONED US. TORTURED US.
BUT NOW, SEALED IN YOUR DIMENSION, YOU WILL NEVER HARM ANYONE AGAIN.
WHARRROOOOMMMM
YOUR CHILDREN... MY FAMILY... WILL STAND GUARD AGAINST YOU FOR THE REST OF ETERNITY.

‹UUNNHH...‹

AZAR! TRIGON'S BLAST...

RAVEN FACTOID NUMBER SEVEN. BY RAVEN. IF ANYONE EVER ASKS WHAT SET OFF THE 1906 SAN FRANCISCO EARTHQUAKE...

...PLEASE RESIST ANSWERING "RAVEN'S INTERDIMENSIONAL DOOM-DEMON FATHER."

ALTHOUGH TRUE, ABSOLUTELY NOBODY IS GOING TO BELIEVE YOU.

WINTERS, THE ANSWER IS NO. I AM NOT INTERESTED.

13 HOURS LATER.

YOU DON'T EVEN KNOW WHY I ASKED YOU HERE.

IT DOES NOT MATTER. I AM AN EMPATH. THEREFORE, I KNOW WHO AND WHAT YOU ARE.

YOU ARE A LIAR. YOU AMORAL. YOU WOULD AN INNOCENT TO G YOUR WAY. I FIND Y DESPICABLE.

I CAN'T DISAGREE WITH ANYTHING YOU SAID, BUT--

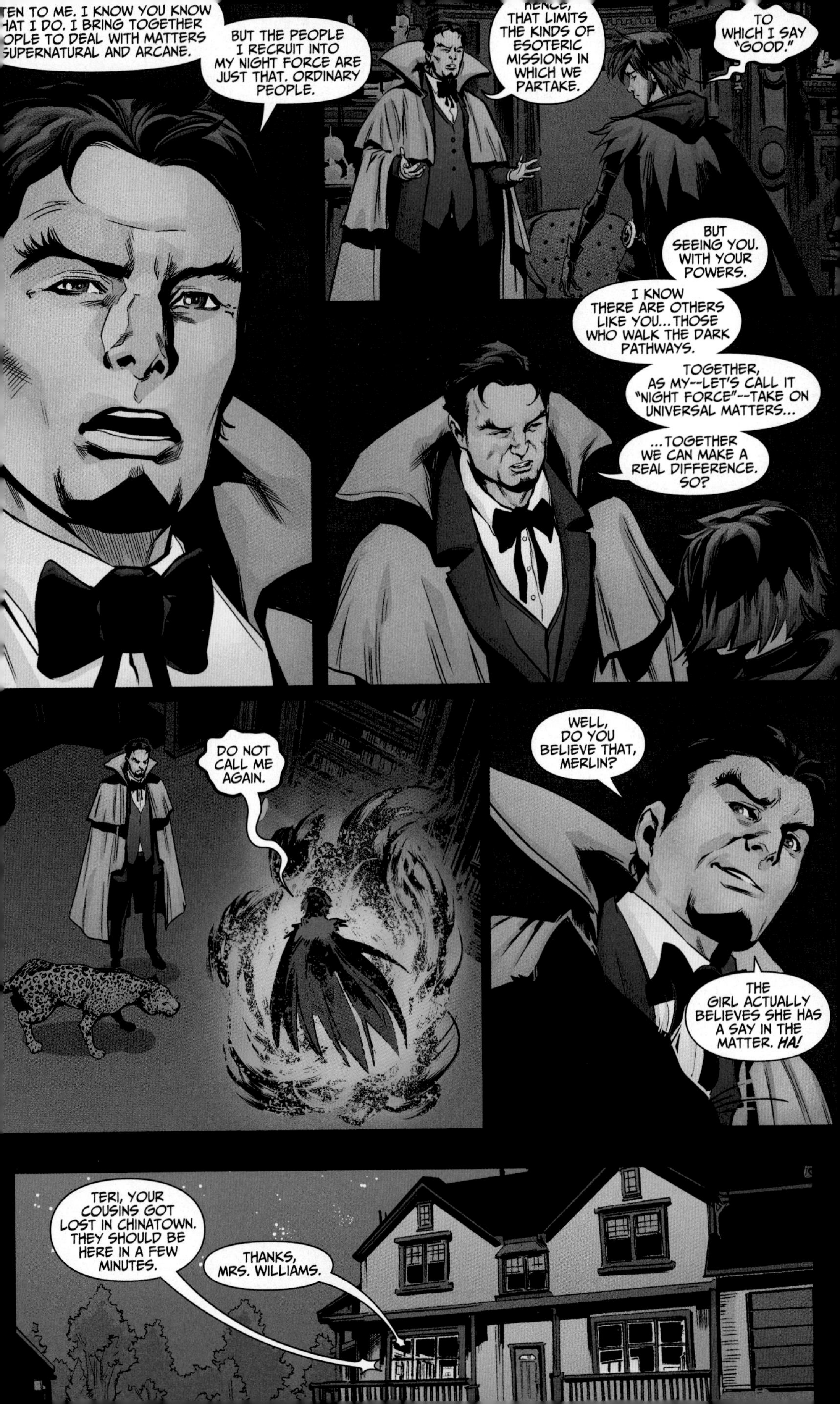

TEN TO ME. I KNOW YOU KNOW HAT I DO. I BRING TOGETHER OPLE TO DEAL WITH MATTERS SUPERNATURAL AND ARCANE.
BUT THE PEOPLE I RECRUIT INTO MY NIGHT FORCE ARE JUST THAT. ORDINARY PEOPLE.
HENCE, THAT LIMITS THE KINDS OF ESOTERIC MISSIONS IN WHICH WE PARTAKE.
TO WHICH I SAY "GOOD."
BUT SEEING YOU. WITH YOUR POWERS.
I KNOW THERE ARE OTHERS LIKE YOU...THOSE WHO WALK THE DARK PATHWAYS.
TOGETHER, AS MY--LET'S CALL IT "NIGHT FORCE"--TAKE ON UNIVERSAL MATTERS...
...TOGETHER WE CAN MAKE A REAL DIFFERENCE. SO?
DO NOT CALL ME AGAIN.
WELL, DO YOU BELIEVE THAT, MERLIN?
THE GIRL ACTUALLY BELIEVES SHE HAS A SAY IN THE MATTER. *HA!*
TERI, YOUR COUSINS GOT LOST IN CHINATOWN. THEY SHOULD BE HERE IN A FEW MINUTES.
THANKS, MRS. WILLIAMS.

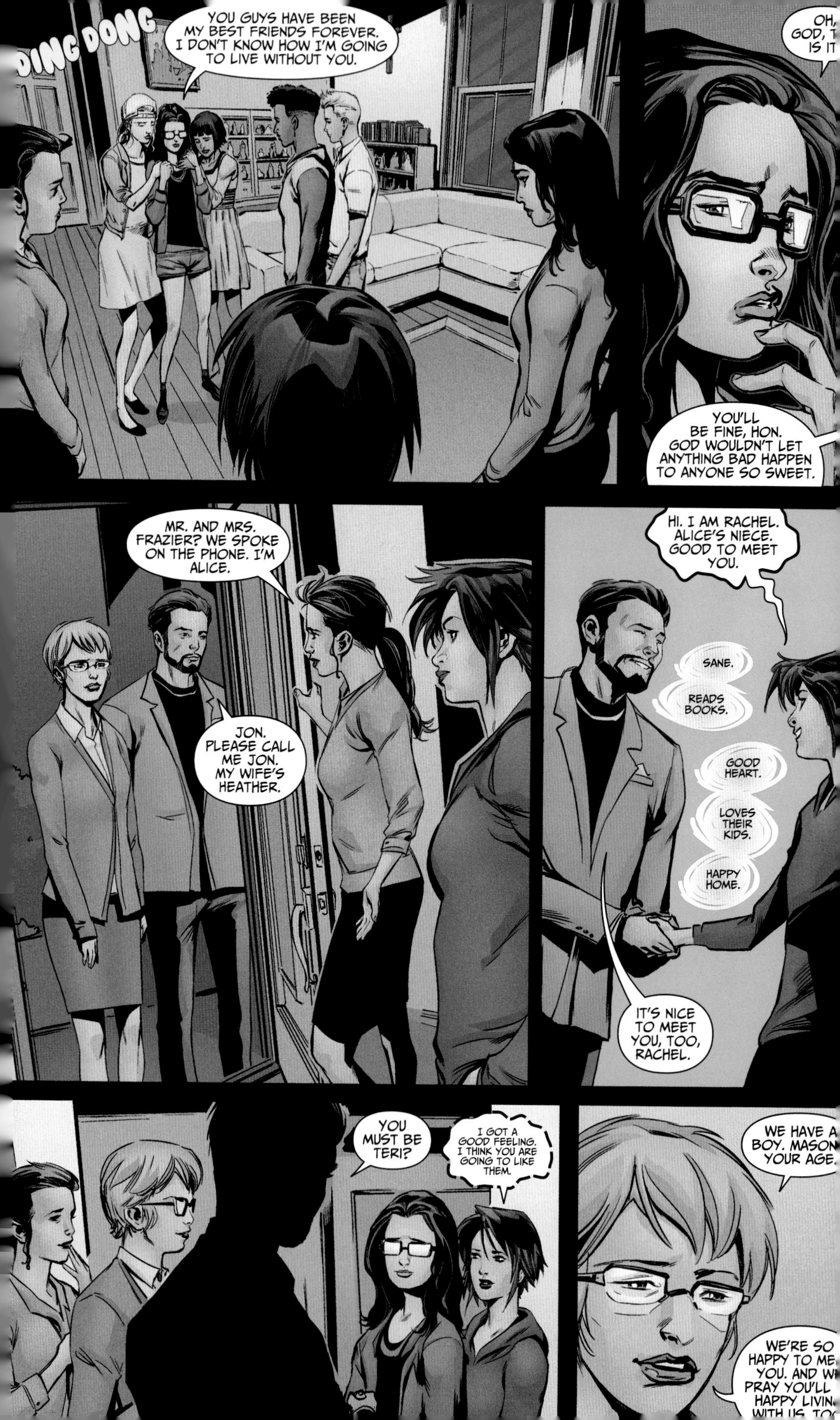
DING DONG
YOU GUYS HAVE BEEN MY BEST FRIENDS FOREVER. I DON'T KNOW HOW I'M GOING TO LIVE WITHOUT YOU.
OH, GOD, T IS IT
YOU'LL BE FINE, HON. GOD WOULDN'T LET ANYTHING BAD HAPPEN TO ANYONE SO SWEET.
MR. AND MRS. FRAZIER? WE SPOKE ON THE PHONE. I'M ALICE.
JON. PLEASE CALL ME JON. MY WIFE'S HEATHER.
HI. I AM RACHEL. ALICE'S NIECE. GOOD TO MEET YOU.
SANE.
READS BOOKS.
GOOD HEART.
LOVES THEIR KIDS.
HAPPY HOME.
IT'S NICE TO MEET YOU, TOO, RACHEL.
YOU MUST BE TERI?
I GOT A GOOD FEELING. I THINK YOU ARE GOING TO LIKE THEM.
WE HAVE A BOY. MASON YOUR AGE.
WE'RE SO HAPPY TO ME YOU. AND W PRAY YOU'LL HAPPY LIVIN WITH US. TO

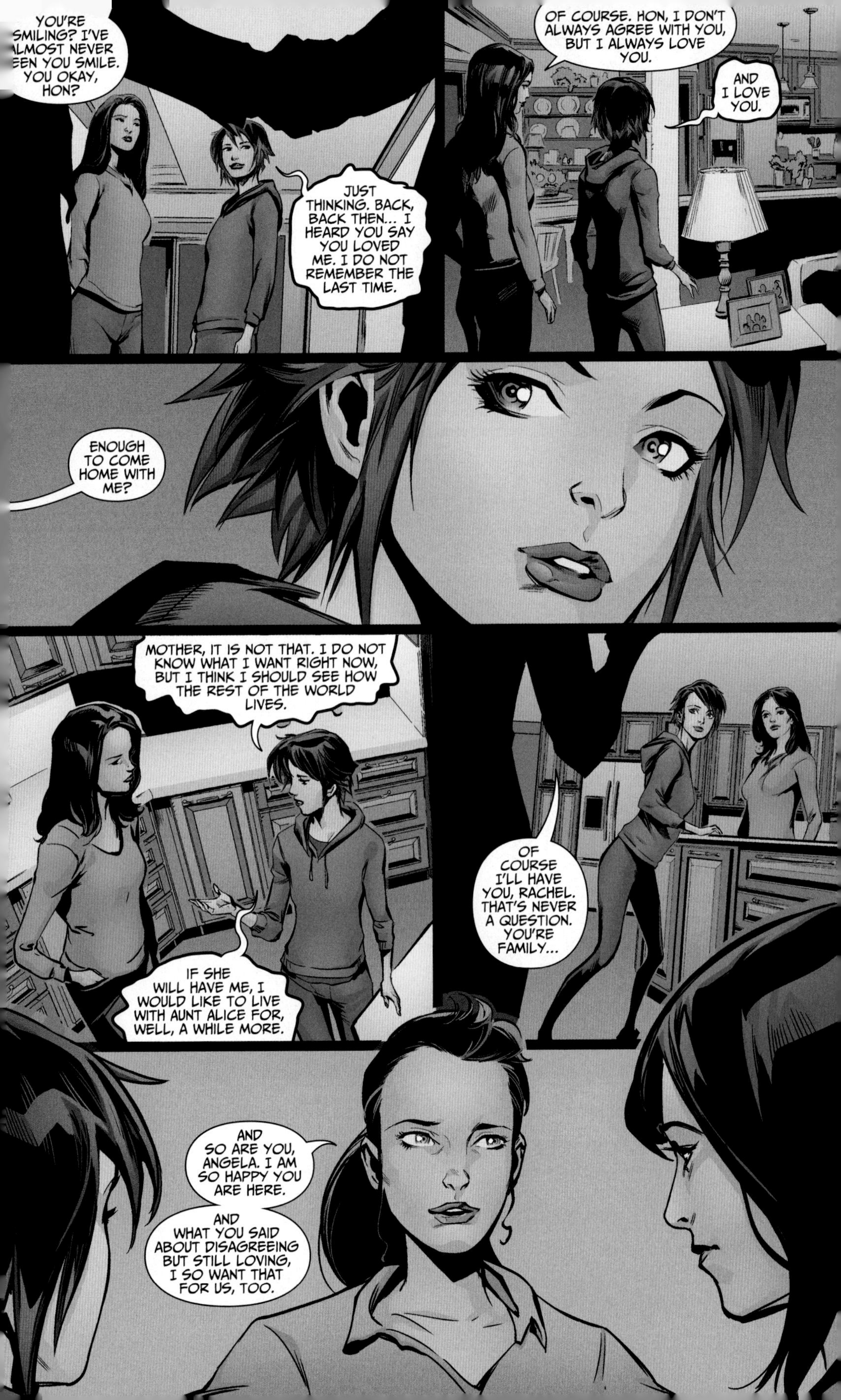
YOU'RE SMILING? I'VE ALMOST NEVER SEEN YOU SMILE. YOU OKAY, HON?
JUST THINKING. BACK, BACK THEN... I HEARD YOU SAY YOU LOVED ME. I DO NOT REMEMBER THE LAST TIME.
OF COURSE. HON, I DON'T ALWAYS AGREE WITH YOU, BUT I ALWAYS LOVE YOU.
AND I LOVE YOU.
ENOUGH TO COME HOME WITH ME?
MOTHER, IT IS NOT THAT. I DO NOT KNOW WHAT I WANT RIGHT NOW, BUT I THINK I SHOULD SEE HOW THE REST OF THE WORLD LIVES.
IF SHE WILL HAVE ME, I WOULD LIKE TO LIVE WITH AUNT ALICE FOR, WELL, A WHILE MORE.
OF COURSE I'LL HAVE YOU, RACHEL. THAT'S NEVER A QUESTION. YOU'RE FAMILY...
AND SO ARE YOU, ANGELA. I AM SO HAPPY YOU ARE HERE.
AND WHAT YOU SAID ABOUT DISAGREEING BUT STILL LOVING, I SO WANT THAT FOR US, TOO.

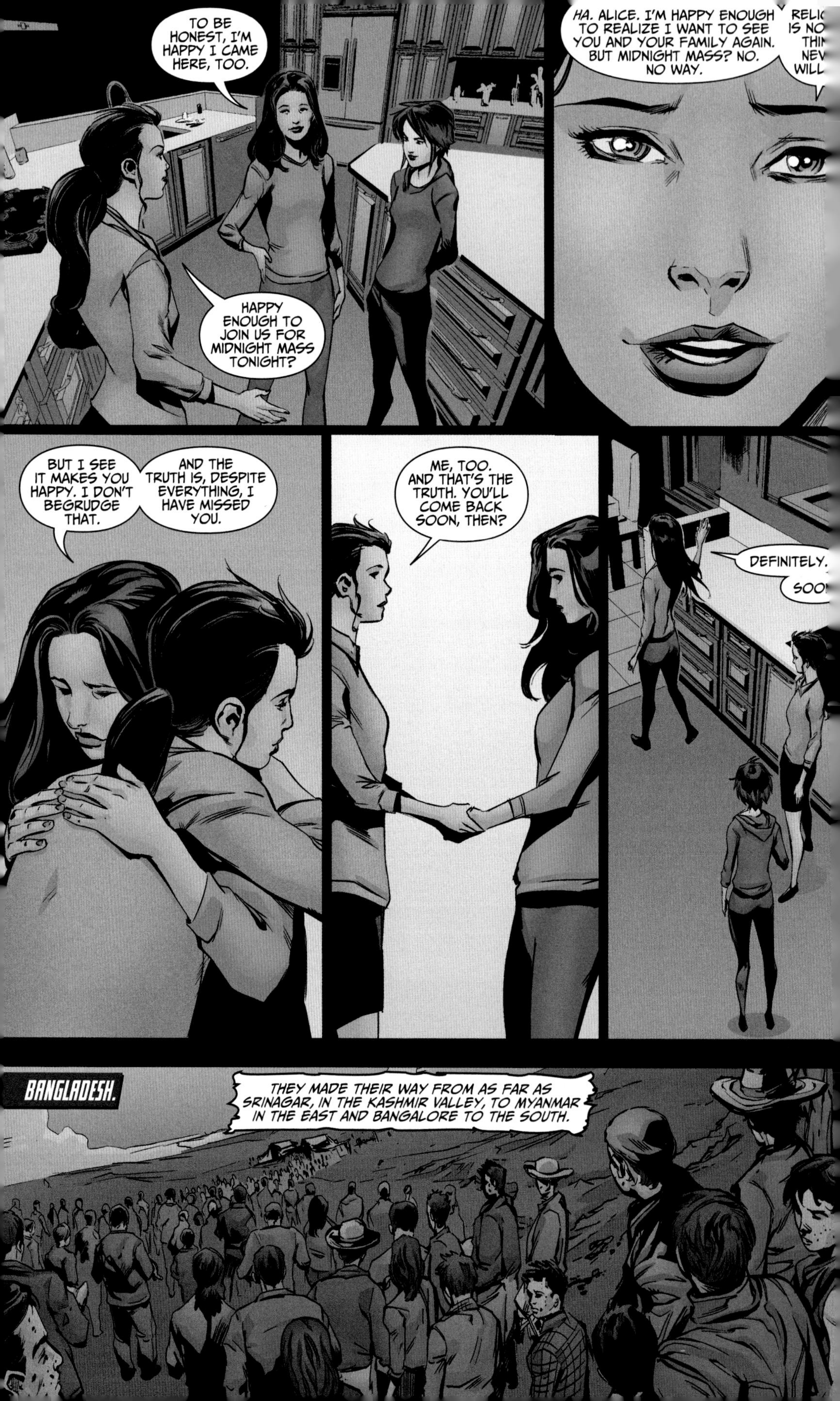
TO BE HONEST, I'M HAPPY I CAME HERE, TOO.
HAPPY ENOUGH TO JOIN US FOR MIDNIGHT MASS TONIGHT?
HA. ALICE. I'M HAPPY ENOUGH TO REALIZE I WANT TO SEE YOU AND YOUR FAMILY AGAIN. BUT MIDNIGHT MASS? NO. NO WAY.
BUT I SEE IT MAKES YOU HAPPY. I DON'T BEGRUDGE THAT.
AND THE TRUTH IS, DESPITE EVERYTHING, I HAVE MISSED YOU.
ME, TOO. AND THAT'S THE TRUTH. YOU'LL COME BACK SOON, THEN?
DEFINITELY.
BANGLADESH.
THEY MADE THEIR WAY FROM AS FAR AS SRINAGAR, IN THE KASHMIR VALLEY, TO MYANMAR IN THE EAST AND BANGALORE TO THE SOUTH.

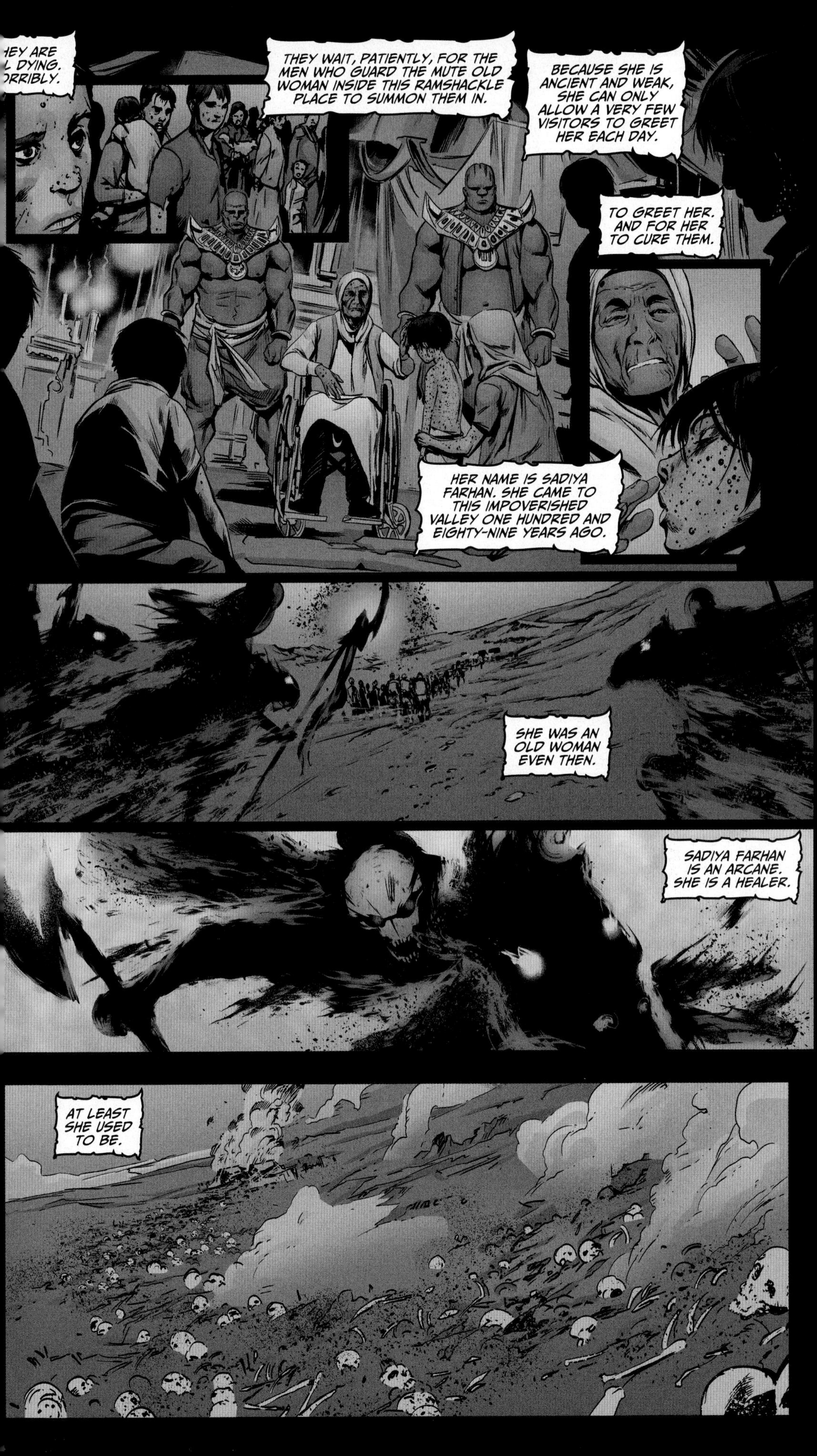
HEY ARE
L DYING.
ORRIBLY.
THEY WAIT, PATIENTLY, FOR THE MEN WHO GUARD THE MUTE OLD WOMAN INSIDE THIS RAMSHACKLE PLACE TO SUMMON THEM IN.
BECAUSE SHE IS ANCIENT AND WEAK, SHE CAN ONLY ALLOW A VERY FEW VISITORS TO GREET HER EACH DAY.
TO GREET HER. AND FOR HER TO CURE THEM.
HER NAME IS SADIYA FARHAN. SHE CAME TO THIS IMPOVERISHED VALLEY ONE HUNDRED AND EIGHTY-NINE YEARS AGO.
SHE WAS AN OLD WOMAN EVEN THEN.
SADIYA FARHAN IS AN ARCANE. SHE IS A HEALER.
AT LEAST SHE USED TO BE.

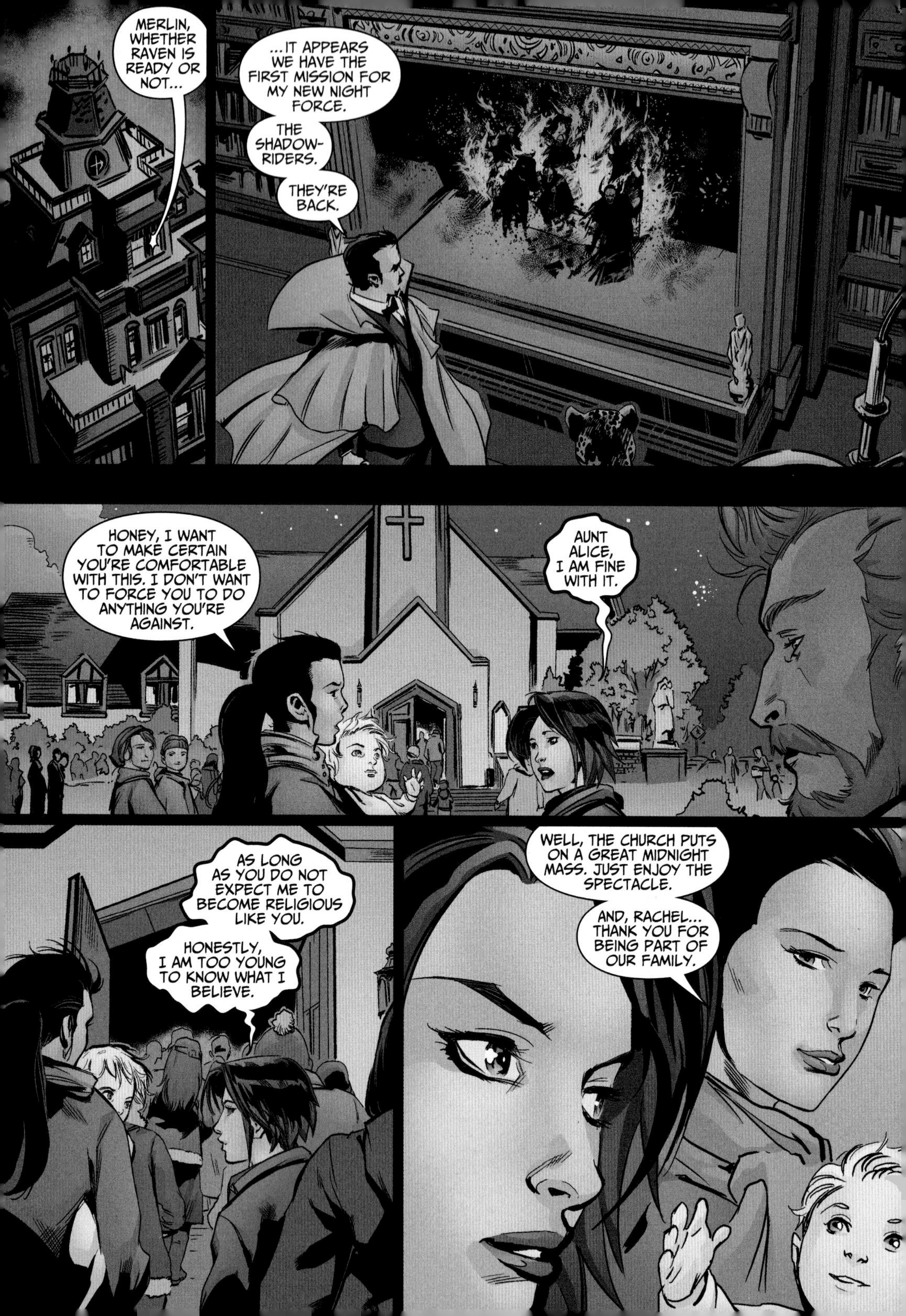
MERLIN, WHETHER RAVEN IS READY OR NOT...
...IT APPEARS WE HAVE THE FIRST MISSION FOR MY NEW NIGHT FORCE.
THE SHADOW-RIDERS.
THEY'RE BACK.
HONEY, I WANT TO MAKE CERTAIN YOU'RE COMFORTABLE WITH THIS. I DON'T WANT TO FORCE YOU TO DO ANYTHING YOU'RE AGAINST.
AUNT ALICE, I AM FINE WITH IT.
AS LONG AS YOU DO NOT EXPECT ME TO BECOME RELIGIOUS LIKE YOU.
HONESTLY, I AM TOO YOUNG TO KNOW WHAT I BELIEVE.
WELL, THE CHURCH PUTS ON A GREAT MIDNIGHT MASS. JUST ENJOY THE SPECTACLE.
AND, RACHEL... THANK YOU FOR BEING PART OF OUR FAMILY.

RAVEN: DAUGHTER OF DARKNESS #1 variant cover by BILL SIENKIEWICZ

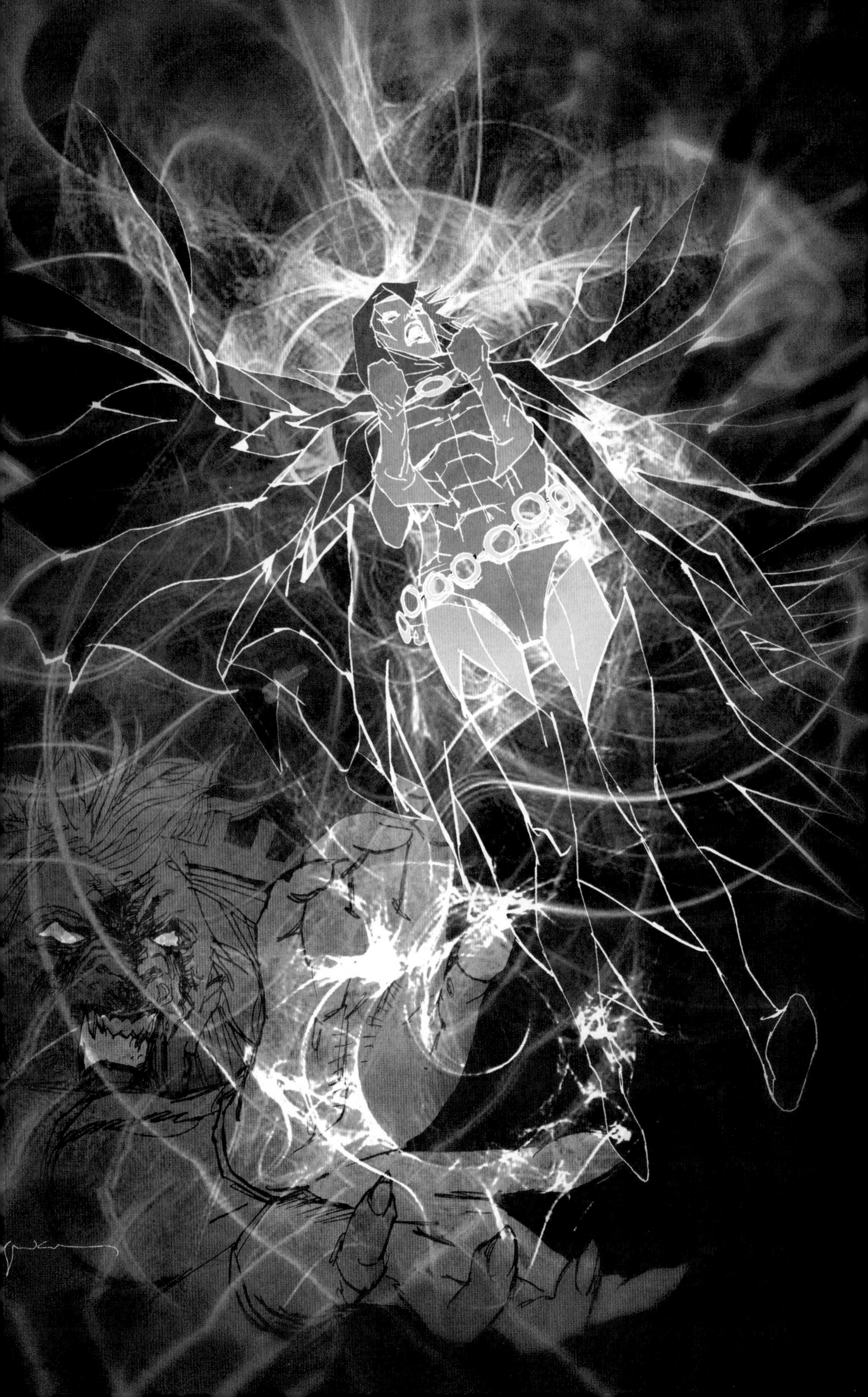

RAVEN: DAUGHTER OF DARKNESS cover sketches and inks by YANICK PAQUETTE

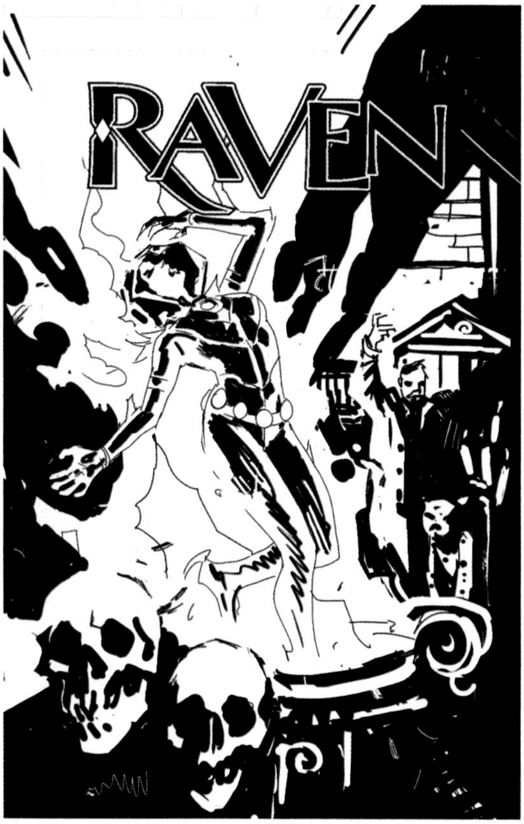
RAVEN

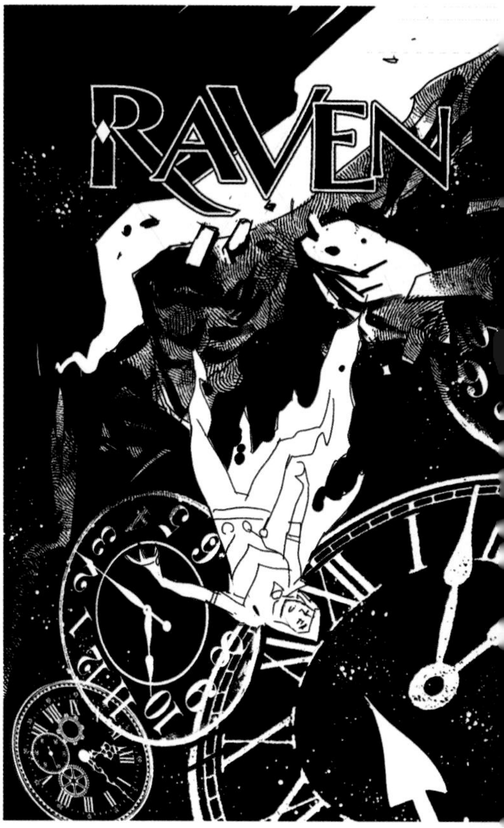
RAVEN

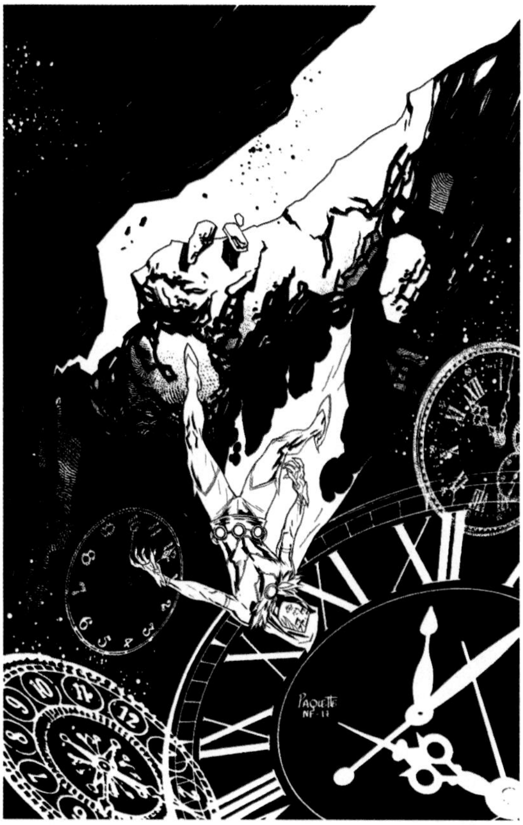
PAQUETTE NF-17

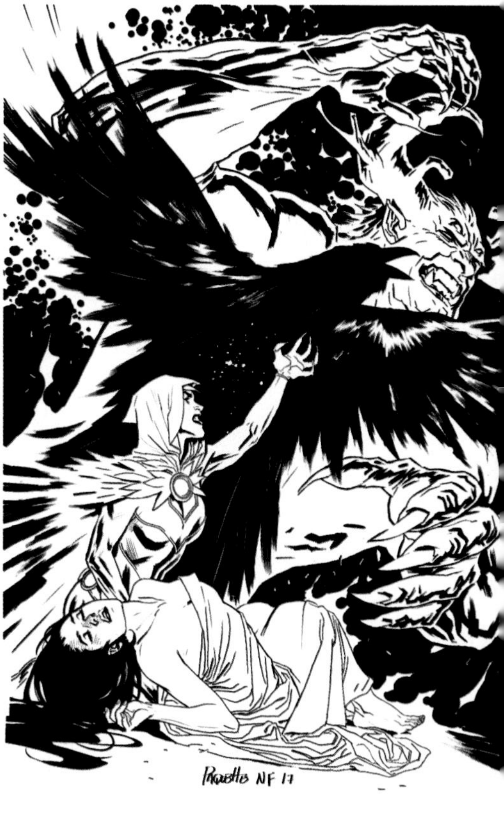
Paquette NF 17

RAVEN: DAUGHTER OF DARKNESS #5 cover pencils by EMANUELA LUPACCHINO

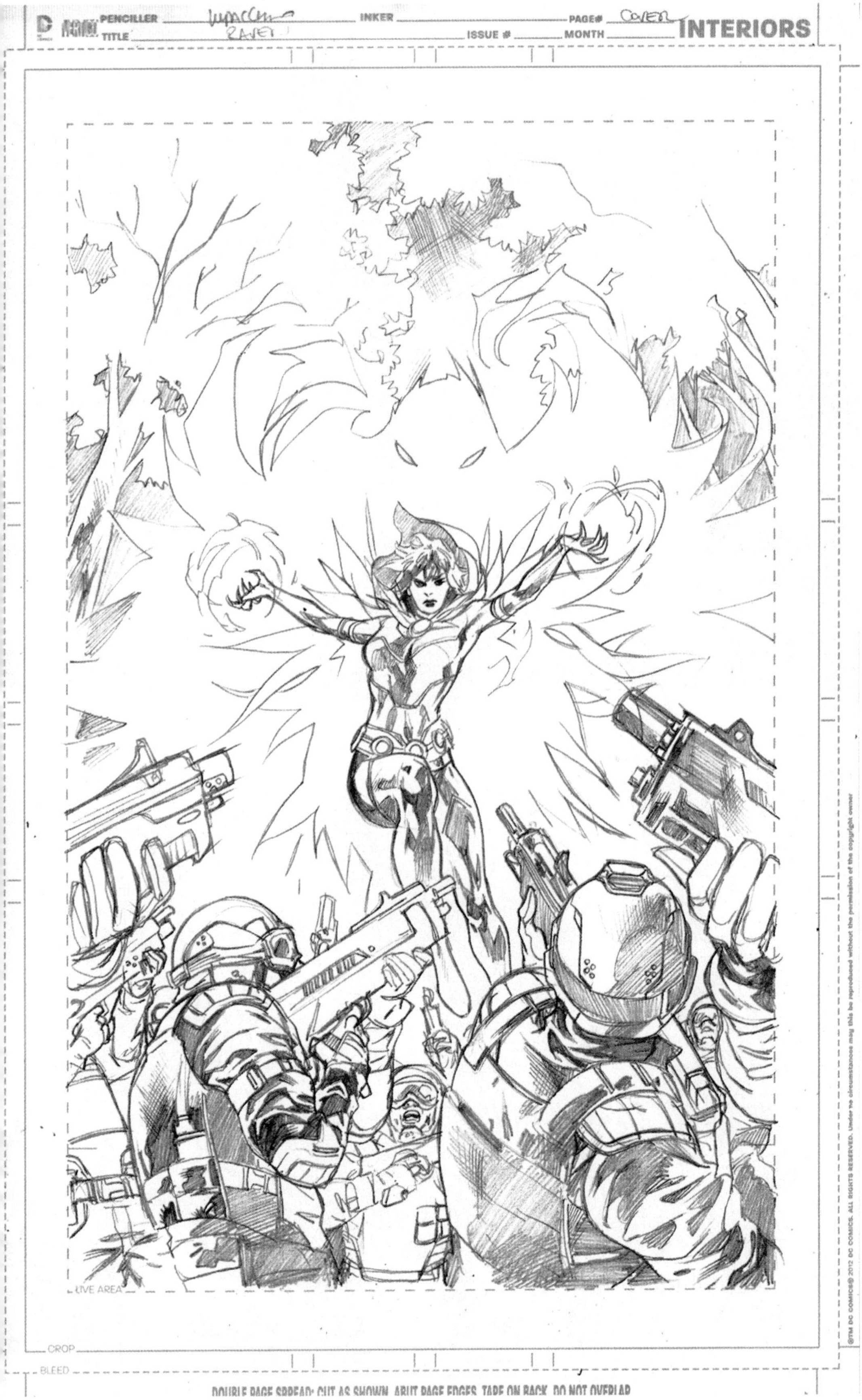
PENCILLER
TITLE
INKER
ISSUE #
PAGE#
MONTH
INTERIORS
LIVE AREA
CROP
BLEED

RAVEN: DAUGHTER OF DARKNESS #6 cover inks by GUILLEM MARCH

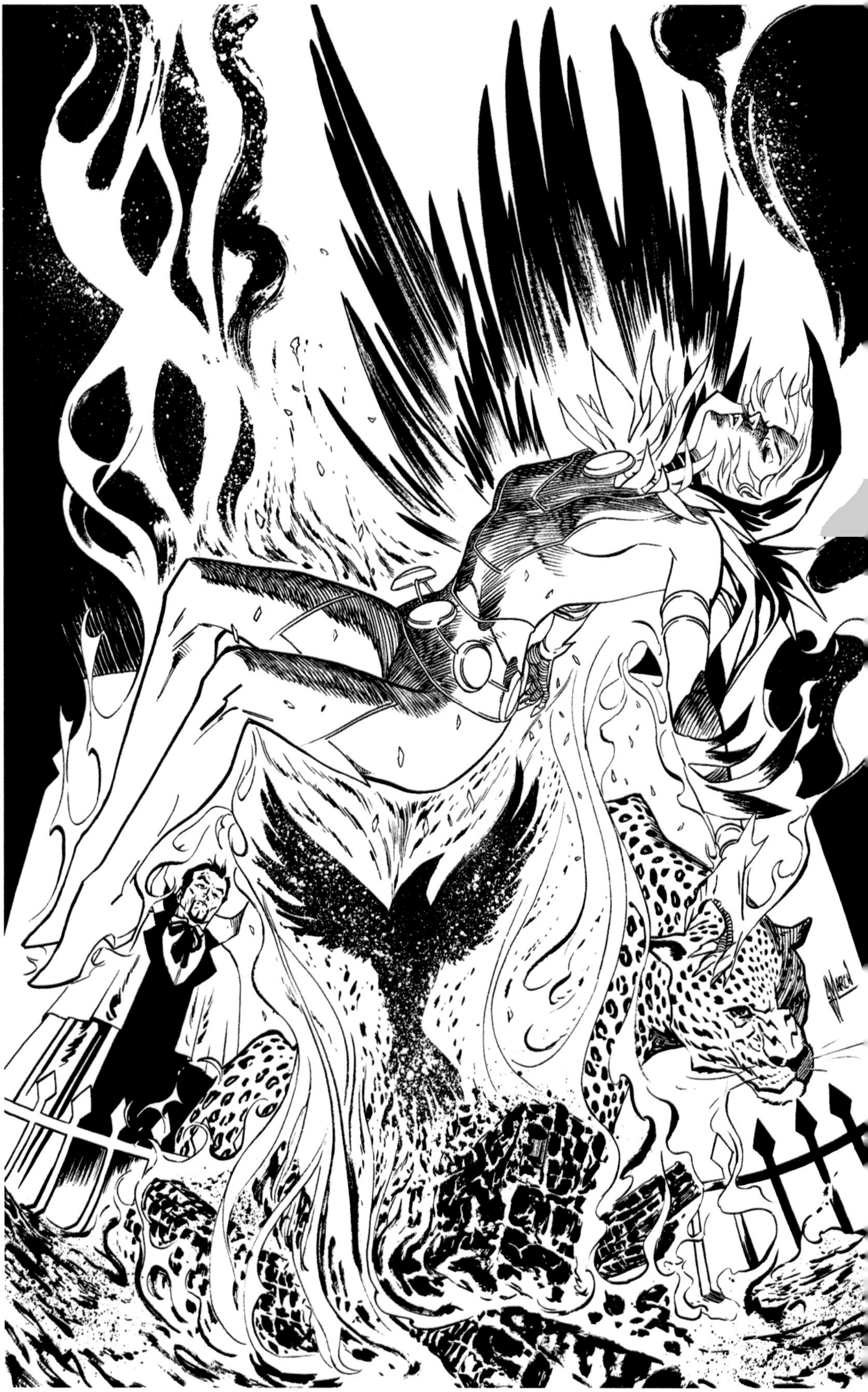
MARCH

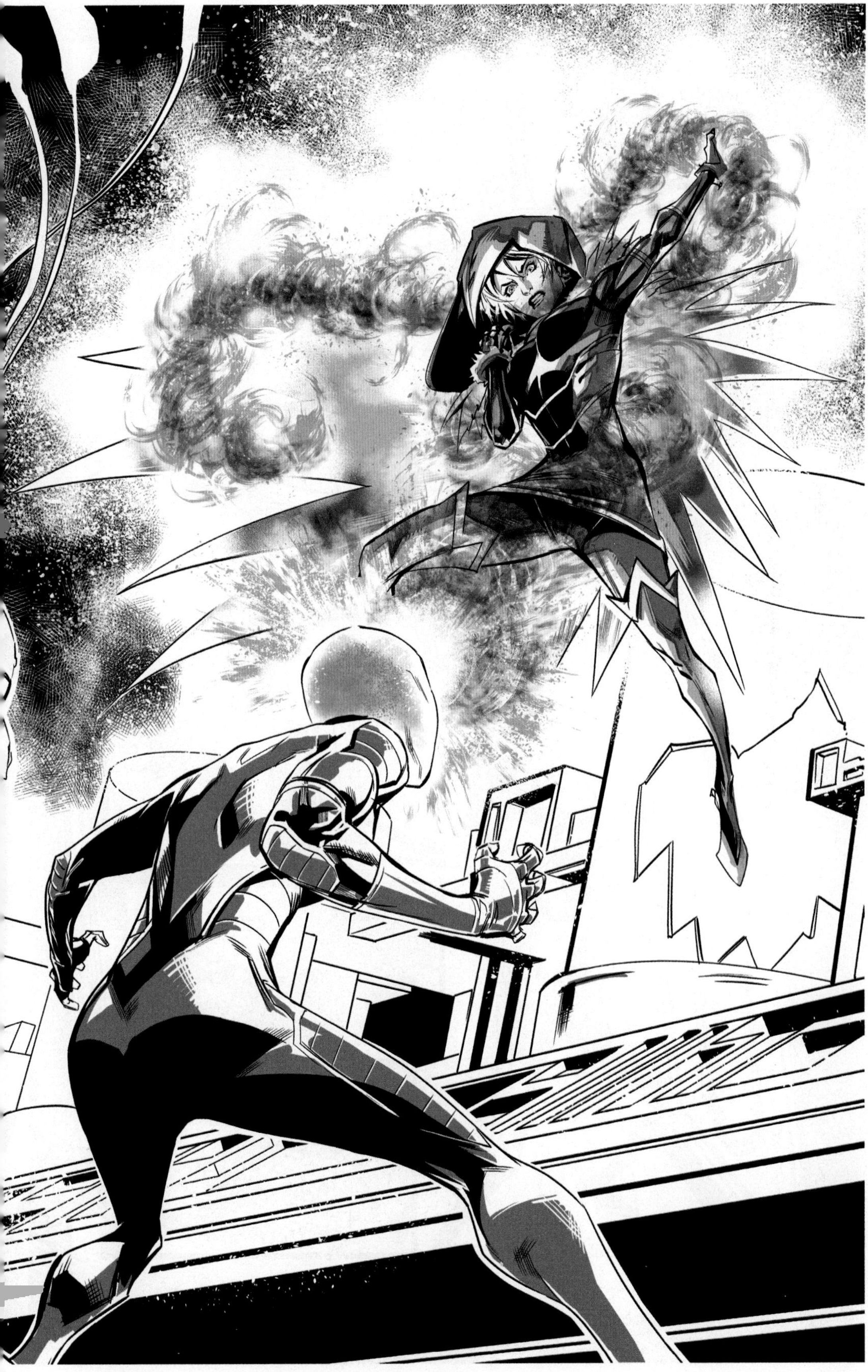

RAVEN: DAUGHTER OF DARKNESS #3 page 9 inks by POP MHAN

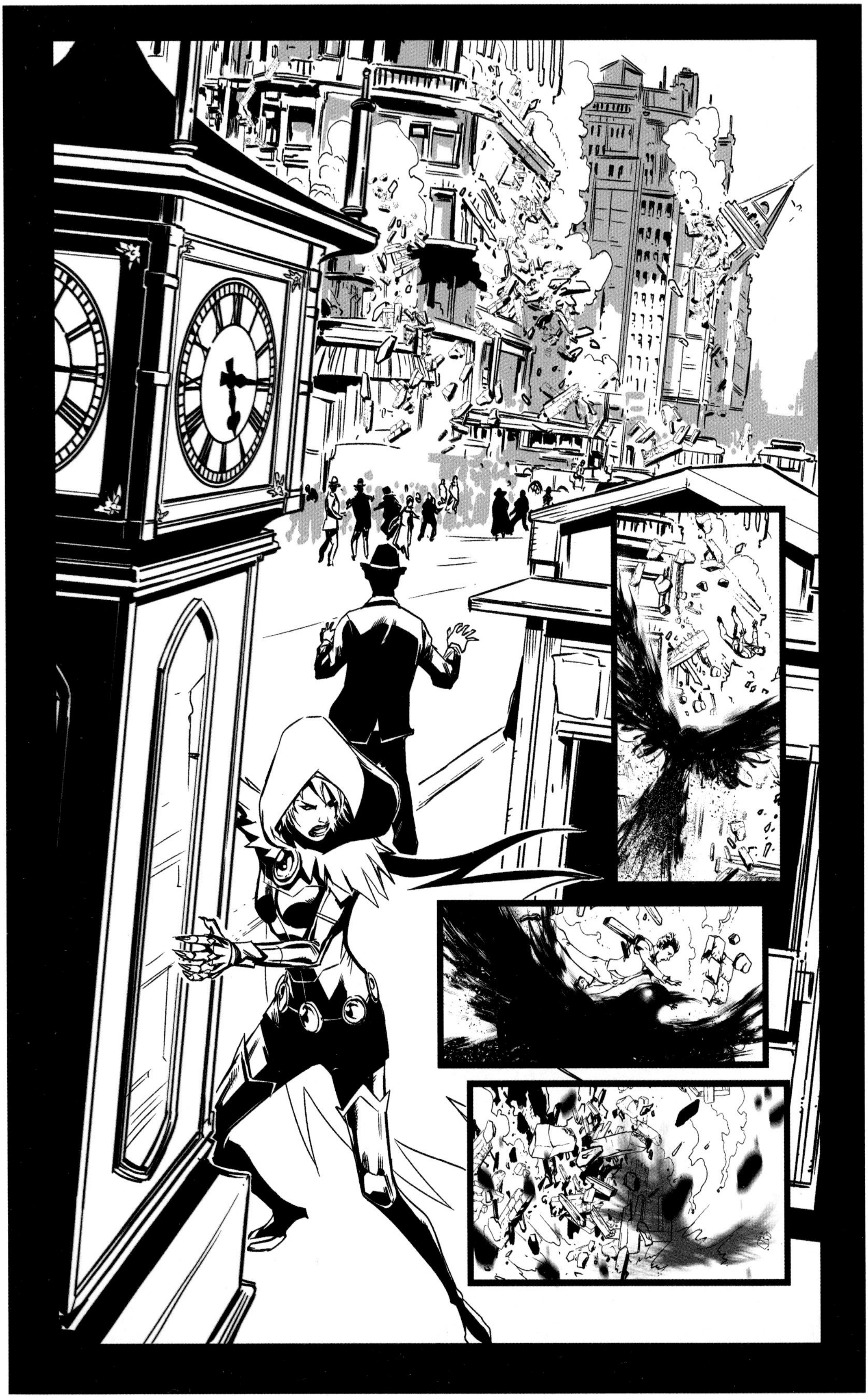